DOCUMENTATION REQUIREMENTS
IN NON-ACUTE
CARE FACILITIES
& ORGANIZATIONS

I would like to extend a special thanks to my mother, Mary E. Horn, for her hours of editing this manuscript as well as to my husband, Edmund, for his unfailing support and encouragement

Acknowledgement of contributors

A special thank you to all of my colleagues who shared their knowledge and expertise, especially the following:

Patricia Aldredge, RHIT
Gwen Harris, RHIA
Octavia Kelly-Gaston, RHIA
Josephine Omangi, RHIA
Lisa Pichinson, RHIA
Laureen Rimmer, RHIA
Elinor Taylor, RHIA
Antoinette Tolbert, RHIA
Calla Waldon, RHIT, CCS

DOCUMENTATION REQUIREMENTS IN NON-ACUTE CARE FACILITIES & ORGANIZATIONS

Barbara J. Manger, MPA, RHIA, CCS
Kean University, Union, NJ

The Parthenon Publishing Group
International Publishers in Medicine, Science & Technology

NEW YORK   LONDON

Published in the USA by
The Parthenon Publishing Group Inc.
One Blue Hill Plaza
PO Box 1564, Pearl River
New York 10965, USA

Published in the UK and Europe by
The Parthenon Publishing Group Limited
Casterton Hall, Carnforth,
Lancs. LA6 2LA, UK

Library of Congress Cataloging-in-Publication Data
Manger, Barbara J. Horn.
    Documentation requirements in non-acute care facilities and
    organizations / Barbara J. Manger.
        p.   cm.
    Includes bibliographical references and index.
    ISBN 1-84214-001-9
    1. Medical records–Management–United States.
    2. Medical records–Standards–United States. I. Title.

    RA 976.M27 2001
    651.5'04261'021873–dc21

                                                    00-056681

British Library Cataloguing in Publication Data
Manger, Barbara J.
    Documentation requirements in non-acute care facilities and organizations
    1. Medical records
    I. Title
    651.5'04261

    ISBN 1842140019

Printed and bound by J.W. Arrowsmith Ltd., Bristol, UK

CONTENTS

Chapter 1

INTRODUCTION

At the conclusion of this chapter you should be able to:

Compare and contrast alternative approaches to medicine and describe the trends in the uses of these approaches

Describe the trends in hospital utilization over a period of time

Describe the effects of managed care on the practice of medicine

Identify essential elements of medical record documentation and describe how they benefit medical care

Describe the challenges to confidentiality in settings outside of acute care

Identify the coding systems commonly utilized, and describe the impact of legislation and regulation on coding practices

HEALTH-CARE ENVIRONMENT

If we look at the provision of health care in the past, we do not have to go back too far to see that the health-care arena of today has changed greatly. When we look at the dollars expended on health care now and in the past, we will see that there is a shift in the venue. A hospital used to be the hub of the health-care industry. We now see that this focus is changing and the dollars expended in the hospital setting, in comparison to the total dollars, is decreasing (Table 1-1).

Table 1-1 National health dollars for selected expenditures and calendar years (in billions)[1]

Type of expenditure	1980	1985	1990	1995	1997
National expenditure	$247.3	$428.7	$699.4	$993.7	$1092.4
Hospital care	102.7	168.3	256.4	347.2	371.1
Physician services	45.2	83.6	146.3	201.9	217.6
Dental services	13.3	21.7	31.6	45.0	50.6
Other professional services	6.4	16.6	34.7	53.6	61.9
Home care	2.4	5.6	13.1	29.1	32.3
Nursing-home care	17.6	30.7	50.9	75.5	82.8

We can also see from the information presented in Table 1-2 below that the individual's use of health-care services has changed as well. Patients are frequenting hospitals less often while seeking attention in the physician's office more often.

Table 1-2 Personal health-care use (average episodes per person per year)[2]

	Mid-1960s	Mid-1970s	Mid-1980s	Mid-1990s
Hospital admissions	13	14	10	9
Physician visits	4.5	4.9	5.4	6.1

Although significant efforts have been made to reduce the cost of health care resulting in many of these changes, a study released by the Health Care Financing Administration (HCFA) in 1998 found that health-care spending in the United States is expected to more than double by 2007. It is expected to rise to $2.1 trillion in 2007 from $1 trillion in 1996. The report states that the growth in spending in private sector health is expected to outpace public health spending growth over the next 5 years.

ALTERNATIVE MEDICINES[3]

The medical establishment is paying special attention to alternative treatment in a response to skyrocketing use by mainstream Americans of such approaches as acupuncture, massage therapy, chiropractic, naturopathy, tai-chi, yoga and over-the-counter herbs and supplements. More Americans sought treatment from alternative medicine practitioners last year than visited a primary-care physician, according to a survey published by the *Journal of the American Medical Association* in November 1998[4].

The trend is alarming to some traditional medical practitioners who say the acceptance of untested and unproven alternative medicine therapies must stop. This trend is not surprising. People are much more sensitive to a concept of health that involves more than just their body, but total well-being – mental, physical and social – and not just an absence of disease. The medical profession classically has tended to focus on the treatment of illness rather than the maintenance of good health.

Some patients seek alternatives only when they discover that conventional medicine does not have much to offer them if they have a chronic problem such as back pain or chronic fatigue syndrome.

Managed-care doctors have less time to spend with their patients in contrast to some alternative practitioners who might spend a great deal of time. Managed care is a big contributor to the shift of patients to alternative practitioners.

It is because of all of these significant changes that the health information professional is increasingly finding employment in environments outside of the hospital. It is, therefore, necessary for educational programs in this area to move away from the focus on acute care and include more pertinent information on the non-acute care settings.

This text will provide a vast array of information on documentation practices in non-acute care settings. Although certain aspects of health information will not change from one venue to the next, some requirements are quite different due to the type of care rendered.

Most chapters are structured with the following sections:

> Overview and introduction
> Type of care rendered
> Patient population
> Legal and regulatory issues
> > Licensing
> > Accreditation
> > Federal regulations
> Documentation guidelines
> Retention and storage
> Challenges for the HIM professional
> Performance improvement
> Sample forms

Certain chapters will refer you elsewhere on some of these topics if they have been previously covered in an earlier chapter.

DOCUMENTATION AND WHY IT IS IMPORTANT[5]

Medical record documentation is required to record pertinent facts, findings and observations about an individual's health history including past and present illnesses, examinations, tests, treatments and outcomes. The medical record documents the care of the patient and is an important element contributing to high-quality care. The medical record facilitates:

- The ability of the physician and other health-care professionals to evaluate and plan the patient's immediate treatment, and to monitor his/her health care over time
- Communication and continuity of care among physicians and other health-care professionals involved in the patient's care
- Accurate and timely claims review and payment
- Appropriate utilization review and quality-of-care evaluations
- Collection of data that may be useful for research and education

HCFA provides guidelines for documentation which are applicable to all types of medical and surgical services in all settings. Generally, these principles state that documentation should meet the following criteria:

- The record is complete and legible
- Documentation for each encounter includes:
  - Reason for the encounter
  - Relevant history
  - Physician exam findings
  - Prior diagnostic test results
  - Assessment and impression
  - Plan for care
  - Date and legible identity of provider
- Inference of rationale for diagnostic and ancillary services ordered and provided
- Identification of appropriate health risks
- Patient response to treatment and prognosis
- Supportive documentation for billed ICD-9-CM and CPT codes

CONFIDENTIALITY

One issue that has come to the forefront as patients seek services outside of the hospital – they are often being treated at a variety of facilities either simultaneously or in rapid succession. There is a need for coordination of information flowing from one setting to the next to provide adequate quality of care.

In the drive to provide this information, care must be taken to uphold the patient's right to privacy and the protection of confidentiality. The provider–patient bond is the most important relationship in the health-care arena. Even with the changes occurring in the marketplace, the trust engendered in these encounters should remain constant. Health-care providers have a duty to patients to ensure their medical records are held in confidence and are disclosed only in appropriate situations. According to the Medical Group Management Association, the health-care provider must be held accountable for the protection of health information. Anyone who improperly discloses confidential medical records should face civil and criminal penalties. Policy makers should adopt confidentiality measures that apply to everyone. They therefore are instrumental in promoting national legislation which will provide uniformity in confidentiality laws. National uniformity will give physicians one set of standards and will make compliance feasible.

These statutes should specifically define improper disclosure of medical records. Federal policy should identify where disclosure is unlawful and attach appropriate penalties to identified improper disclosure.

CODING AND REIMBURSEMENT

In all health-care settings, reimbursement is often based on coded information submitted on the bill for service rendered. A variety of reimbursement schemes are in place or planned and these are discussed in the chapters to follow. Enough cannot be said of the importance of complete and accurate coding. Insurance companies are spending large amounts of money on systems to track the claims history of their clients in order to establish rates as well as the fees they will pay out. Previously, they never had the tools to thoroughly track coding accuracy. Edit checks were rudimentary, i.e. invalid code as principal diagnosis, inappropriate code for gender or age, principal diagnosis not valid reason for admission. However, more sophisticated coding systems are now in place which will be able to locate problematic codes previously missed. Inpatient coders are not as proficient in CPT as they were in ICD-9-CM because until a few years ago many were not required to do CPT coding in their facilities. CPT codes are much more descriptive and precise than ICD-9-CM and are, therefore, preferable to those analyzing the data. Coders will need the tools to increase their proficiency in using these coding systems, i.e. automation, encoders, electronic coding references and sophisticated coding edits[6].

Coding professionals are seeing their work reviewed internally and externally on a much more frequent basis. Much of this stems from the increased focus of the federal government on issues of fraud and abuse. The Office of the Inspector General (OIG) of the United States proposed a rule to implement the Healthcare Integrity and Protection Data Bank (HIPDB) in the October 1998 Federal Register. The HIPDB stems from a provision in the Health Insurance Portability and Accountability Act (HIPAA) and establishes a health-care fraud and abuse data collection system and data bank. According to the rule, data collected on providers, practitioners, and supplies will include the following:

- Adverse federal and state civil judgements regarding the delivery of a health-product or service
- Federal and state criminal convictions involving the delivery of a health-care product or service
- Federal and state licensing and certification agency actions
- Exclusion from federal and state health-care programs
- Other adjudicated actions or decisions as established through regulations by Health and Human Services (HHS)

The OIG also published new guidelines for its program establishing protocols for voluntary disclosure of Medicare and Medicaid fraud to the government in the Federal Register (10-30-98). The Provider Self-Disclosure Protocols are effective now, and replace a pilot program established as part of the OIG's 1995 Operation Restore Trust project. While self-disclosure will not defend the provider from civil and criminal prosecution under the False Claims Act, the OIG states that it may recommend such disclosure to prosecuting agencies as possibly mitigating material that could prevent provider exclusion from federal health-care programs like Medicare and Medicaid. Traditionally, health-care providers have been reluctant to voluntarily disclose possible fraud out of fear of federal prosecution. The OIG intends this program to encourage providers to pursue their ethical concerns with non-compliance in federal health-care programs[7].

PROFESSIONAL PRACTICE STANDARDS

For the new health information professional, there are many sources of information available to provide guidance. One excellent source of information is the American Health Information Management Association (AHIMA) which can cite many written materials some of which they publish themselves. One group of these documents is called the Professional Practice Standards Manuals which are available for all different types of health-care facilities. These include:

- Ambulatory care
- Long-term care
- Mental health
- Substance abuse
- Inpatient settings

Should you find yourself employed in any one of these settings as a Health Information Manager, the information contained within the appropriate manual will be useful in answering many basic questions which new professionals, and often seasoned ones, have.

The professional standards manual is an excellent reference guide that will allow you to systematically evaluate areas within your department that need improvement. In each book there are eight major categories of responsibilities that health information managers need to address. These are outlined below.

Content of the Health Record speaks of the importance of the timeliness and quality of health information documentation.

Health-Care Data contains standards related to the following:
- The collection and processing of health information
- The quality and timeliness of computerized patient data and health statistics
- The procedures and policies used to organize information flow
- How information will be displayed and reported
- Elements necessary with classification systems

Confidentiality section works to establish policies and procedures that will safeguard patient information from unauthorized disclosure and assures that health-care professionals who have the need to know information to complete their jobs are the only ones who have access without authorization.

Health Information Management is a new section that discusses information in which many HIM directors have not been involved in the past. The standards covered in this section were often relegated to the direction of the data-processing area of the facility.

Record Retention and Retrieval is one of the most costly and important of all the responsibilities in the HIM department today, especially ambulatory care, as computerized patient information is not yet a reality.

Management and Supervision covers information which is applicable to all HIM professionals who will have responsibilities for managing operations and personnel.

External Requirements and Standards will help you evaluate whether you are prepared to acquire and measure the necessary regulatory and accreditation information for your department.

Quality Management Systems discusses the use of quality improvement, quality assurance and utilization review management functions within the HIM department.

THE MANAGEMENT ROLE

When first employed in a management position in a HIM department, every new manager will inherit a group of employees, all with their own temperament and agendas, and their functions. The new manager will be expected to manage these people and be responsible for the quality and timeliness of their work. There will be many policies and procedures that are existing and systems that are already in place.

Depending on the priorities established by the individual's administrator and the organization, the new manager will begin by trying to maintain and improve the department's services and the documentation in the medical record.

The demands upon the health information manager in a health-care facility are great. There is never enough time to complete all of the priorities, so when the new position is entered, there will always be problems or areas that need improvement. All facilities and organizations are in a perpetual state of self-improvement through assessment and performance-improvement programs. Many organizations are involved in re-engineering, which is defined as 'the fundamental rethinking and radical redesign of business processes to achieve dramatic improvements in critical, contemporary measures of performance, such as cost, quality, service and speed'[8]. It is not downsizing by eliminating positions or flattening the organization, although these may be the end results because of streamlining the processes.

As we enter a new millennium we see that the premises by which health care in general is defined, delivered and paid for are being challenged and revised. A new paradigm, managed health care, has replaced the old paradigm, fee-for-service independent practice. Pressures influencing this paradigm shift include not only the general recognition of the need to contain costs and minimize inefficiencies and waste, but also the growing acceptance that health-care processes can achieve maximum effectiveness if they follow 'best practice' standards that have been designed by practitioners based upon scientific consensus regarding health-care outcomes.

MEDICAL RECORD STORAGE

Regardless of the type of facility an HIM professional will be working in, there will be a medical record containing the documentation pertaining to all patients assessed and/or treated. These records will be produced in hard copy, meaning on paper, or using an electronic format, or in a combination of both types. Let us briefly address a few issues which are present in these formats.

There are unlimited efforts to eliminate the paper record. They are often cumbersome and difficult to locate even with the best efforts at record organization. Paper records only allow one person at a time to access information unless copies are made which would be costly. They also consume a lot of storage space as one visit may generate seven pieces of paper. Use of paper records often leads to duplication of documentation and greater time consumption for the health-care provider at this task. Paper documentation for physicians averages 23 minutes per visit[9].

Electronic records have already been implemented in many health-care organizations and are being seriously considered by many others as a means of conquering the multitude of problems which exist with the paper record. One major advantage is that the information in this format is widely available from office or home so that the provider does not necessarily have to be in the same location as the record to access the information. This allows increased monitoring of patient information, easier access to labs, and increased communications between all health-care providers and allied health services.

Although this may seem like a panacea for the ills of record information, many physicians are still reluctant to institute the electronic record. To get support, stress the following benefits:

7

- Saves time
- Supports entire care team
- Increases productivity
- Increases collaboration with patient and/or family (value to the patient)
- Information is sharable for collaboration with health-care team, specialists, etc.
- Eliminates duplication
- Information security *is* possible
- Collects and processes information at point of care

For the near future, there will continue to be issues presented dealing with information access and security; however, these very issues are the focus of many groups involved in promoting and developing the computerized record. Discussions with those who have electronic systems in place will be useful in identifying and avoiding many issues as well as prospectively planning for unavoidable problems.

In conclusion, this text will provide a comparative look at documentation practices in many health-care arenas. Whether the records at these sites are computerized or on paper, it is essential to understand the differences between the various sites and their requirements for documenting health information to support quality care.

References

1. National Statistics Group. www.hcfa.gov.10-29-98. Baltimore, MD: Health Care Finance Administration
2. Williams SJ, Torrens PR. *Introduction to Health Services,* 5th edn. Albany, NY: Delmar Publishers, 1999
3. McVicar N. Surging popularity of alternative medicine makes AMA take skeptical notice. *Newark (NJ) Star Ledger* 1998;November 11
4. Eisenberg DM, Davis RB, Ettner S, *et* al. Trends in alternative medicine use in the United States 1990–1997: results of a follow-up national survey. *J Am Med Assoc* 1998; 280:1569–75
5. *Guidelines for Evaluation and Management Services.* www.hcfa.gov/medicare/mcarpti.htm. Baltimore, MD: Health Care Financing Administration, November 1997
6. Sweet B. Coding for managed care. *Adv Health Inf Prof* 1997;7:no. 11
7. *Legislation Update.* Medical Group Management Association. www.mgma.org/ legislation/fraud /10-31-98.html. 1998
8. Hammer M, Champy J. *Reengineering the Corporation.* New York: Harper Collins Publishers, 1993:32
9. Ng L. *The Paper Medical Record and The Electronic Medical Record.* Presented at Franciscan Health System, Trenton, NJ, 1998;September 28

Additional suggested reading

Abdelhak M, *et al. Health Information: Management of a Strategic Resource.* Philadelphia: W.B. Saunders, 1996

Glondys B. *Documentation Requirements of the Acute Care Records.* Chicago: American Health Information Management Association, 1996

HIM Practice Standards: Tools for Assessing Your Organization. Chicago: American Health Information Management Association, 1998

Peden AH. *Comparative Records for Health Information Management.* Albany, NY: Delmar Publishers, 1998

Chapter 2

AMBULATORY CARE

At the conclusion of this chapter you should be able to:

> Define ambulatory care and identify multiple types of facilities which are classified as ambulatory-care facilities

> List the accreditation and regulatory agencies which set standards for care and reimbursement

> Discuss the required elements of documentation and the possible outcomes of incomplete documentation

> Discuss the quality-control measures required by the Joint Commission on Accreditation of Healthcare Organizations

INTRODUCTION AND OVERVIEW

Ambulatory care is a term which covers a wide range of services for non-institutionalized patients. The large majority of ambulatory care is provided by office-based physicians[1]. The types of care available have increased over the last decade to allow patients to receive care outside of the costly hospital setting.

Ambulatory care is an alternative to inpatient hospitalization. A definition would be the provision of health-care services to outpatients and others who do not require admission to hospital as inpatients.

The shift in the predominant provision of health care from inpatient to ambulatory services has occurred for many reasons. Government influences, such as prospective payment systems at both the state and federal levels, have made organizational survival dependent on the ability of a health-care facility to minimize costs while maintaining the quality demanded by both the regulatory environment and the consumer. As the overall insurance industry has made the transition from indemnity-based programs to managed care, they have become the gatekeepers to patient access to health services. Both government and private reimbursement methods have provided the financial incentives to decrease inpatient hospital stays which results in an increased use of ambulatory services. All of these initiatives have developed in response to the overwhelming increases in the cost of health care and the continued effort to maintain or decrease these costs. In addition to these financial endeavors, changes and advances in science and technology have resulted in the decreased need for long hospital stays as health and medical issues are resolved or relieved more quickly or are addressed on an ambulatory or outpatient basis.

TYPE OF CARE RENDERED

Ambulatory care is provided in a variety of settings which include but are not limited to the following:

- Hospital-based services
- Hospices
- Urgi-centers (facilities established for urgent walk-in services)
- Managed-service organizations
- Neighborhood health centers
- Eldercare centers
- Physician group practices
- Health maintenance organizations
- Surgi-centers (ambulatory surgical centers)
- Industrial employee health services
- School health services

Many of these will be covered in separate chapters throughout this text.

LEGAL AND REGULATORY ISSUES

Licensing

Licensing for many ambulatory organizations is required at the state level by the Department of Health or an equivalent agency. Where required, individual health-care providers must also be licensed to operate within a particular state by the agency or bureau deemed responsible for this process such as the Medical Examiners Board (NJ) for physicians or state-level consumer affairs agencies having separate divisions for professionals such as nurses, pharmacists and chiropractics.

Accrediting agencies

The voluntary process of accreditation, which demonstrates a facility's compliance with a set group of standards, is available to ambulatory-care organizations through several organizations. Among those most commonly utilized are:

- Association for Accreditation of Ambulatory Health Care (AAAHC)
- Joint Commission on Accreditation of Healthcare Organizations (JCAHO)
- American Osteopathy Association (AOA)
- National Commission on Quality Assurance (NCQA)
- National Commission on Correctional Health Care (NCCHC)
- Commission on Accreditation of Rehabilitation Facilities (CARF)

The accreditation process is similar in many of these agencies. The facility applies to the organization within the allotted time frame requesting a survey of their facilities. The facility then completes a preliminary self-survey during which they are able to assess their level of compliance and make necessary corrections and improvements before the actual on-site survey is conducted. This site visit is most often conducted by a team of surveyors who spend 3–5 days at the facilities reviewing documentation such as policies, procedures, medical records and meeting minutes, as well as visually inspecting the facility for compliance with applicable standards. Depending on the outcome of the survey, the facility is granted either full accreditation for 3 years, accreditation for a lesser period of time with recommendations for improvement, or denied accreditation pending resolution of deficiencies.

Federal regulations

The Health Care Financing Administration (HCFA) is the federal agency responsible for overseeing both the Medicare program and the federal government's role in state-run Medicaid Programs. Their emphasis is primarily on quality improvement and utilization of services[2]. To be eligible for reimbursement by the federal health programs, facilities must comply with the Conditions of Participation, through which certification is granted for having met the applicable standards.

In an effort to standardize the collection of data using standard data definitions, the National Committee on Vital and Health Statistics created the Uniform Ambulatory Care Data Set in 1989 to meet agency data needs of government, research and the private sector (Table 2-1). Not all of this data must be collected in the medical record although it is recommended. Other documents may contain the required elements as long as there is a system to link all of the data required in the data set on the same patient.

Table 2-1 Uniform ambulatory care data set

Patient data items	Personal identification
	Residence
	Birth date
	Sex
	Race/ethnic background
	Living arrangement (optional)
	Marital status (optional)
Provider data items	Provider name and identification number
	Provider address
	Profession
Encounter data items	Date of encounter
	Place (if different from provider info)
	Patient reason for encounter
	Services provided including diagnostic, therapeutic and preventive
	Disposition
	Charges
	Expected source of payment

DOCUMENTATION GUIDELINES

In the ambulatory-care setting, the medical record is always open (incomplete) and continuous when it is expected that the patient will be returning. To manage efficiently the documentation of services provided by different health-care providers, the record is often source-oriented; that is, organized by the provider. You will find that each caregiver or provider records his own information. It is particularly challenging when services provided are not physically located at the same site. If the recording system is not carefully coordinated and monitored each provider might record only what is important to him or her. Another adverse result would be that the information of various providers is not tied together. This becomes apparent when you begin to scrutinize data elements and discover redundant, as well as missing, data.

In one particular study of ambulatory-care forms at a facility which has requested to remain anonymous, a review was conducted of forms completed by physicians. At this particular facility, the medical record functions had not previously been under the direction of an organized health information department but rather had been decentralized and maintained in close proximity to the practicing physician. Of the 350 forms reviewed, only 68 of those forms contained patient diagnosis, 57 contained allergy (to drugs) information and only 42 contained current medication. After this information was shared, the physicians in the facility confirmed their commitment to improve their documentation practices.

Inconsistent documentation can lead to several problems in patient care. Someone searching for information might miss essential data recorded on only some of the forms if that same information is, in fact, required on several forms. Inefficient arrangement of information will also increase the time needed to retrieve the information. If providers are unaware of their own responsibility for documenting patient information, essential data may be omitted because of an assumption that someone else will do the collection.

HCFA provides guidelines for documentation which are applicable to all types of medical and surgical services in all settings where federal reimbursement is sought. Generally, these principles state that documentation in the record should be complete and legible and that each encounter should include the following:

- Reason for the encounter
- Relevant history
- Physician exam findings
- Prior diagnostic test results
- Assessment and impression
- Plan for care
- Date
- Legible identity of provider
- Inference of rationale for diagnostic and ancillary services ordered and provided
- Identification of appropriate health risks
- Patient response to treatment and prognosis
- Supportive documentation for billed diagnostic and procedural coding schemes

Specific requirements for documenting care

Because accreditation and licensing comes from many different agencies and organizations, requirements for documentation may differ depending on the particular organization. There are many commonalities which represent good documentation practices. Stated below is an outline of the requirements of the National Commission on Quality Assurance (NCQA) which accredits many of the ambulatory-care facilities:

- Patient identification

- Biographical data to include address, employer, home and work telephone number, marital status
- Dated author identification on all entries
- Legibility to someone other than the writer
- Problem list to include significant illnesses and medical conditions
- Presence or absence of known allergies and adverse reactions are prominently noted
- History for patients seen three or more times
- Substance use documentation for patient 14 years and older
- Laboratory and other studies ordered
- Diagnosis consistent with findings
- Treatment plans consistent with diagnoses
- Notation regarding follow-up care, calls or visits with notation of time of return
- Unresolved problems from previous visit(s) indicate follow-through at next visit
- Evidence of review by primary-care physician of consultations, laboratory report and other reports filed in record
- Up-to-date immunization record
- Evidence that the patient is not placed at inappropriate risk at any time

Freestanding ambulatory care facilities are also required to document the following:

- Chief complaint/reason for visit
- Significant advice given to patient by telephone is entered in patient record

An example of a freestanding facility encounter record is shown in Exhibit 2-1. Many freestanding facilities contract with corporations to provide urgent care for work-related injuries. As these cases are covered under Workers' Compensation regulations, it is essential that appropriate information be provided to satisfy the claim and alert the employee to the time frame of disability. To demonstrate such information, two forms are included as Exhibits 2-2 and 2-3.

It is common practice for each provider to document narrative information using the SOAP format. This requires documentation of **S**ubjective information, **O**bjective findings, the **A**ssessment and the **P**lan.

RETENTION AND STORAGE

The statute of limitations for the retention of records in ambulatory-care facilities is set by the state in which the facility is licensed.

It is not unusual to find a variety of filing systems in use in one organization at different sites. This is due to a significant number of mergers in the past decade. When this occurs, a decision needs to be made which will weigh the advantages and disadvantages of combining the filing systems which would require conversion of non-conforming systems to the chosen one.

CHALLENGES OF HIM PROFESSIONALS

The role of the health information professional is constantly in transition as a result of the changes in the health-care industry. These changes include not only new technology and regulations, but the need to update departmental systems to meet the mandates of corporate mergers and acquisitions. Although the health information professional originated in the inpatient hospital setting, the opportunities outside of hospitals continue to expand with the changing health-care arena. Managers will need to have the skills necessary to assist with development of systems of good documentation of patient care and should become involved in this role for both inpatients and outpatients.

In addition the HIM professional must ensure that they have adequate input on policy development which concerns:

- Record content and format
- Release of information to care providers and other authorized users
- Confidentiality of data practices
- Collection of appropriate data for statistical purposes

PERFORMANCE IMPROVEMENT AND QUALITY ASSURANCE ACTIVITIES

In an effort to integrate performance measures into the accreditation process the Joint Commission on Accreditation of Healthcare Organizations instituted their ORYX initiative. (ORYX is not an acronym, but was chosen because it is different from any term currently used in the industry and, therefore, reflects the magnitude of anticipated changes in the years ahead.) The JCAHO ORYX initiative is required for hospitals, long-term care organizations, integrated health-care delivery networks, health plans and provider-sponsored organizations (1997) as well as behavioral health- and home-care organizations (1998).

Performance and quality statistics are based on the data collected and referred to as a unit of service. Units computed most often in ambulatory care include the following:

- Encounter: face-to-face contact
- Professional contact: includes phone contact, specimen examination, etc.
- Outpatient visit: total of all services
- Occasion of service: singular identifiable component, i.e. X-ray

With today's organizational mergers, many problems arise when different facilities collect information using different units of measurement. It becomes difficult, if not impossible, to make comparisons and merge information. In addition, there are often problems in using records for various studies because of differences in format, completion and legibility.

There are a number of quality-control mechanisms that are required by the JCAHO[3]:

- Coordinated scheduling
- Follow-up on cancelled/broken appointments
- Timely diagnosis review and reporting
- Systematic evaluation of outpatient admitted for surgery
- Dissemination of clinical information to follow-up physician
- Drug profiles and usage
- Blood usage on ambulatory-care patients
- Language of the 'majority'

Clinical data collection and coding systems

There are various classification systems used to record patient data in ambulatory care. They include:

- ICD-9-CM which is to be replaced by ICD-10, already in use in some countries. The purpose of this system is to group illnesses into a universal classification system, for the purpose of trending mortality and morbidity rates
- CPT-4 which is designed to improve the specificity necessary to reflect physician time involved in providing services and the level of difficulty involved in determining the diagnosis and treatment
- HCPCS which is built off the CPT coding system by HCFA to promote uniform reporting and statistical data collection of medical procedures, supplies, products and services

References

1. Raffel MW, Raffel NK. *US Health System*. Albany, NY: Delmar Publishers, 1994
2. Abdelhak M, *et al. Health Information: Management of a Strategic Resource*. Philadelphia: W.B. Saunders, 1996
3. Cofer J. *Health Information Management*, 10th edn. Berwyn, IL: Physician Record Co., 1994

Additional suggested reading

Ambulatory Care Documentation. Chicago: Ambulatory Care Section, American Health Information Management Association, 1997

Peden AH. *Comparative Records for Health Information Management*. Albany, NY: Delmar Publishers, 1998

Standards for Accreditation. Washington, DC: National Commission on Quality Assurance, 1998

Personal communications

Casarella, Deborah, RHIA, Health Care Support and System Administration Manager, Pinnacle Medical Group, New Brunswick, NJ, February 1998

Trezza, Judy, RHIA, Director of Medical Records, HIP of New Jersey, New Brunswick, NJ, April 1997

SAMPLE FORMS IN AMBULATORY CARE

Exhibit 2-1 ENCOUNTER RECORD

FREESTANDING MEDICAL CARE CENTER

ENCOUNTER RECORD

NAME: RECORD #

ADDRESS: ENCOUNTER DATE:

DOB: H:

AGE: W:

SEX:

DRUG ALLERGIES:

MEDICATIONS:

BP:____/_____   P: _____ R:_____   LMP ____/____/_____   LAST TET:___/___/____   WT:_____

NURSING ASSESSMENT:

_____RN

HISTORY:

PHYSICAL FINDINGS:

IMPRESSION

LAB/X-RAY FINDINGS   TREATMENT PLAN AND MEDICATIONS

CALL BACK

REFER/ADMIT TO: REVISIT: ____PRN _____ DAYS _____ MOS

WRITTEN REFERRAL COMPLETED: Y   N   N/A

SIGN: _____MD

Exhibit 2-2 EMPLOYER REFERRAL FORM

FREESTANDING FACILITY
EMPLOYER REFERRAL FORM
INITIAL INJURY REPORT

COMPANY _____

AUTHORIZED BY _____ | TEL. NO. _____

SIGNED _____ | DATE _____

EMPLOYEE NAME
POSITION _____

SERVICE REQUESTED (Please check):
☐ Worker's Compensation Treatment
☐ Pre-employment/Annual physical: ☐ Perm/Regular ☐ Temp
☐ Second Opinion/Disability Exam
☐ Illness Evaluation at Employer's Request
☐ Other _____

EMPLOYMENT STATUS:
☐ Cleared for Employment – no activity restrictions
☐ Cleared for Employment – with activity restrictions as follows:
☐ Should not work until further information is obtained

INITIAL INJURY REPORT

Date of first symptom/injury _____
Nature of illness/injury

_____

_____ X-RAY TAKEN? _____

Related to employment: Yes ☐ No ☐ Undetermined ☐
If yes, how did patient say injury occurred

_____

Probable period of treatment: _____
Does illness/injury prevent working? Yes ☐ No ☐
If so, for how long? _____

Signed _____MD   Date _____

Exhibit 2-3 INJURY STATUS REPORT

FRONT DESK COMPLETES INFORMATION IN BOX   CASE REFERENCE #

NAME	SOCIAL SECURITY #	EMPLOYEE SIGNATURE	TIME IN
EMPLOYER	PHONE #	FAX #	TIME OUT
DATE OF INJURY	DATE OF VISIT	INFO VERIFIED AS COMPLETE AND ACCURATE	

A. Chief complaint: (initial visit must state how work related)

B. Findings: C. Diagnosis:

D. Treatment plan/test ordered (referrals must be authorized):

E. Medications:

F.   Duty status: Return to work date:
     ☐ Full duty
     ☐ Restricted duty (complete section G) _____☐ Projected
     ☐ Unable to work   ☐ Determined

G. Authorized activity level

Capability		Activity	Weight limit	Time/frequency limitations	H. Other comments
Yes	No				
☐	☐	Sitting		_____	
☐	☐	Standing		_____	
☐	☐	Walking		_____	
☐	☐	Carrying	_____	_____	
☐	☐	Bending		_____	
☐	☐	Lifting	_____	_____	
☐	☐	Squatting		_____	**I. NEXT APPOINTMENT**
☐	☐	Pushing/pulling _____		_____	
☐	☐	Grasping/handling		_____	Date _____ Time _____
☐	☐	Reaching above shoulder		_____	
☐	☐	Climbing (except to/from job)		_____	

Treating Physician _____
                          Signature   Print Name

Fax sent to: ☐ Employer ☐ MCO Photocopies to: ☐ Case Manager ☐ Billing

Completed by: _____ Date _____

Chapter 3

HOSPITAL-BASED AMBULATORY CARE

At the conclusion of this chapter you should be able to:

> Describe the major categories of ambulatory care provided in the hospital setting
>
> List the most common agencies offering accreditation to hospital-based ambulatory care services
>
> Describe the required elements of documentation for clinical records
>
> Identify customary retention methods of records in these settings

INTRODUCTION AND OVERVIEW

Within the hospital complex there are most often many services provided which are not inpatient services, but rather services where a patient is expected to return to their own living circumstances and not remain overnight. These services are of a wide variety but can generally be categorized into one of the four areas covered in this chapter.

The four major categories of the hospital-based ambulatory care setting are:

1. Ancillary Services
2. Organized Outpatient Department (a/k/a primary-care center)
3. Emergency Department
4. Ambulatory Surgery Department

TYPE OF CARE RENDERED

'Ancillary Service' is a term given to services provided which are independent of evaluation and management services (general medical examinations). These include testing services as requested, or ordered, by physicians in the outpatient department or in their private offices. The patient is usually required to have a written request (an order or prescription) signed by the physician. There are exceptions to this, however. In order to encourage continued health monitoring, most facilities permit self-referral for many screening tests such as mammograms.

Physicians are required to include a tentative or working diagnosis or reason for testing. The patient most often registers as an outpatient and is seen by hospital technical staff (see Exhibit 3-1). Depending on the services requested, they also may be seen by a physician employed by the facility for a particular specialty.

The facility will usually only maintain copies of the reports and send the original reports back to the requesting physician for inclusion in the patient's medical record (see Exhibits 3-2 and 3-3).

Procedures are often already coded on a check-off type of form or included in the computer's database so that when the charge is posted the code is assigned. This is done when procedure codes are linked to descriptions of services and their associated charges in the chargemaster of the facility.

Traditionally, the 'Organized Outpatient Department' of a hospital would refer to the hospital's clinic system (Table 3-1). However, many hospitals without clinic systems will often refer to their network of ancillary services as their outpatient department. Historically clinics are only found in teaching hospitals and urban areas (low-income areas without primary physicians.) Clinics are separate from emergency departments and handle non-urgent patients. They include primary and specialty care in all disciplines, i.e. family practice, orthopedics, cardiology, etc. The medical or family practice clinic will make necessary referrals to specialty services. Patients may also be referred by the emergency department for follow-up care directly to the specialty departments.

Table 3-1 Outpatient service usage statistics[1]

Visits in 1996	67 million
Covered by insurance	80%
Most common payment type	Fee for service (followed by HMO)
Most common source of payment	Government (47%)

The hospital 'Emergency Department' is designed and staffed to treat patients in need of emergency or urgent care provided on an as-needed basis (Table 3-2). Patients are treated for symptoms, illnesses and injuries which can either be readily resolved or the patient is referred for further care. This can be provided as an inpatient after admission to the same facility, or the patient is referred by transfer to another facility for services not provided at the emergency facility or referred to a clinical or private physician.

Table 3-2 Emergency room usage statistics[1]

Visits in 1996	90 million
Most common problem	Injury treatment (40%)
Most common source of payment	78% covered by insurance

A chronic problem with overcrowding is often the result of too many people who use the emergency department as their primary-care physician because they have no other means of care or they have no insurance or money to pay for non-emergency services. The emergency department cannot turn them away without assessing their problem.

Emergency Department records are considered a form of ambulatory-care record because most of the patients seen are not admitted, but are sent home. These records must permit the recording of intensive medical intervention over a relatively brief period of time. Because of this they are well organized and include little need for long narrative reports. Instead they often consist of a collection of check-off and fill-in areas for rapid recording of vital information.

The 'Ambulatory Surgery Department', also called the 'Same Day Surgery Unit', is different from the outpatient department in that the procedures performed on patients in this unit are actually operative procedures. It is intended for patients who need surgical intervention in a fully equipped operating room with minor postoperative observation, but do not require an overnight stay (usually). Patients receiving these services are often registered by much the same procedure as inpatients.

PATIENT POPULATION

Patients referred to, or seeking, hospital-based ambulatory care services are either self-referred or referred by their primary physician or managed-care organization. It is expected that patients using these ambulatory services will more likely than not return to their primary residence. An exception to this would be emergency room patients in need of further care and evaluation who need admission to the inpatient setting.

LEGAL AND REGULATORY ISSUES

Licensing

Ambulatory services which are based in hospitals and medical centers are included in the licensing of the overall facility. This license to operate as a medical facility would be obtained from the state in which the facility is located unless it is a federal facility in which case the facility would operate under the regulatory environment of the federal government.

Accrediting agencies

As with licensing, the accreditation processes of hospital-based ambulatory services are incorporated into the process of accrediting the facility. Accreditation is sought from the Joint Commission on the Accreditation of Healthcare Organization (JCAHO), the American Osteopathy Association (AOA), and in some cases further accreditation status is sought for the ambulatory services from the Association for the Accreditation of Ambulatory Health Care (AAAHC).

RELEASE OF INFORMATION

Unless the ambulatory-care service is organized as a separate department which manages its own medical records, the requests for health information are usually processed and responded to by the Health Information Management Department along with the requests for inpatient information. Like all health information, the state and federal rules pertaining to confidentiality apply to the release of ambulatory records as they would inpatient hospital records.

DOCUMENTATION GUIDELINES

The Emergency Department record starts with triage of the patient (except ambulance arrivals). Triage is an assessment of the patient's condition to determine the urgency of his/her need for treatment. In a situation where many patients may arrive at the same time, there must be this system to assess which patient has the greatest need, as delays in prompt care can be critical to the well-being and survival of the patient (see Exhibits 3-4 and 3-5).

With emergency department records, documentation is essential in determining the level of care provided which is the basis for reimbursement.

In many facilities the emergency room clerical staff analyze the record for completeness, often within 24 hours of the visit. They are specifically looking for the presence and completeness of the chief complaint, history, physical exam, disposition, signatures, diagnosis and times recorded on all entries.

Hospital ambulatory-care organizations (clinics) are required to use an encounter summary or problem list which includes the significant diagnoses, conditions, procedures, known adverse drug reactions and current medications. When this inform-ation is collected onto one form, all health-care providers evaluating and treating the patient in the clinic setting are able to see the significant issues which have been resolved and which are ongoing allowing them to make more accurate clinical decisions. Exhibits 3-6 through 3-12 are examples of forms used in the hospital-based clinic setting.

RETENTION AND STORAGE

The Emergency Department record usually stays with the patient while the patient is being serviced in the emergency area. If the patient is admitted, the record becomes part of the inpatient record. Records of patients not admitted are usually filed by date and held in the ER for a specific period of time.

Many facilities hold the emergency room records in the ER (often for 4–6 weeks). This allows the records to be immediately available should the patient return; however, if coding for reimbursement is not performed in the emergency department, this would cause a significant delay in billing. After the initial holding period, they are then usually forwarded to the 'Health Information Management' (HIM) department for permanent filing. Most HIM departments continue to maintain them (alphabetically) by date order in a special filing section of the department. Hospitals with true unit filing systems will interfile the emergency record in the patient's medical record folder containing other health information such as inpatient admissions and outpatient encounters.

Regardless of the filing system in use, the information available to the ER is for life and death situations and therefore must be retrievable.

CHALLENGES OF HIM PROFESSIONALS

An interesting role of the health information management professionals would be his or her department's assigned duties during an emergency room disaster drill (or actual disaster event). The drill is performed to allow the hospital staff to be fully prepared to handle the care and treatment of casualties of a large-scale incident, such as a plane crash or plant explosion. These drills, which are often unannounced, bring a large number of patients into the emergency department in a relatively short amount of time. Responsibility of the HIM staff usually centers around information collection, i.e. registration and record number assignment. It is astounding how quickly patients will be processed; therefore it is recommended that advance preparations be made, i.e. having pre-numbered charts made up in advance for this purpose. There is no way of knowing how many will be needed so you have to balance between how many you can afford to store and put aside and what the maximum number of casualties might be. An additional problem will arise as patients are quickly triaged, treated and released if no further care is needed. In order to alleviate an overcrowded situation, patients with minor injuries (or no obvious trauma) may be requested to leave even though registration may not be complete as to receiving full names, billing information, etc.

Coding is usually another area of responsibility for the health information management department. Procedure codes can often be tied in to the chargemaster for automatic posting; however, review of services provided is recommended to insure that all appropriate codes for procedures as well as diagnostic codes are applied (see Exhibits 3-13, 3-14 and 3-15).

Coding in ambulatory services areas and the emergency department is often done by clerical personnel who have received minimal coding education or on-the-job training.

Ambulatory surgery records are most often coded in the health information management department since they are treated as inpatient records, often following the same format and processing guidelines.

PERFORMANCE IMPROVEMENT AND QUALITY ASSURANCE ACTIVITIES

Some of the performance improvement activities which take place in the hospital-based ambulatory care settings include assessment of waiting time in outpatient, ancillary and emergency departments as well as monitoring the record availability for patients who have been seen at the facility in the past.

Reference

1.   Ambulatory medical care in 1996. *Public Health Reports.* 1998;113:184

Additional suggested reading

Abdelhak M, *et al. Health Information: Management of a Strategic Resource.* Philadelphia: W.B. Saunders, 1996

Cofer J. *Health Information Management*, 10th edn. Berwyn, IL: Physician Record Co., 1994

Peden AH. *Comparative Records for Health Information Management.* Albany, NY: Delmar Publishers, 1998

Personal communications

Gaston-Kelly, Octavia, RHIA, Director of Health Information Services, Newark Beth Israel Medical Center, Newark, NJ, December 1998

Omangi, Josephine, RHIA, Manager, Outpatient Medical Records, Newark Beth Israel Medical Center, October 1998

SAMPLE FORMS IN HOSPITAL-BASED AMBULATORY CARE

Exhibit 3-1 OUTPATIENT REGISTRATION SHEET

OUTPATIENT RECORD

LAST NAME, FIRST, MI			ADDRESS						TELEPHONE			MED MAN RELIGION

APT. #	CITY			STATE	ZIP CODE		RESIDENT CD	SOC. SEC. #		BIRTHDATE		AGE	SEX

ROOM	BED	ACM	SERV.	STATUS	PREV. NBIMC	OTHER HOSP.			ADDRESS			DISCH DATE	TIME

ADM. BY	DATE OF ADM.	TIME	ENCOUNTER #	UNIT #		AREA							COMP

PATIENT'S EMPLOYER	ADDRESS		TELEPHONE	EXTENSION

CITY	STATE	ZIP CODE	OCCUPATION	FATHER'S NAME	MOTHER'S MAIDEN NAME

GUARANTOR	ADDRESS		TELEPHONE	TEL-WORK

APT. #	CITY	STATE	ZIP CODE	RELATIONSHIP	GUARANTOR SOC. SEC.

GUARANTOR'S EMPLOYER	ADDRESS		TELEPHONE	EXTENSION

CITY	STATE	ZIP CODE	OCCUPATION	IN-HOUSE TRANSFER 1. 2. 3.

NEXT OF KIN	ADDRESS		TELEPHONE	TEL-WORK

APT. #	CITY	STATE	ZIP CODE	RELATIONSHIP	

FC	PLAN	PLAN NAME	SERV	CODE	EFF. DATE	PTB	SUBSCRIBER	REL	POLICY/ID #	GRP/PRES #
FC	PLAN	PLAN NAME	SERV	CODE	EFF. DATE	PTB	SUBSCRIBER	REL	POLICY/ID #	GRP/PRES #
FC	PLAN	PLAN NAME	SERV	CODE	EFF. DATE	PTB	SUBSCRIBER	REL	POLICY/ID #	GRP/PRES #
FC	PLAN	PLAN NAME	SERV	CODE	EFF. DATE	PTB	SUBSCRIBER	REL	POLICY/ID #	GRP/PRES #
FC	PLAN	PLAN NAME	SERV	CODE	EFF. DATE	PTB	SUBSCRIBER	REL	POLICY/ID #	GRP/PRES #

OTHER INSURANCE MAILING ADDRESS	CITY	STATE	ZIP CODE	TELEPHONE

TYPE OF SERVICE	INFO SOURCE	RTN PHYSICAL	AUTO ACCIDENT	DATE

DIAG CODE	DIAGNOSIS

PHYSICIAN NAME	PHYSICIAN NAME	PHYSICIAN NAME

REMARKS

Exhibit 3-2 DIAGNOSTIC RADIOLOGY REPORT

REPORT:

_____   _____M.D.
         DATE   RADIOLOGIST

EXAM(S) REQUESTED:	REQUEST DATE	AGE	DOB	SEX	X-RAY NO.			
	PREV. X-RAY HERE		CLASS: □ I/P □ ER					
			□ REF. □ PAT		DATE COMPLETED			
	□ AMBUL. □ PORT. □ STRETCHER □ OR							
REASON FOR EXAM: (MUST BE COMPLETED)	NAME				FILMS USED	14X17	11X14	10X12
						8X10	9X9	105MM
	ADDRESS				TECH NOTES:			
ALLERGIES □ YES □ NO PREGNANT □ YES □ NO	DOCTOR:							
□ PRE-OP	FC: □ BCBS □ MCARE □ MCAID □ SELF				TECH. SIGNATURE			
□ EMERGENCY_____ MD	□ COMP □ COMML □ EMPLOYEE							

DIAGNOSTIC RADIOLOGY

Exhibit 3-3 SURGICAL PATHOLOGY REPORT

☐ PHOTO	DATE OF OPERATION	DATE RECEIVED	(LEAVE BLANK) PATH NO.
SURGEON /uHC	RESIDENT		

PRE-OPERATIVE DIAGNOSIS:

POST-OPERATIVE DIAGNOSIS:

OPERATIVE PROCEDURE:

PREVIOUS SPECIMEN IN N.B.I.M.C.? ☐ NO ☐ YES—WHEN

SPECIMENS:	1.
PLEASE	2.
LABEL	3.
ALL	4.
SPECIMEN	5.
CONTAINERS	6.

CLINICAL DATA:
(A REPORT WILL NOT BE GIVEN UNLESS THIS SECTION IS COMPLETED)

GYN. ONLY: **L.M.P.**   **Hormones:**   **Radiation:**

COMPLETED BY: M.D.

☐   ☐   ☐   ☐   *DO NOT WRITE BELOW THIS LINE*   ☐   ☐   ☐   ☐   ☐
1   2   3   4   S   S6Mo. D   T.R. T.C.

CODE:

MICROSCOPIC:

DIVISION OF PATHOLOGY   **SURGICAL PATHOLOGY**

Exhibit 3-4 EMERGENCY DEPARTMENT RECORD

DEPARTMENT OF EMERGENCY MEDICINE

E.D No.	Med. Rec. No.	Triage Form	Date	Time	Registrar ID	Phys Code	DX Code

Emergency Department:	Emergent 201-8052	Urgent 201-8045	Semi Urgent-NP 201-8079	Semi Urgent-P 201-8067	Non Urgent 201-8029	M/S	N/C 201-7797	Birthdate	Sex	Age	Mar

PESS:	On. Cris. 089-9755	Onc. Scr. 089-9754	Psy. Eval 089-9757	PES F/U 089-9758	Off. Scr 089-9756	Stab 4 089-9759	Stab 8 089-9760	Stab 12 089-9761	Stab 24 089-9762	Employee on Duty Yes No	Religion	Race

PATIENT

Patient Name - Last, First, MI	Address			Telephone-Home
City	State	Zip Code	Soc. Sec. No.	Telephone-Work
Guarantor (Bill to) Name:	Address			Telephone-Home
City	State	Zip Code	Relationship	Telephone-Work
Nearest Relative (for Emergency Notification)	Address			Telephone-Home
City	State	Zip Code	Relationship	Telephone-Work
Employer (Pt or Guardian)	Address			Telephone
City	State	Zip Code	Occupation	Deposit

INSURANCE

Payor Code	Payor Name		Plan Name
Policy Holder Name/Sub/HOH		Policy Holder's Relationship to Patient	Grp/Pers No.	Policy #
Payor Code	Payor Name		Plan
Policy Holder Name/Sub/HOH		Policy Holder's Relationship to Patient	Grp/Pers No.	Policy #
Insurance Claim Mailing Address	City	St	Zip Code	Grp Name on Card

Mode of Arrival	Police Notified	Precinct No	Time	Accident Type
		Name	Badge No.	
Date	Time	Place		

DISPOSITION

❏ DOA ❏ AMA ❏ ME Notified ❏ Accepted ❏ Released Transfer To: _____ Accepted By: _____
❏ DIE ❏ Walk Out Name: _____

Admit To: _____ Physician: _____ ❏ Private # of Valuables: ❏ None ❏ Family ❏ Safe
Time: _____ Room: _____ ❏ Service _____ ❏ Self ❏ Police ❏ Other

Final Diagnosis: ❏ Treat/Release Time Discharge/ Transfer _____ am pm ❏ Stable ❏ Improved ❏ Other

Return to work/school: An appointment has been made for you in the _____ clinic on _____ at _____
❏ Yes ❏ No When: _____ Please contact your primary care physician (PCP) for follow-up by: _____

FOLLOW-UP

Diagnosed and treated in my presence and under my supervision:

_____ Student/Resident Signature _____ Print   _____ Attending Physicians Signature _____ Print

Discharge RX (Dose; Frequency; Duration)
_____
_____

❏ Dose of Antibiotic Given in E.D. ❏ Medication Given in E.D. That Makes Driving Dangerous ❏ Tetanus Toxoid Given in E.D.

I hereby acknowledge that I have received and understand both written and verbal recommendations and instructions pertaining to my condition. I understand that I have had emergency treatment only. I will arrange for follow-up care as instructed above.

UP

_____ Signature   _____ Relationship (if other than patient)

_____ Discharged By: MD or RN (witness)   _____ Disch. Inst. #

EMERGENCY DEPARTMENT RECORD (continued)

RELEASE — REFUSAL OF TREATMENT

I refuse to allow and specifically forbid anyone to _____ , as such medical procedure or treatment is contrary to my wishes. The risks attendant to such refusal have been fully explained to me as (M.D. fill in) _____
_____ , and I fully understand that my refusal for such procedure or treatment may seriously imperil my health and/or my life (the life of _____) or may result in serious disability. I herewith release the Newark Beth Israel Medical Center, its physicians, nurses, employees, and agents from any and all liability for respecting and following my express wishes and directions.

Signed _____ Relationship _____

Witness _____ Date _____

RELEASE — SELF DISCHARGE AGAINST MEDICAL ADVICE

I herewith assume full responsibility for my own care and custody (the care and custody of _____), having demanded my (his/her) discharge from this hospital contrary to the advice of the Emergency Department physician(s) who have been evaluating/treating me (him/her). The risks attendant to my decision have been fully explained to me as (M.D. fill in) _____
and I understand that my decision may seriously imperil my (his/her) health and/or life or may result in serious disability. I herewith release the Newark Beth Israel Medical Center, its physicians, nurses, employees, and agents from any and all liability.

Signed _____ Relationship _____

Witness _____ Date _____

CONSENT FOR MEDICAL TREATMENT

I hereby consent to the rendering of care to the patient indicated on the reverse side, which may include routine diagnostic procedures and such medical treatment as the attending physician(s) or others of the hospital's medical staff consider to be necessary, including but not limited to: drawing blood samples (both venous and arterial); starting intravenous lines; taking X-rays; administering oxygen; cleaning and suturing open wounds; cessation of bleeding using standard techniques; splinting/casting of possible bone, joint, or soft tissue injuries; administering routine medications considered necessary for evaluation/treatment of the patient's condition. It is understood that this consent does not include any operation or diagnostic procedure beyond routine necessary tests; if such operation or procedures are required at a later time, I understand that I will be asked to give special consent for these. I understand that the patient has the right to refuse consent to any proposed procedure or therapeutic course. I understand that the practice of medicine is not an exact science and that diagnosis and treatment may involve risks of injury, or even death. I acknowledge that no guarantees have been made to me as to the result of examination or treatment in this hospital. I realize that among those who attend patients at this medical center are medical, nursing, and other health care personnel in training who, unless otherwise requested, may be present during patient care as part of their education. I agree to hold free and harmless the medical center's employees and physicians who rendered this care.

GUARANTEE OF PAYMENT

For and in consideration of the services rendered, I do hereby guarantee to pay to the Newark Beth Israel Medical Center and to the Emergency Department Physicians the full and entire amount of any and all bills rendered for said patient which are not covered by the patient's medical insurance.

I have been given the opportunity to read this form and ask any questions I may have. I understand that I may ask for further explanation at any time.

Signed _____ Relationship _____

Witness _____ Date _____

CONSENT FOR PAYMENT AND RELEASE OF INFORMATION

If I, as patient or guarantor, am covered by Blue Cross, Blue Shield, Medicare, Medicaid, Commercial insurance, Health Maintenance Organizations (HMO's), or any other insurance, I authorize the insurance carrier(s) to make payments for the services that I or the patient received or will receive from Newark Beth Israel Medical Center and their physicians. By physicians, I mean those from whom I received or will receive services in relation to this hospital encounter (spell of illness) which includes, but is not limited to the Medical Center's attending physicians, the NBIMC Emergency Doctors' Panel, and the Medical Center's Radiologists group. I permit a copy of this authorization to be used in place of the original.

I consent and authorize the Medical Center, the Medical Center's attending physicians, NBIMC Emergency Doctors' Panel, the Medical Center's Radiologists group, and any other physician from whom I or the patient received or will receive medical attention in regard to this hospital encounter (spell of illness) to release to Medicare, Medicaid, Blue Cross, Blue Shield, Commercial insurance, HMO's, or any other medical plan or its authorized agents any information regarding any diagnosis, prognosis, or treatment or other aspects of my stay at the Medical Center or outpatient services received from the Medical Center (including such as may have been related to drug or alcohol abuse or treatment for same) that is necessary for them to make payment on this or related claims. I understand that this consent is subject to revocation at any time, except to the extent that action has been taken in reliance thereon and will expire without express revocation after all bills rendered to me have been paid in full.

Signed _____ Relationship _____

Witness _____ Date _____

EMERGENCY DEPARTMENT RECORD (continued)

❑ CBC	❑ CHEMISTRY	❑ URINE	❑ ABG	❑ OTHER TESTS
TIME _____	TIME _____	ßHCG _____	TIME _____	❑ SGOT ❑ ßHCG
RBC _____	Na _____	AZ _____	FIO$_2$ _____	❑ SGPT ❑ T Bili
WBC _____	K _____	pH _____	pH _____	❑ Alk. Phos ❑ D Bili
Hgb _____	CO$_2$ _____	SpGr _____	PCO$_2$ _____	❑ Culture
Hct _____	Cl _____	Alb _____	BE _____	❑ Gram Stain
PLT _____	BS _____	Gluc _____	HCO$_3$ _____	❑ Other_____
Segs _____	BUN _____	Acct _____	PO$_2$ _____	❑ Other_____
Bands _____	Creat _____	Bld _____	O$_2$Sat _____	❑ Other_____
Lymphs _____	CK _____	Leuk _____	COHg _____	❑ PULSE OXIMETRY
Baso _____	MB _____	WBC _____	MetHgb _____	TIME %
Eos _____	LDH _____	RBC _____	Na _____	1 _____
Other _____	LD$_1$ _____	Epi _____	K _____	
Other _____	Amylase _____	Bact _____	Hgb _____	2 _____
Other _____	Lipase _____	Casts _____		3 _____

X-RAY	X-RAY	X-RAY	DATA REVIEWED
			❑ Run Sheet
			❑ Transfer/NH Forms
			❑ Previous ED Chart
			❑ NBIMC Med. Record

EKG Time:	Rate:	Rhythm:	Other:	❑ Previous X-Ray
EKG Time:	Rate:	Rhythm:	Other:	❑ Other_____

Assessment/Medical Decision Making

_____

_____

_____

_____

_____

_____

_____

_____

_____

_____

_____

_____

Dictation #

TIME	ORDERED BY	PHYSICIAN ORDERS	ROUTE/SITE	TIME	NURSE

E.D. NO.	MEDICAL RECORD NO.	PATIENT'S LAST NAME - LAST, FIRST	BIRTH DATE	AGE	SEX	DATE	E.D. RM. NO.

EMERGENCY DEPARTMENT RECORD (continued)

Location _____
Arrival _____
Triage _____
Nursing _____

Reason for Today's Visit: _____
_____

❏ NBIMC

PMD: _____ ❏ Other   Clinic: _____   Last ED Visit: _____

Vital Signs		Present Medications:	Allergies:
Time	_____	_____	_____
Temp	_____	_____	_____
Pulse	_____	_____	_____
R	_____	_____	_____
BP	_____	_____	_____
WT	_____	_____	_____

LMP _____   Last Tetanus _____   Wrist ID _____   Nurse's Signature _____   Print _____

HISTORY OF PRESENT ILLNESS/ROS (Gen'l, Eyes, ENT, Resp, CV, GI, GU, Musc/Skel, Skin, Neuro, Psych, Hema/Immuno, Endo)

Time: _____
_____
_____
_____
_____
_____

PAST MEDICAL HISTORY

❏ CAD _____   ❏ CHF _____
❏ HTN _____   ❏ DM _____
❏ CVA _____   ❏ HIV _____
❏ Asthma _____   ❏ COPD _____
❏ _____
❏ _____

SOCIAL HISTORY

YES   NO
❏   ❏   Smoke _____
❏   ❏   Alcohol _____
❏   ❏   IVDA _____
❏   ❏   Drugs _____
Other _____

FAMILY HISTORY

❏ DM _____
❏ HTN _____
❏ Cardiac _____
❏ CA _____
❏ Asthma _____
❏ _____

PHYSICAL EXAM/ROS CATEGORIES: (Gen'l, Eyes, ENT, Resp, CV, GI, GU, Musc/Skel, Skin, Neuro, Psych, Hema/Immuno, Endo)

Time: _____
_____
_____
_____
_____
_____
_____

Time	Procedures/Re-evaluation/Communications
_____	_____
_____	_____
_____	_____
_____	_____
_____	_____
_____	_____
_____	_____
_____	_____

Patient Endorsed to Dr. _____ who accepts responsibility for the further evaluation and treatment of this patient.

_____   _____   _____
Time   Signature   Print

E.D. NO.	MEDICAL RECORD NO.	PATIENT'S LAST NAME - LAST, FIRST	BIRTH DATE	AGE	SEX	DATE	E.D. RM. NO.

Exhibit 3-5 EMERGENCY DEPARTMENT ADULT TRIAGE ASSESSMENT FORM

DEPARTMENT OF EMERGENCY MEDICINE

ADULT TRIAGE / ASSESSMENT FORM

ADDRESSOGRAPH

DATE	TIME	MODE OF ARRIVAL	❏ WALKING ❏ WHEELCHAIR	❏ CARRIED ❏ ALS ❏ BLS	ED #	MR #

NAME			AGE	SEX M F	PMD / HMO (PCP)

PREHOSPITAL TREATMENT
❏ NONE ❏ CERVICAL COLLAR ❏ BACKBOARD ❏ SPLINT/SITE _____ ❏ OTHER_____
❏ IV _____ ❏ MEDS _____ ❏ O₂ _____ L / MIN. VIA _____

CHIEF COMPLAINT	VITAL SIGNS	T	P	R	BP
	MEDS				

ASSESSMENT	
	ALLERGIES
	PMH

TRIAGE INTERVENTIONS ❏ NONE	LAST ED VISIT	LAST TETANUS ❏ N/A ❏ > 5 YRS ❏ < 5 YRS. ❏ UNKNOWN	LMP

TRIAGE ASSESSMENT

TRIAGE CATEGORY	❏ EMERGENT I ❏ URGENT II ❏ SEMI-URGENT III	TRIAGE RN SIGNATURE

RN ASSESSMENT TIME	VITAL SIGNS	T	P	R	BP	RA LA	LOCATION

SYSTEMS ASSESSMENT

AIRWAY & BREATHING
- ❏ PATENT
- ❏ UNLABORED
- ❏ LABORED

R   LUNGS   L
- ❏   CLEAR   ❏
- ❏   DIMINISHED   ❏
- ❏   ABSENT   ❏
- ❏   WHEEZES   ❏
- ❏   RALES   ❏
- ❏   RHONCHI   ❏

MENTAL STATUS
- ❏ A & OX _____
- ❏ RESPONDS TO VERBAL
- ❏ RESPONDS TO PAIN
- ❏ UNRESPONSIVE
- ❏ LOSS OF CONSCIOUSNESS   DURATION _____
- ❏ SEIZURE ACTIVITY
- ❏ FLEXION / DECORTICATE
- ❏ EXTENSION / DECEREB.
- ❏ OTHER _____

ABDOMEN ❏ N/A
- ❏ SOFT
- ❏ NONTENDER
- ❏ RIGID
- ❏ TENDER
- ❏ DISTENDED
- ❏ BS
- ❏ PAIN _____
- ❏ VOMITING _____
- ❏ DIARRHEA _____
- ❏ GYN SX _____
- ❏ GU SX _____

EXTREMITIES ❏ N/A

	UPPER R L		LOWER R L
❏ ❏	PAIN	❏ ❏
❏ ❏	PALLOR	❏ ❏
❏ ❏	PARALYSIS	❏ ❏
❏ ❏	PARASTHESIA	❏ ❏
❏ ❏	EDEMA	❏ ❏
❏ ❏	ECCHYMOSIS	❏ ❏
❏ ❏	DEFORMITY	❏ ❏

CIRCULATORY / SKIN
- ❏ NORMAL   ❏ CLAMMY
- ❏ PALE   ❏ DIAPHORETIC
- ❏ CYANOTIC   ❏ WARM
- ❏ JAUNDICE   ❏ HOT
- ❏ DRY   ❏ COOL
- ❏ MOIST   ❏ COLD
- ❏ CAPILLARY REFILL _____
- ❏ DISTAL PULSES
  - RUE _____
  - LUE _____
  - RLE _____
  - LLE _____
- ❏ OTHER _____

PUPILS ❏ N/A

R		L
❏	PERRL	❏
❏	PINPOINT	❏
❏	DILATED	❏
❏	REACTIVE	❏
❏	SLUGGISH	❏
❏	BRISK	❏
❏	NON-REACTIVE	❏

_____ SIZE _____

VISUAL ACUITY ❏ N/A
OD _____ OS _____

P U P I L   S I Z E
2
3
4
5
6
7
8
9

CHEST PAIN ❏ N/A
- CHARACTER _____
- LOCATION _____
- RADIATES TO _____
- DURATION _____
- ❏ DIAPHORESIS   ❏ SOB
- ❏ NAUSEA   ❏ VOMITING
- ❏ DIZZINESS
- ❏ REPRODUCIBLE c̄

INTERVENTIONS BY PT. _____

PAIN SCALE
0 _____ 10
NO PAIN ⌊⌊⌊⌊⌊⌊⌊⌊⌊⌊⌋ WORST PAIN
WORST____ NOW____

NECK / BACK ❏ N/A
- ❏ PAIN
- ❏ LOCATION _____
- ❏ PT. DENIES
- ❏ RADIATES TO _____

RN SIGNATURE _____

WHITE - ORIGINAL   CANARY - FILE COPY

EMERGENCY DEPARTMENT ADULT TRIAGE ASSESSMENT FORM (continued)

IV THERAPY						MEDICATIONS				
TIME	SITE	SOLUTION	GAUGE	RATE	BY	TIME	MEDICATION	DOSE	ROUTE	INIT.

TOTAL INTAKE AND OUTPUT			
INTAKE IV	INTAKE PO	OUTPUT URINE	OUTPUT OTHER

INTERVENTIONS

TIME   TIME

_____ O₂ VIA _____ @ _____ L/MIN   _____ TO X-RAY FOR _____ RETURNED _____
_____ O₂ SAT-RA _____ , O₂ _____   _____ LABS SENT _____
_____ PEAK FLOW _____   _____ WOUND DRESSED _____
_____ ABG SITE _____ BY _____   _____ ACE SPLINT SLING/SITE _____
_____ MONITOR RHYTHM _____   _____ ICE & ELEVATION/SITE _____
_____ EKG - SHOWN TO _____   _____ C COLLAR: APPLIED/REMOVED BY _____
_____ FOLEY (Size/Return) _____   _____ BACKBOARD REMOVED BY _____
_____ NGT (Size/Return) _____   _____ SIDERAILS UP AND LOCKED _____
_____ ACCUCHECK (60-120) _____   _____ RESTRAINTS _____
_____ OTHER _____   _____ OTHER _____

ONGOING ASSESSMENT/TREATMENT/RESPONSE

TIME	VITALS	NOTES

Exhibit 3-6 PEDIATRIC HEALTH HISTORY – AGE 6–12 YEARS

DATE: _____ INFORMANT: _____ PRIMARY LANGUAGE: _____ PVT. PHYSICIAN: _____	 *ADDRESSOGRAPH*

ALLERGIES (CHECK IF YES AND DESCRIBE)

	PENICILLIN		OTHER DRUGS:
	FOODS:		
	NONE KNOWN		OTHER:

CHILDHOOD ILLNESS

	CHICKEN POX		BRONCHITIS/ASTHMA		CONVULSIONS
	ANEMIA		VISION PROBLEM		OTHER

HOSPITALIZATIONS INCLUDE SIGNIFICANT BIRTH HISTORY, I.E. NICU

DATE	PROBLEM	FACILITY

FAMILY HISTORY

MOTHER'S AGE: FATHER'S AGE:

	ASTHMA		DIABETES		TUBERCULOSIS
	CONVULSIONS		HIV/AIDS		BIRTH DEFECT
	CANCER		HYPERTENSION		OTHER
	EARLY DEATH		SICKLE CELL DISEASE		

SIGNATURE _____TITLE _____ DATE _____

SOCIAL HISTORY

PRIMARY CARETAKER	
SUPPORT SYSTEM	
SCHOOL	
PERFORMANCE	

SIGNATURE _____ TITLE _____ DATE _____

ANTICIPATORY GUIDANCE/DEVELOPMENT

DATE & INITIAL	6–8 YEARS	DATE & INITIAL	9–11 YEARS
	KNOWS NAME, ADDRESS, PHONE NO.		RELATES TO A PEER GROUP
	CAN CONTACT POLICE/FIRE DEPT		INVOLVED IN SPECIAL INTEREST OR ACTIVITY
	BIKE IS LIGHTED/HELMET		AWARENESS OF TOBACCO, DRUG AND ALCOHOL ABUSE
	BASIC TRAFFIC LAWS KNOWN		BEGINNING AWARENESS OF PUBESCENT SEXUALITY
	HAS SOME RESPONSIBILITY		MENARCHE
	AWARENESS OF TOBACCO, DRUG AND ALCOHOL ABUSE		

Signature _____Title _____Date _____

Signature _____Title _____Date _____

Signature _____Title _____Date _____

Doc:hisphy6-12

Exhibit 3-7 PEDIATRIC HEALTH HISTORY – ADOLESCENT

DATE: _____	
INFORMANT: _____	
PRIMARY LANGUAGE: _____	
PVT. PHYSICIAN: _____	*ADDRESSOGRAPH*

ALLERGIES (CHECK IF YES AND DESCRIBE)

	PENICILLIN		OTHER DRUGS:
	FOODS:		
	NONE KNOWN		OTHER:

CHILDHOOD ILLNESS

	CHICKEN POX		BRONCHITIS/ASTHMA		VISUAL PROBLEMS
	ANEMIA		CONVULSIONS		OTHER
	PNEUMONIA				

IMMUNIZATIONS

LAST TETANUS		ADVERSE REACTION	
LAST MMR		ADVERSE REACTION	
LAST TB TEST		RESULTS	

HOSPITALIZATIONS INCLUDE SIGNIFICANT BIRTH HISTORY, I.E. NICU

DATE	PROBLEM	FACILITY

FAMILY HISTORY

MOTHER'S AGE: _____   FATHER'S AGE: _____

	ASTHMA		DIABETES		TUBERCULOSIS
	CONVULSIONS		HIV/AIDS		MENTAL RETARDATION
	CANCER		HYPERTENSION		OTHER
	EARLY DEATH		SICKLE CELL DISEASE		

SIGNATURE _____ TITLE _____DATE _____

SOCIAL HISTORY

PRIMARY CARETAKER	
SUPPORT SYSTEM	
SCHOOL	
GRADE	
PERFORMANCE	

ACTIVITIES

AFTER SCHOOL	
HOBBIES	
GROUP	

HABITS

	TOBACCO	ALCOHOL	DRUGS
PERSONAL			
FRIENDS			
FAMILY			

SEXUALITY

	MALE	FEMALE
ACTIVE		
CONTRACEPTIVE		
PARENTHOOD		
HX OF STD		
AGE AT MENARCHE		

SIGNATURE _____TITLE _____ DATE _____

Doc:hisphy6-12

Exhibit 3-8 PEDIATRIC HEALTH HISTORY – AGE 0–5 YEARS

DATE: _____	
INFORMANT: _____	
PRIMARY LANGUAGE: _____	
PVT. PHYSICIAN: _____	ADDRESSOGRAPH

ALLERGIES (CHECK IF YES AND DESCRIBE)

	PENICILLIN		OTHER DRUGS:
	FOODS:		
	NONE KNOWN		OTHER:

PRENATAL HISTORY: (CHECK)

	GRAVIDA		PARA		AB		PLACENTA
	HYPERTENSION		BLEEDING		MEDICATION		OTHER
	ALCOHOL/DRUGS		DIABETES		STD		
	PRENATAL CARE AT THIS FACILITY			MONTH PRENATAL CARE STARTED			

BIRTH HISTORY

GESTATIONAL AGE		WKS	WEIGHT	
TYPE OF DELIVERY			COMPLICATIONS	
BORN AT THIS FACILITY	Y	N	IF NOT, WHERE	

NEONATAL HISTORY

	JAUNDICE		CYANOSIS		DEFECT
	RESPIRATORY		CONGENITAL INFECTION		OTHER

CHILDHOOD ILLNESS

	CHICKEN POX		BRONCHITIS/ASTHMA		PNEUMONIA
	ANEMIA		O.M. x 3 LAST YEAR		OTHER
	CONVULSIONS		LEAD		

SIGNATURE _____ TITLE _____ DATE _____

HOSPITALIZATIONS

DATE	PROBLEM	FACILITY

FAMILY HISTORY

ASTHMA	DIABETES	TUBERCULOSIS
CONVULSIONS	HIV/AIDS	SICKLE CELL DISEASE
CANCER	HYPERTENSION	OTHER
EARLY DEATH	MENTAL RETARDATION	

SOCIAL HISTORY

PRIMARY CARETAKER	
SUPPORT SYSTEM	
DAYCARE/SCHOOL/SITTER	

SIGNATURE _____TITLE _____DATE _____

ANTICIPATORY GUIDANCE RECORD

(Please date and sign when health education has been provided.)

2–4 weeks	Crying; straining at BMs; feeding; vitamins Sibling rivalry; bathing; stimulation; bulb syringes; car seat	12 mos	Negative; manipulative behavior; discipline; care of minor illness/injuries SAFETY: pot handles; pets, car seat
Date:	Sign:	Date:	Sign:
2–3 mos	Temperature taking; fever control; vomiting; diarrhea; babysitters SAFETY: Car seat; rolling over; aspiration	15–18 mos	Temper tantrums; toilet training; speech; toothbrush; snacks vs. junk food SAFETY: Stoves; street; poisons, Ipecac, pica; car seat
Date:	Sign:	Date:	Sign:
4 mos	Solid foods; teething/drooling; lead paint; vitamins SAFETY: Car seat; no nuts, small toys, etc.	24 mos	TV; peers/sharing; night fears; nutrition/vitamins; review fever and injury care SAFETY: Review above
Date:	Sign:	Date:	Sign:
6 mos	Fear of strangers; separation anxiety; shoes; junior foods; cups; Tylenol dose SAFETY: Car seat; plants; electrical outlet/wires	3–4 years	Chewing; dentist; sexual identification; nursery school/day care; update Tylenol dose SAFETY: Strangers; bikes; guns; seat belts
Date:	Sign:	Date:	Sign:
9 mos	Setting limits/discipline; spoon; normal drop in appetite; weaning from bottle SAFETY: Climbing; stairs; fans/heaters; car seat	5 years	Independence/separation; responsibilities; allowance; fears and fantasies, manners SAFETY: Prepare for school commute
Date:	Sign:	Date:	Sign:

Doc:hisphy

Exhibit 3-9 VACCINE ADMINISTRATION RECORD

VACCINE ADMINISTRATION RECORD

DEPT/LOCATION _____   **ADDRESSOGRAPH**

Vaccine	Date given	Age	Inject. site*	Location or dept	Vaccine manuf.	Lot # & exp. date	Given by (init.)	Parent/ guardian/ Pt. initial
DT/DTP 1								
DT/DTP 2								
DT/DTP 3								
DT/DTP/DTaP 4								
DT/DTP/DTaP 5								
DTP-HIB 1								
DTP-HIB 2								
DTP-HIB 3								
DTP-HIB 4								
HIB 1								
HIB 2								
HIB 3								
HIB 4								
OPV IPV 1								
OPV IPV 2								
OPV IPV 3								
OPV IPV 4								
MMR 1								
MMR 2								
HBIG								
HEP B 1								
HEP B 2								
HEP B 3								
HEP B Booster								
Varicella 1								
Varicella 2								

SITE LEGEND: RA = right arm, A = left arm, RT = right thigh, LT = left thigh, PO = oral
(arm is preferred site for ambulatory patients)

INITIAL	SIGNATURE VACCINE ADMINISTRATOR	INITIAL	SIGNATURE PARENT/ PATIENT/GUARDIAN

(Side A)

VACCINE ADMINISTRATION RECORD (continued)

Vaccine	Date given	Age	Inject. site*	Location or dept	Vaccine manuf.	Lot # & exp. date	Given by(init.)	Parent/ guardian/ Pt. initial
MEASLES								
RUBELLA								
PNEUMOVAX								
INFLUENZA								
INFLUENZA								
INFLUENZA								
INFLUENZA								
INFLUENZA								
INFLUENZA								
Td 1								
Td 2								
Td 3								
MANTOUX								
OTHER								

SITE LEGEND: RA = right arm, A = left arm, RT = right thigh, LT = left thigh, PO = oral
(arm is preferred site for ambulatory patients)

(Side B)

Exhibit 3-10 PEDIATRIC PATIENT SUMMARY LIST

ALLERGIES _____

LOCATION OF OTHER SIGNIFICANT INFORMATION _____

		PROBLEM/HEALTH MAINTENANCE LIST						
#	ENTRY DATE	HEALTH MAINTENANCE OR PROBLEM (CHRONIC OR EPISODIC)	RECURRENCE DATES					
			1	2	3	4	5	6

Exhibit 3-10 PEDIATRIC PATIENT SUMMARY LIST

PEDIATRIC PATIENT SUMMARY LIST (continued)

MEDICATION LIST			
DATE ORDERED	NAME OF MEDICATION	DOSE/FREQUENCY/ROUTE	DATE D/C

HOSPITALIZATIONS/SURGICAL PROCEDURES		
DIAGNOSIS	DATE(S)	HOSPITAL

SPECIALTY SERVICES			
	DATE		DATE

doc:PEDSSUML

Exhibit 3-11 IMMUNIZATION SCREENING HISTORY

	DATE						
1	Has your child ever had a reaction to a shot before?						
	Fever under 104 degrees?						
	Fever over 104 degrees?						
	Mild local tenderness/redness?						
	Uncontrolled high pitch cry?						
	Seizure/convulsions (fits/falling out)?						
	Acute anaphylactic reaction occurring seconds to minutes after shot?						
	Rash/hives?						
	Difficulty breathing?						
	Shock/unconsciousness?						
2	Does child/family member have a history of convulsions?						
3	Does your child have any allergies to:						
	Eggs (MMR)?						
	Neomycin (MMR)?						
	Streptomycin (OPV)?						
	Thimersal (HIB)?						
4	Is your child or anyone in household						
	Immunosuppressed?						
	Receiving steroid treatment?						
	Receiving chemotherapy?						
	Have AIDS or HIV infection/ARC						
5	Has your child had any infections within the past month?						
6	Today's temperature (nurse's notes)						
7	Females 11–19: Was LMP normal?						
	NURSE'S SIGNATURE	Initials	Initials	Initials	Initials	Initials	Initials
	LEGEND 0 = NO X = YES						

Exhibit 3-12 FAMILY PLANNING EDUCATION FORM

T.O.P. PATIENT'S FAMILY PLANNING EDUCATION AND FOLLOW-UP	
	ADDRESSOGRAPH

Education

1. Post TOP follow-up appointment _____ _____
   TIME   PLACE

2. Does patient verbalize understanding of importance of follow-up? ☐ YES ☐ NO

3. Method reviewed   ☐ Yes   ☐ No

4. Method desired _____

5. Did patient review literature given in clinic?   ☐ Yes   ☐ No

6. Does patient verbalize understanding of options?   ☐ Yes   ☐ No

7. Does patient verbalize understanding of method chosen?   ☐ Yes   ☐ No

8. Comments: _____
_____
_____
_____
_____
_____

Signature _____ Date _____

Follow-up Documentation For Patients Returning to XYZ Outpatient Department

Appointment date _____

Did patient keep appointment?   ☐ Yes   ☐ No

Comments: _____
_____
_____
_____
_____

Signature _____ Date _____

Exhibit 3-13 SURGICAL PATHOLOGY CHARGEMASTER

☐ PHOTO	DATE OF OPERATION	DATE RECEIVED	(LEAVE BLANK) PATH NO.	
SURGEON /WHC	RESIDENT			
PRE-OPERATIVE DIAGNOIS:				
OPERATIVE PROCEDURE:				

PREVIOUS SPECIMEN IN N.B.I.M.C.? ☐ NO ☐ YES—WHEN

PHYSICIAN PRACTICE SERVICES
Pathology Chargemaster

34715

PATIENT NAME _____

PATIENT BARCODE

AGE _____ DATE OF SERVICE _____ - _____ -

REFERRING PHYSICIAN _____

PLACE OF SERVICE	○ NI	○ NP	○ 8I	○ XI		DEPARTMENT	○ DL	○ LB	○ SG	○ XI
PROVIDER	○ AT	○ CD	○ EZ	○ JK	○ LB	○ ME ○ VC	○ X1	○ X2	○ X3	○ X4

QTY PROCEDURES   DIAGNOSES

1 2 3 4

QTY	Code	Procedure
○ ○ ○ ○	○ 88300	Surg. Exam Gross Only
○ ○ ○ ○	○ 88302	Surg. Exam for Identification
○ ○ ○ ○	○ 88304	Surg. Exam Diagnostic
○ ○ ○ ○	○ 88305	Surg. Exam Large
○ ○ ○ ○	○ 88307	Surg. Exam Complete
○ ○ ○ ○	○ 88309	Surg. Exam Comprehensive
○ ○ ○ ○	○ 88311	Decalcification
○ ○ ○ ○	○ 88312	Spec. Stain Group I
○ ○ ○ ○	○ 88313	Spec. Stain Group II
○ ○ ○ ○	○ 88318	Histochemistry - Chemical
○ ○ ○ ○	○ 88319	Histochemistry - Enzyme
○ ○ ○ ○	○ 88321	Consultation (Slide)
○ ○ ○ ○	○ 88329	O.R. Consultation
○ ○ ○ ○	○ 88331	O.R. Frozen Section
○ ○ ○ ○	○ 88332	O.R. Add. Section Each
○ ○ ○ ○	○ 88342	Peroxidase Exam
○ ○ ○ ○	○ 88346	Immunofluor. Exam Tissue

○ ○ ○ ○

Code	Diagnosis	Code	Diagnosis
○ 658.40	Amniotic Infection - Unsp	○ 202.80	Malignant Lymphomas, NOS
○ 217	Benign Neoplasm of Breast	○ 632	Missed Abortion
○ 211.3	Benign Neoplasm of Colon	○ 396.9	Mitral and Aortic Valve Disease
○ 219.1	Benign Neoplasm of Corpus Uter	○ 558.9	Non-Infect Gastroenteritis/Col
○ 174.9	Cancer of Breast / Female	○ 792.2	Nonspecific Abnormal Findings
○ 233.1	Ca in Situ of Cervix Ut	○ 792.9	Other Nonspecific Abnormal Fin
○ 669.72	Cesarean Delivery	○ 795.4	Other Nonspecific Abnormal His
○ 610.1	Diffuse Cystic Mastopathy	○ 799.9	Other Unknown and Unspecified
○ 535.60	Duddentitis w/o HMRGH	○ 136.3	Pneumocystic Pneumonia
○ 622.1	Dysplasia of Cervix	○ 605	Redundant Prepuce and Phimosis
○ 218.9	Fibroid Uterus	○ 519.9	Respiratory Disease - Chronic
○ 785.4	Gangrene	○ 634.91	Spontaneous Abortion, Incomplete
○ 535.50	GSTR/DDNTS NOS w/o HMRHG	○ V25.92	Sterilization
○ 996.83	Heart Transplant	○ 635.92	TOP, Comp
○ 474.12	Hypertrophy of Adenoids	○ 635.91	TOP, Inco
○ 474.10	Hypertrophy of T/A	○ 635.90	TOP, Unsp
○ 474.11	Hypertrophy of Tonsils	○ 633.1	Tubal Pregnancy
○ 996.81	Kidney Transplant	○ 550.90	Unilateral Hernia
○ 214.9	Lipoma, Unspecified Site	○ 621.9	Unspecified Disorder of Uterus
○ 785.6	Lymphadenopathy		

Additional Procedure _____

Additional Diagnosis _____

Physician Signature _____

32560-3

Exhibit 3-14 PEDIATRIC AMBULATORY-CARE SERVICE REPORT

PEDIATRIC PRIMARY CARE 216	DATE OF SERVICE

TREATING PHYSICIAN _____

DESCRIPTION	CPTCODE	CDM	QTY
PROCEDURES			
OUTPATIENT OFFICE VISIT – NEW			
Clinic Visit – Initial	99201	0001	
Expanded H & E – Straight Forward	99202	0002	
Detail H & E – Low Complexity (30 min)	99203	0003	
Comp H & E – Moderate Complexity (45 min)	99204	0004	
Comp H & E – High Complexity (60 min)	99205	0005	
OUTPATIENT OFFICE VISIT – FOLLOW-UP			
Clinic Visit – Follow-up	99211	0009	
Problem Focus – H & E Straight Forward (10 min)	99212	0010	
Expanded H & E – Low Complexity (15 min)	99213	0011	
Detailed H & E – High Complexity (25 min)	99214	0012	
Comp H & E – High Complexity (40 min)	99215	0013	
EMERGENCY VISIT			
Emergency Visit	90058	0006	
Prolonged Visit (level 4)	99354	0007	
Prolonged Visit (level 5)	99245	0008	
PREVENTIVE SERVICES – NEW			
Preventive Visit – Under 1 year	99381	0014	
Preventive Visit – 1–4 years	99382	0015	
Preventive Visit – 5–11 years	99383	0016	
Preventive Visit – 12–17 years	99384	0017	
Preventive Visit – 18 years+	99385	0018	
PREVENTIVE SERVICES – ESTABLISHED			
Preventive Service – Under 1 year	99391	0019	
Preventive Service – 1–4 years	99392	0020	
Preventive Service – 5–11 years	99393	0021	
Preventive Service – 12–17 years	99394	0022	
Preventive Service – 18 years+	99395	0023	
OUTPATIENT CONSULTATIONS			
Consultation Level 1	99241	0024	
Consultation Level 2	99242	0025	
Consultation Level 3	99243	0026	
Consultation Level 4	99244	0027	
Consultation Level 5	99345	0028	

FORM 123 – 1998

Exhibit 3-15 EMERGENCY DEPARTMENT CHARGE TICKET

Date: _____
Time: _____
Dr.#: _____

Diagnosis 1: _____
Diagnosis 2: _____
Diagnosis 3: _____

Signature: _____

DESCRIPTION	CODE		√	DESCRIPTION	CODE		√	DESCRIPTION	CODE		√
EYE				**LACERATIONS – SIMPLE** (hands, feet, trunk, scalp, extremities)				**LEVELS OF SERVICE**			
EYE EXAM	92002	120		0 – 2.5 cm	12001	195		LEVEL 1	99281	70	
EYE EXAM CORNEAL ABRASION	92018	175		2.6 – 7.5 cm	12002	260		LEVEL 2	99282	100	
FB REMOVAL/CONJUCTIVA-SCLERA	65210	143		7.6 – 12.5 cm	12004	310		LEVEL 3	99283	160	
FB REMOVAL/CORNEA	65222	160		12.6 – 20.0 cm	12005	400		LEVEL 4	99284	280	
FB EXTERNAL EYE	65205	115		20.1 – 30.0 cm	12006			LEVEL 5	99285	390	
EAR				**SIMPLE** (face, mouth, mucous membranes)				CRIT CARE 1ST HOUR	99291	450	
FB REMOVAL	69200	110		0 – 2.5 cm	12001	195		CRIT CARE ADDITIONAL 30 MIN.	99292	230	
REMOVAL EMPACTED CERUMEN	69210	110		2.6 – 5.0 cm	12013	290		**PROLONGED SERVICE**			
I & D EXT. EAR ABSCESS HEMATOMA	69000	160		5.1 – 7.5 cm	12014	330		INITIAL 30 – 74 MINUTES	99354	140	
NOSE				7.6 – 12.5 cm	12015	480		EACH ADDITIONAL 30 MINUTES	99355	115	
FB REMOVAL	30300	120		12.6 – 20.0 cm	12016	550		**OUTPATIENT VISIT**			
EPISTAXIS/CAUTERY	30901	156		**LAYERED** (scalp, trunk, extremities)				LEVEL 1	99201	80	
EPISTAXIS/CAUTERY/PACKING ANT	30903	220		0 – 2.5 cm	12031	295		LEVEL 2	99202	130	
EPISTAXIS/CAUTERY/PACKING POST	30905	330		2.6 – 7.5 cm	12032	380		LEVEL 3	99203	160	
NAILS				7.6 – 12.5 cm	12034	420		LEVEL 4	99204	220	
EVAC. SUBJUNGUAL HEMATOMA	11740	125		12.6 – 20.0 cm	12035	500		LEVEL 5	99205	300	
NAIL AVULSION	11730	180		20.1 – 30.0 cm	12036	650		**SPECIAL PROCEDURES**			
EXCISION OF NAIL	11750	332		**LAYERED** (feet, hands, genitalia, neck)				ARTERIAL PUNCTURE	36600	65	
DEBRIDEMENT OF NAIL	17000	120		0 – 2.5 cm	12041	330		BLADDER CATH. STRAIGHT	53670		
BURN CARE				2.6 – 7.5 cm	12042	410		BLADDER CATH. BALLOON	53675	180	
1ST DEGREE	16000	120		7.6 – 12.5 cm	12044	450		AEROSOL INHAL. BRONCHODILATOR	94660	85	
2ND: 0 – 1% BSA W/WO DEBRIDEMENT	16020	130		12.6 – 20.0 cm	12045	540		CHEST TUBE	32020	625	
2ND: 1 – 9% BSA W/WO DEBRIDEMENT	16025	215		**LAYERED** (face, mouth, mucous membranes)				THORACENTESIS	32000	305	
2ND: >9% BSA W/WO DEBRIDEMENT	16030	290		0 – 2.5 cm	12051	360		CRICOTHYRODIOTOMY	31605	640	
FRACTURES				2.6 – 5.0 cm	12052	440		GASTRIC INTUBATION; LAVAGE	91105	140	
CLAVICLE	23500	340		5.1 – 7.5 cm	12053	510		LUMBAR PUNCTURE	62270	280	
SCAPULA	23570	440		7.6 – 12.5 cm	12054	580		PARACENTESIS	49080	285	
PHALANX, MID; FINGER	26720	236		12.6 – 20.0 cm	12055	680		PERITONEAL LAVAGE	49420	330	
PHALANX, DISTAL, FINGER	26750	225		20.1 – 30.0 cm	12056	840		PERICARDIOCENTESIS	33010	390	
PHALANX, TO (EACH)	28510	183		**COMPLEX** (wound, revision, debridement, complex (trunk))				PROCTOSCOPY	45300	115	
RADIAL HEAD	24650	355		0 – 2.5 cm	13100	356		GASTROSTOMY TUBE REINSERTION	43760	165	
RADIAL SHAFT – CLOSED	25500	355		2.5 – 7.5 cm	13101	495		INDIRECT LARYNGOSCOPY	31505	130	
FINGER, JOINT	26740	260		**COMPLEX** (scalp, arms, legs)				ASPIRATION PUNCTURE BLADDER	51000	115	
PHALANX, TOE (EACH)	28510	183		0 – 2.5 cm	13120	380		BLOOD OCCULT STOOL	62270	17	
GREAT TOE	28490	185		2.5 – 7.5 cm	13121	450		EAR OR PULSE OXIMETRY	94760	35	
METATARSAL	28470	285		**COMPLEX** (face, hands, feet)				PEAK EXPIRATORY FLOW RATE (PERF)	94160	35	
METACARPAL	26600	260		0 – 2.5 cm	13131	534		IPECAC/CHARCOAL & OBSERVATION	99175	165	
SKULL – CLOSED	21300	350		2.5 – 7.5 cm	13132	740		DEBRIDEMENT; SKIN, PARTIAL	11040	90	
STERNUM – CLOSED	21820	285		**COMPLEX** (eyelids, nose, ears, lips)				DEBRIDEMENT; SKIN, FULL	11041	115	
VERTEBRAL BODY – CLOSED	22310	465		0 – 1.0 cm	13150	440		DEBRIDEMENT; NAIL	11700	120	
ANKLE	27808	465		1.0 – 2.5 cm	13151	580		GASES, BLOOD PH ONLY	82800	28	
FOOT	28430	315		2.5 – 7.5 cm	13152	940		INJ: ANES, OTHER PERIPH NERVE/BRANCH	64450	55	
FIBULA	27780	400		**COMPLEX** (any area)				VENTIALATION, ASSIS/MANAGE	94656	260	
HUMERAL HEAD	23600	465		> 7.5 cm	13300	930		**CARDIAC/CPR**			
RADIAL HEAD	23600	465		**IMMOBILIZATION**				CPR	92950	640	
TIBIA	27750	495		ANKLE TO FOOT	29540	136		RHYTHM EKG MONTIORING	93042	45	
ULNA SHAFT	25530	380		ELBOW, WRIST	29260	135		EKG – INT/REP	93010	45	
WRIST	25600	380		KNEE	29530	136		TRACEAL INTUBATION	31500	295	
RADIAL SHAFT – CLOSED	25500	355		LOW BACK	29720	135		DEFIBRILATONIC/CARDIOVERSON	92960		
INCISION AND DRAINAGE				NECK	21899	130		TEMPORARY PACEMAKER INTERNAL	33210	650	
I & D ABSCESS: SIMPLE	10060	145		SHOULDER	29240	135		TRANSCUTANEOUS PACEMAKER	92953	170	
I & D ABSCESS: COMPLEX (local/packing)	10061	360		FINGERS/HAND	29130	130		ROUTINE VENIPUNCTURE	36415	42	
PILONIDAL CYST: COMPLEX (local/packing)	10081	390		SHORT ARM SPLINT	29125	175		VENOUS CUTDOWN	36425	255	
HEMATOMA	10140	90		LONG ARM SPLINT	29105	210		CENTRAL VENOUS CATHETER	36489	260	
FELON	26011	345		SHORT LEG SPLINT	29515	175		CENTRAL VENOUS CATH. – CUTDOWN	36491	315	
SUBUNGUAL HEMATOMA	11740	125		TOES	29550	130		THROMOLYSIS INTRAVENOUS INFUSION	92977	577	
I & D BARTHOLIN ABSCESS	56420	250		RIB STRAPPING	29200	130		**UNLISTED PROCEDURES**			
FB REMOVAL SUB-CUT/MUSCLE				**ARTHROCENTESIS**				CONSCIOUS SEDAT, IV, IM, INHAL	99141		
FB SUBCUTANEOUS – SIMPLE	10120	145		SMALL JOINT AREA	20600	100		CON. SEDATION, ORAL, RECT, NAS	99142		
FB SUBCUTANEOUS – COMPLEX	10121	360		INTERMEDIATE JOINT	20605	100					
FB MUSCLE, SIMPLE	20520	345		MAJOR JOINT (SHOULDER, KNEE)	20610	105					
FB MUSCLE, COMPLEX	20525	520									
FB RECTUM	46608	230									
FB REMOVAL IUD/VAGINAL	58301	185									

EMERGENCY DEPARTMENT CHARGE TICKET (continued)

DESCRIPTION	CODE		√	DESCRIPTION	CODE		√	DESCRIPTION	CODE		√
HEAD & NECK				SPINE & PELVIS				LOWER EXTREMITIES			
FACIAL BONES	70150	28		CERVICAL – 2 VIEW	72040	23		FEMUR	73550	25	
NASAL BONES	70160	21		CERVICAL – 4 VIEW	72050	30		KNEE – 2 VIEWS	73560	26	
SINUSES 1-2 VIEWS	70210	23		THORACIC – 2 VIEW	72070	22		TIBIA & FIBULA	73590	23	
NECK SOFT TISSUE	70360	16		LUMBRO-SACRAL – 2 VIEW	72100	25		ANKLE – 3 VIEWS	73610	23	
MANDIBLE	70100	21		LUMBAR COMPLETE	72110	35		FOOT – 2 VIEWS	73620	21	
ORBITS	70200	28		HIP – 2 + VIEWS	73510	21		TOES	73660	18	
SKULL <4 VIEWS	70250	26		HIPS 2 VIEW W/ AP PELVIS	73520	35		CALCANEUS	73650	21	
CHEST				PELVIS	72170	20		ABDOMEN			
CHEST – 1 VIEW	71010	18		SACRUM & COCCYX	72220	28		ABDOMEN – 1 VIEW (KUB)	74000	23	
CHEST – 2 VIEW	71020	24		SACROILIAC	72200	28		ABDOMEN – 3+ VIEWS	74010	30	
RIBS 2 VIEWS	71100	24		UPPER EXTREMITIES				ABDOMEN – COMPLETE	74020	33	
RIBS UNILATERAL/PA CHEST	71101	35		CLAVICLE	73000	18		IVP	74400	45	
STERNUM	71120	28		SHOULDER 1 VIEW	73020	21		DISLOCATION			
				SHOULDER COMPLETE	73030	23		A/C SEPARATION	23540	335	
				SCAPULA COMPLETE	73010	23		RADIAL HEAD	24640	210	
				A/C – BILATERAL	70350	22		PATELLA	27560	420	
				HUMERUS – 2+ VIEWS	73060	21		IP (FINGER)	26770	340	
				ELBOW AP & LAT	73070	21		MP (FINGER)	26700	345	
				ELBOW – 3+ VIEWS	73080	21		IP (TOE)	28660	190	
				FOREARM	73090	21		MP (TOE)	28630	290	
				WRITS – 2 VIEWS	73100	21		SHOULDER, W/O ANES.	23650	440	
				HAND – 3 VIEWS	73120	21		SHOULDER, W/ANES.	23655	565	
				HAND MIN. 3 VIEWS	73130	21		ELBOW, W/O ANES.	24600	510	
				FINGERS	73140	19		ELBOW, W/ANES.	24605	545	
								OTHER			

Chapter 4

PHYSICIAN PRACTICE

At the conclusion of this chapter you should be able to:

> Define the multiple venues in which physicians practice medicine and discuss the reasons for shifts which have occurred in these venues

> Identify multiple HMO models

> Identify the accrediting and licensing agencies which set standards and regulate the physician office setting

> Identify professional affiliation organizations commonly sought by practicing physicians

> Discuss the elements of documentation in this setting recommended and/or required by agencies such as HCFA and NCQA

> Discuss unique confidentiality issues often found in this setting

> Discuss the role of the health information management professional as well as challenges which are unique in this setting

> Identify credentials available to coding employees and organizations which sponsor them

INTRODUCTION AND OVERVIEW

Physicians are the primary providers of health care. It is through their evaluation and decisions that a patient's care follows a set path.

This chapter deals mainly with physicians and their practices whether they are the only physician at the office or are in a multi-physician arrangement.

Solo practices are difficult to uniformly characterize. Many are subspecialists who provide secondary care on referral from primary-care practitioners. Under managed care these subspecialists are facing reduced income. Some provide both primary and secondary care since they have insufficient work in their own specialties to achieve their desired income. Most solo practitioners perform a number of office functions which include office administration of staff members. They are increasingly affiliated with managed-care organizations as a source of referral. There is often a belief by patients that the care provided by solo practitioners is more personal and that these professionals care more about their patients and have a better patient–provider relationship. They also often have a better relationship with the community served since there is more interaction with the patients they serve.

Group practice has been growing in popularity in recent years (Table 4-1). This is where three or more physicians share income, expenses, facilities, equipment, medical records and support personnel in the provision of service. Traditionally, ownership was by the physicians themselves; however, in recent years there has been an increase in group practices corporately owned or owned by other health-care organizations such as hospitals and health maintenance organizations.

Table 4-1 Physician group statistics[1]

	No. of groups	*No. of physicians*
1980	10,762	88,290
1985	19,787	210,811

Health maintenance organizations (HMO) have expanded greatly in both number and organization. Several HMO models exist today. These include the following:

Group model In this set-up the HMO contracts directly with a specific physician group to provide care to the HMO members. The physicians are not employees of the HMO, but are either employees or partners in their own physician group.

Staff model In this arrangement the physicians are employed by the HMO.

Network model The HMO contracts with different physician groups as part of its network of services.

Individual practice association model (IPA) This entails a contract between the individual physician who may be in solo practice but is part of a physician association and the HMO. The association acts as a negotiating 'agency' for the physician in dealing with the HMO.

Open access model In this model the HMO as gatekeeper is eliminated which means that the primary-care physician no longer needs prior approval from the HMO to refer the patient to a specialist.

Point-of-service HMO model In this model the member is able to go out of the network to obtain health-care services, although he or she has to pay a set percentage out-of-pocket for services received by non-contracted practitioners.

The Health Care Financing Administration (HCFA) has issued a statement that HMO contracts which restrict physician–patient communication violate federal law[2]. It is because of this issue that HMO contracts eased the requirements for exclusive use of their own physicians.

TYPE OF CARE RENDERED

The services offered by physicians in private practice are dependent upon the nature of the physician's specialty. General practitioners and family practitioners provide care needed for ailments of most body systems. Problems of a complex nature are usually referred to physicians who practice within a particular specialty or subspecialty.

LEGAL AND REGULATORY ISSUES

Licensing

Licensing of medical practitioners is required in all states through examination. This process is carried out by the State Department of Health, Board of Medical Examiners or a similar agency responsible for licensing physicians. As of writing, their continued education is required for license renewal in most states but none require re-testing for license renewal.

Specialty physicians often seek board certification to indicate additional education, training and knowledge in their area of expertise.

Accrediting agencies

The Accreditation Association for Ambulatory Health Care (AAAHC) is an agency used most often by group practices. This began in 1979 as the Joint Commission on Accreditation of Healthcare Organizations (JCAHO) dissolved its accreditation program for ambulatory care. Within 1 year, the JCAHO changed its mind and began again to build and offer an ambulatory-care accreditation process. This is why there are two agencies instead of one for ambulatory care.

The purpose of the AAAHC is to organize and operate a peer-based assessment, education and accreditation program for ambulatory health-care organizations. Physician group practices fit this model. Other types of ambulatory-care organizations the AAAHC accredits include ambulatory surgery centers, college and university health centers, and health maintenance organizations.

The standards manuals used by AAAHC are similar to those used by the JCAHO. When organizations are surveyed for accreditation, they receive a 3-year accreditation if they are substantially in compliance and a 1-year accreditation for partial compliance.

There are six professional organizations which are a part of the AAAHC:

- American College Health Association
- American Group Practice Association
- Federated Ambulatory Surgery Association
- Group Health Association of America
- Medical Group Management Association
- National Association of Community Health Centers

The Joint Commission on the Accreditation of Healthcare Organizations (JCAHO) is less often found in physician practices. As physicians, whether in solo practice or group practice, contract or become a part of hospital corporations, the JCAHO may opt to survey the physician offices as part of the hospital's accreditation process. Although physician offices are 'ambulatory' facilities it is not clear if they will be surveyed according the JCAHO ambulatory-care standards or the hospital outpatient standards.

The National Commission on Quality Assurance (NCQA) offers accreditation to those group practices that have managed-care programs.

Affiliated agencies

The Medical Group Management Association (MGMA) is a group that physician offices and corporate administrators of physician offices look up to.

The MGMA is a professional association for physician group practices much like AHIMA is for the HIM professionals. This organization has many resources available to group practices. For a fee you can get reports and information about administrative issues and statistics, policies and procedures, and statistics about other group practices, sizes and other valuable information for benchmarking purposes.

The Group Practice Improvement Network (GPIN) is another professional association that group practices are affiliated with. This association is comprised of 58 group practices of various sizes in the United States. It began in 1992 and its mission is to improve the quality and value of medical group practice through a shared learning network focusing on the following:

- Better clinical outcomes
- Improved access to care
- Greater ease of consumer use
- Cost effectiveness
- High satisfaction for users of health-care systems, their families and the community

This organization has two annual meetings where presentations about administrative and clinical issues are given, as well as the findings of results from study groups during the year.

Federal regulations

Although licensure of physicians is at a state level, most physicians, whether practicing alone or in a group, receive payment by the federal government for care rendered to patients participating in federal health-care programs. These include such programs as Medicare, an insurance program for the elderly or disabled, and Medicaid, the federal insurance program for those with limited or no income which is run at the state level. In order to participate or accept reimbursement from federal programs, it is necessary to follow the guidelines established for these programs. The Health Care Financing Administration (HCFA) administrates the Medicare program and requires that all participants adhere to the guidelines set forth in the Conditions of Participation.

A major emphasis for the HIM professional is on coding and billing compliance with the current focus on fraud and abuse issues. It is expected that after the Y2K (year 2000) issues are resolved, the Office of the Inspector General (OIG) will accelerate the monitoring and sanctioning of physicians for poor (negligent) or inaccurate (fraudulent) billing practices.

Other legal issues

Another interesting legal issue that should be considered is a physician's obligation to the patient in providing and continuing treatment. The physician is obligated:

- To treat the patient as long as the patient's condition requires treatment or until the physician properly withdraws or discharges the patient

- To inform patients of proposed treatment and obtain consent
- To caution patients against unneeded or undesirable surgery

There is an implied contract between the physician and the patient which starts when the physician begins the examination (or treatment) of the patient (not when the appointment is initially made by the patient). This contract or relationship cannot be terminated without the patient being formally discharged from care that is no longer needed or by written notification.

There is on occasion a desire or need on the part of the practitioner to dissolve the relationship with the patient. However, this must be done with care in order to avoid any allegations of abandonment. When this termination leads to a disruption of continuity of care, the patient may try to claim abandonment. A physician found to have abandoned a patient may face disciplinary action by the state medical board and medical malpractice liability for any injury the patient may incur.

Relationships are terminated for various reasons:

- Physician relocates geographically
- Patient relocates (and therefore terminates relationship himself)
- Physician terminates because of continued non-compliance with medical advice

With this last circumstance, the physician who continues the relationship places himself at legal risk and the patient at medical risk.

Meticulous documentation in the medical record is essential to protect the physician including dated entry explaining desire to terminate and, if appropriate to circumstances, a complete, concise record of the chronology of patient non-compliance as supporting evidence.

A letter (see Exhibit 4-1) should be sent to the patient (in consultation with legal counsel) which specifically states:

- The reason(s) for termination
- Effective date (which must be sufficient enough for patient to seek medical care elsewhere: minimum 30 days)
- Availability of emergency care for the term of notice
- Advice to contact local medical society for referral if desired
- Offer to supply new physician with medical information to facilitate continuity of care upon receipt of patient authorization (exhibit letter)

The letter should be sent certified mail/return receipt requested with a copy retained by the physician's office. (It is recommended that this letter be reviewed by facility attorney prior to use.)

If the patient is insured through an HMO agreement, the HMO contract may specify steps which must be undertaken for this process.

RELEASE OF INFORMATION

It is wise to have all employees in physician offices, as well as other health-care settings, sign confidentiality statements. This demonstrates a proactive effort on the part of the organization to maintain secure and private patient information. Private practice physicians are often unaware of legalities of release of information.

Mostly requests are from patients, physicians' offices and insurance companies. The number of attorney requests and subpoenas can be high, depending upon the specialties of the physicians in the practice and the litigious nature of the specialty.

There are continued problems with confidentiality as many support personnel have access to the records and are often not aware of the laws concerning release of information.

It is almost routine for a physician's office to call and remind a patient with an upcoming appointment or to call the patient with test results. One must consider the possibility that this information may be overheard by someone the patient may not be willing to share the information with. It is therefore advisable for the office to have the patient give permission for telephone notifications, especially since the physician's office personnel cannot be sure to whom they are talking over the phone (see Exhibit 4-2).

DOCUMENTATION GUIDELINES

The use of medical records in a physician group setting is similar to the outpatient department discussed previously; however, the hospital's medical records are not available to the physician in his office setting.

Most group practices have one unit record, but there are a few that have separate records. With separate records comes the dilemma of how information about the patient will get communicated to the other physicians. Separate record systems can be a significant risk management issue.

Other problems that occur with separate records are:

- Knowing which offices should receive incoming copies of dictations, reports and correspondence
- Trying to control release of information, because many support staff act independently
- Cost of maintaining separate files, duplication of services, file folders and shelving to hold files

The flow of medical records in a physician group practice begins with the scheduling of an appointment. An outguide or notice prints in the record department identifying a patient who will be having a visit on a given day. When it is prescheduled, the record is batched and processed usually 1 or 2 days before the actual office visit. With add-on appointments, the record must be retrieved and processed individually. This would increase the cost of handling.

The record is delivered to the appointment location prior to the visit. In the physician's office the record is prepared, service sheets are attached, and the office notes are stamped with the date and the physician's name. In some organizations the medical record department completes this function, whereas in others, the physician's support staff are responsible.

Following the office visit, the record either stays in the physician's office area, waiting for test results to come back, or the record is sent to transcription, where the transcriptionists transcribe the office notes, and return the records with the dictation to the physician's office.

Issues confronted by the health information department with this type of work flow:

- Record availability decreases
- Records move but outguides are not updated
- Labor costs increase due to number of records out of the department
- Posting of loose reports is delayed, as records are not in the department

Specific requirements for documenting care

Documentation should include:

- Chief complaint
- Information relevant to above
- Services rendered
- Patient education
- Discussions regarding risks and benefits

For each encounter document (see Exhibit 4-3):

- Date
- Reason for encounter
- Appropriate history and physical exam
- Review of lab, X-ray, other ancillary data
- Assessment
- Plan for care (including discharge if appropriate)

In some physician offices, in an effort to have an up-to-date history and patient complaint, the patient is often requested to complete a questionnaire which can then be used as the history at each visit (see Exhibit 4-4).

NCQA standards requirements include:

- Problem list
- Allergies
- History
- Diagnoses consistent with findings
- Treatment plans
- No evidence of the patient being placed at risk
- An identification name or number on every page
- Biographical data
- Author identification
- Dated entries
- Legible entries
- Notations on use of tobacco, alcohol or drugs (14 years or older)
- Ordering of appropriate laboratory and ancillary services
- Consistency of diagnosis with findings
- Consistent treatment plan
- Notations on follow-up care, calls or visits as well as time of return

- Attention to previously unresolved problems
- Information such as consultations and labs are initialed by provider as evidence of review
- Up-to-date immunization records for children

RETENTION AND STORAGE

Although state statutes may dictate the period for retention of medical records to be as few as 7 years, AHIMA recommends that medical records be maintained for a period of not less than 10 years. Records of minors must be retained until the patient reaches majority +2 years in some states or for a period equal to the statute of limitations for adult records that is applied beyond the last visit.

In physician group practices, records are either sequenced in straight chronological order, or divided into sections, to aid in finding information. Many physician office HIM professionals feel that records filed by patient name are more convenient. This allows physicians to pull records needed without having to ask for assistance in getting a medical record number or pulling to file. This method of filing does have its drawbacks as the files will not expand uniformly. As with any other filing system, when setting up the file, room for expansion should be allowed. When filing alphabetically, it is more difficult to assess the amount of expansion space needed as all letters do not expand uniformly. Frequency information is available in most health information text books and has been included below for quick reference.

Table 4-3 Frequency distribution of the alphabet[3]

A	3.00%	I	0.38%	Q	0.17%
B	9.38%	J	2.59%	R	5.05%
C	7.18%	K	4.24%	S	10.20%
D	4.84%	L	4.85%	T	3.37%
E	1.87%	M	9.50%	U	0.24%
F	3.72%	N	1.85%	V	1.24%
G	5.05%	O	1.52%	W	6.31%
H	7.38%	P	4.93%	X,Y,Z	1.14%

Documents of progress notes in the physician's office are very often formatted using the 'SOAP' format. This format organizes the information into the following areas: subjective, objective, assessment and plan. Many offices choose to use the problem-oriented medical record (POMR). Basically the POMR is organized by clinical problem. All information is organized specifically for one patient problem and a solution is sought for that problem.

Handwriting is often one of the biggest problems of all physician records. Dictated and transcribed information is more effective as it is often more complete and certainly more legible; however, timeliness is an essential issue.

Off-site storage

As paper-based medical records become crowded and unmanageable, physician offices often seek alternative storage methods for storing inactive medical records. Off-site storage is one option. (Some states, i.e. NJ, require that the DOH be notified prior to ambulatory-care facilities using off-site storage.) Questions to consider when considering this method should include:

- Are they bonded?
- Is this their main business?
- How are the records stored?
- How accessible will the records be (available at all times)?
- What is the cost for storage, access and transportation?
- What policies and procedures are in place for security?

Computerization of record information

In a physician group practice, there are many benefits to computerizing patient contact. Medical records are the lifeline of the health-care professional and when records are not available, it causes losses in productivity and potentially quality.

Many organizations have been utilizing computerization for decades. At a large Massachusetts-based organization, the physician uses an encounter form to collect administrative and clinical data from the patient visit. This form is sent to their information services department where it is keyed into the computer. When the patient is seen next, the encounter form displays information from prior visits to provide the physician with essential information about the patient.

Shortcomings to this approach to computerization may include data entry errors, decreased use of knowledge-based systems for drug interaction problems, differential diagnoses, warnings like adverse drug reactions and/or increased operational costs.

Several computer systems are also available for management of physician office visits and related functions. Key consideration when trying to purchase or build a computerized patient record system would be:

- Who the system is being used for – the provider, the administrator, the researchers, third-party payers, managed-care organizations
- How should the data be structured for access and data entry
- What type of patients does the organization see and what type of data needs to be captured for each of these categories of patients
- Appointment scheduling with immediate access to patient histories, future appointments, confirmations, no-shows
- Master Patient Index – maintains inpatient and outpatient database, demographics, insurance and employer information. Tools such as health-care ID cards should minimize duplicate records, redundant data entry and data entry errors
- Managed-care support: payer fee schedules and contractual agreements to establish a centralized point of control

CHALLENGES OF HIM PROFESSIONALS

As a health information manager, your role will be to create policies and systems that will foster the use of medical records for direct patient care and minimize their use for paperwork-related functions.

This can be accomplished by:

- Defining policies for how long records can be retained by offices and departments
- Modifying existing behaviors, so offices order records the same day they will be used or within 1 day of the request
- Separating work-flow processes, like lab follow-up, transcription, completion of disability or worker's compensation forms or other types of paperwork-related functions from the medical record

These simple changes can produce a wealth of improved service levels and decreased costs.

Physician practice sites have reported significant saving from the following activities:

- Computerized record tracking
- Quality improvement activities
- Modification of work flows
- Re-engineering work flows

One of the biggest challenges you will have in the group practice setting is trying to get records to offices for immediate or last minute requests.

With phone calls and add-on visits the physician needs the medical record more than any other time, as often the patient is experiencing a problem or needs their prescription renewed. When records are unavailable in a timely manner, the quality of that patient's care may suffer, and patient satisfaction greatly decreases. Patients are often upset when they hear that their medical records are not available or when their phone calls are returned late.

It is difficult to teach physicians all the requirements of good documentation and the legal requirements of managing health information. Physicians are resistant to receiving direction from anyone in what was once their own 'private practice'. Even in large groups the physicians often have a partnership relationship and therefore are the 'owners' of the practice. Many still have a 'small business' mentality rather than updating the processes of the office to conform with a corporate setting. For example, they at times inadvertently release medical information to a relative, such as the spouse of a patient, as this was commonplace in solo practice of days gone by.

Another challenge faced in managing an HIM department in the group physician setting is that most positions within the department are entry level since the bulk of the work to be done will be pulling and filing records. Because of this, motivation can be a big factor. In addition, functions requiring less than one full-time employee (FTE) must provide a lot of cross-training for coverage, depending upon the size of the department.

PERFORMANCE IMPROVEMENT AND QUALITY ASSURANCE ACTIVITIES

Quality assurance activities are necessary in a group practice setting for the HIM functions to monitor the assessed compliance with NCQA standards. Other accreditation agencies also have monitoring activities as a required function.

The health information department manager needs to have monitors in place that measure turn-around time and quality of essential services:

- On-time record deliveries
- Misfiled record
- Loose filing filed within 24 hours of receipt and posted in the correct records 100 per cent of the time
- Transcribed office notes and letters within acceptable time frame, free of transcription errors
- Number of records out of file
- Office notes dictated or written for every patient office visit
- Recording of phone calls and prescription renewals in medical records

Benchmarking studies are also important. Examples of issues which might be part of these assessments include waiting times for appointments and patient satisfaction surveys.

NCQA requires that managed-care organizations (MCO) conduct reviews of medical records from primary-care practice sites at least every 2 years to determine compliance with established standards and goals.

The MCO should periodically review a reasonable sample of primary-care practitioner medical records to determine conformance with the medical record standards and achievement of performance goals.

Information must be collected and submitted to the National Practitioner Data Bank. These requirements affect physicians, dentists and other health-care practitioners. Hospitals and other health-care entities must report:

- Professional review actions related to professional competence or conduct that adversely affect clinical privileges of a physician or dentist for more than 30 days
- A physician's or dentist's voluntary surrender or restriction of clinical privileges while under investigation for professional competence or conduct or in return for not conducting an investigation
- Revisions to such actions

Practitioners may report other health-care practitioners to the data bank if they identify unprofessional or incompetent activity.

Coding systems

The coding systems used by physician group practices include ICD-9-CM for diagnosis codes and CPT-4 for office visits, procedures, hospital visits and consultations. As the CPT code assignment must be supported by information documented in the record, it is essential that physicians be made aware of the requirements. Some facilities have incorporated coding guidelines into progress records to assist the physician while documenting the office visit (see Exhibits 4-5 and 4-6). Others post guidelines for easy reference (see Exhibit 4-7).

HCPCS is used along with charges for any Medicare and Medicaid patients. This information is included on the HC1500 (Exhibit 4-8) sent to the fiscal intermediaries.

In the group practice setting, physicians use service sheets to record charges. Samples of these sheets are included at the back of the chapter. With emergency room or hospital visits, the physician either keeps a log or uses a form to record for his or her office staff the day's patients who were seen and the services that were rendered.

Copies of admissions sheets are brought back from the hospital and given to the support staff, along with the physician's service. His or her support staff will usually assign the codes and submit the information to the HIM department or billing personnel for data entry. Large groups often have direct data entry at reception areas or small data-processing departments. Service information can also be entered by completing 'charge tickets' including all possible services. This is usually tied in with the appropriate CPT code or chargemaster information (see Exhibits 4-9 and 4-10).

Some physician's offices have the physician do their own coding for hospital services. The problem with this approach is that the physician is not trained in coding systems, and there is potential for over- and undercharging based on incorrect coding. Also, they tend to submit their charges when they have the time, which causes an uneven work flow and delays in submitting charges for the patients.

Coding credentials Certified Coding Specialist/Physician Office (CCS-p) is the latest credential offered by the American Health Information Management Association.

Another credential offered by examination through the American Academy of Procedural Coders is the Certified Procedural Coder (CPC). The exam for this credential deals with reimbursement issues, coding in the physician setting using operative summaries, chargemaster issues, lab, radiology, pathology and therapy coding. Test takers typically have experience in the physician office arena and have completed a series of educational modules available from the organization which provides the certification exam. Module completion is not required, or any other formal education, but recommended. However, in order to sit for the exam, it is required that the candidate have 2 years of work experience in the medical field (any aspect). The exam does not include ICD procedure coding, DRG issues, UB92 billing or Coding Clinic guidelines.

References

1. Havlicek PO, ed. *A Survey of Practice Characteristics*. Medical Groups in the US, 1996
2. Stahl D. Managed care trends: the affect of subacute care. *Nurs Manage* 1997;March
3. Waters KR, Murphy GF. *Medical Records in Health Information*. Germantown, MD: Aspen Systems Corp., 1979

Additional suggested reading

Abdelhak M, *et al. Health Information: Management of a Strategic Resource.* Philadelphia: W.B. Saunders, 1996

Peden AH. *Comparative Records for Health Information Management.* Albany, NY: Delmar Publishers, 1998

Personal communication

Rimmer, Laureen, RHIA, Director of Physician Services, Franciscan Family Care, Trenton, NJ, March 1999

SAMPLE FORMS IN PHYSICIAN PRACTICE

Exhibit 4-1 LETTER FOR TERMINATION OF PHYSICIAN–PATIENT RELATIONSHIP

John Smith, MD
123 His Address
Anytown, State, 12345
123-456-7890

Date

Name of Patient
Address

Dear Mr. (or Mrs.) _____

I find it necessary to inform you that I am withdrawing from further professional attendance upon you for the reason that you have persisted in refusing to follow my medical advice and treatment. Since your condition requires medical attention, I suggest that you place yourself under the care of another physician without delay.

If you so desire, I shall be available to attend you for a reasonable time after you have received this letter, but in no event for more than thirty (30) days.

This should give you ample time to select a physician of your choice from the many competent in this area. With your approval and upon receipt of your written authorization, I will make available to this physician your case history and information regarding your diagnosis and the treatment that you have received while under my care.

Sincerely,

_____MD/DO

Exhibit 4-2 COMMUNICATION RELEASE FORM

I hereby give permission to the office staff of Dr. _____ to notify me by telephone of the following: (Check all that apply)

Yes ☐   No ☐   Appointment reminder, by personal message or recorded message
Yes ☐   No ☐   A message to call the office for test results

Note: At no time will actual test results be left by message

The individuals listed below are authorized to receive the above information on my behalf:

_____

_____

I understand this form is intended to guard my privacy and is not a release of general medical information.

_____   _____
Patient signature   Date

_____
Witness

Exhibit 4-3 PHYSICIAN ENCOUNTER FORM

USE BALL POINT PEN PRINT FIRMLY

FORM 125 CLINICAL VISIT

APPOINTMENT STATUS	CO-PAYMENT		

APPOINTMENT STATUS

☐ SCHEDULED ☐ WRITE-IN ☐ _____
☐ WALK-IN ☐ AFTER HOURS ☐ _____

APPT. TIME	ARR. TIME	APPT. LENGTH
•	•	☐ 15 ☐ 30
•	• A.M.	
	• P.M.	☐ 45 ☐

CO-PAYMENT

☐ PAID
☐ REPEAT VISIT
☐ FEE FOR SERVICE
☐ NO CO-PAY GROUP
☐

BIRTH   YEAR   MONTH   SEX   MED. REC. NO.

(NAME (LAST)   (FIRST)   (M)

IDENTIFICATION NO.   B.C.

TYPE OF VISIT

☐ HEALTH ASSESSMENT
☐ PROBLEM WORK-UP
☐ NEW PATIENT

☐ SOMERSET   ☐ RT. 1
☐ FOLLOW-UP   ☐ _____
☐ PRE/POST NATAL
☐ MH   **2624193**

INJURY

☐ WORK RELATED
☐ DUE TO AUTO ACCIDENT
☐ NO ACCIDENT

PROVIDERS

PRIMARY CARE PROVIDER OF CHOICE   DATE

LABORATORY STUDIES:

PROCEDURES: ☐ ECG   ☐ Suture # _____   ☐ Suture removal   ☐ Procto   ☐ Allergy test

☐ Allergy shot   ☐ Injection   ☐ IV   ☐ Immunization   ☐ Audiogram   ☐ IUD Insert/Rem.

☐ Diaphragm fitted   ☐ Cryosurgery   ☐ Ear Wash   ☐ Cauterization   ☐ Other: _____

RETURN IN   DAYS ☐   WEEKS ☐   MONTHS ☐   AS NECESSARY ☐   TEL: HOME

REFER TO _____   TEL: OFFICE

AGE	HT.	BP ↑	BP ↔	LAST PREG.
TEMP	WT.	PULSE	LMP	LAST PAP.

PROB. NO.	CLINICAL NOTE:

1-MEDICAL RECORDS

PHYSICIAN ENCOUNTER FORM (continued)

PHYSICAL EXAM	WNL	ABN	NOT EXAM	COMMENTS
Head				
Eyes				
Fundi				
Ears				
Nose				
Mouth				
Throat				
Neck				
Lympth				
Skin				
Breasts				
Heart				
Lungs				
Abdomen				
Genitalia				
Pelvic				
Rectal				
Extremities				
Neurological				
Pulses				
Other				
1				
				HEALTH SCREEN PHYSICIAN NOTES:
Date:				Signature:

Exhibit 4-4 PATIENT QUESTIONNAIRE

ASSOCIATES IN UROLOGY
PATIENT QUESTIONNAIRE

NAME _____ DATE _____

PERSONAL:	**CURRENT MEDICATIONS**
Occupation _____	_____
Marital Status: M S W D	_____
Allergies _____	_____
_____	_____

SOCIAL HABITS

Presently   In past

Presently	In past	
_____	_____	Smoke cigarettes, cigars pipe
		Packs/day_____
_____	_____	Use recreational drugs
_____	_____	Drink alcohol
	_____	Occasionally
	_____	Daily
		AMT _____

CHILDHOOD ILLNESSES

_____	Whooping Cough	_____	Measles
_____	German Measles	_____	Mumps
_____	Rheumatic Fever	_____	Asthma

FAMILY HISTORY

Mother ___ Alive ___ Deceased at age _____

Cause of death _____

Father ___ Alive ___ Deceased at age _____

Cause of death _____

Immediate family members with history of:

____Diabetes	_____Heart Disease
____High Blood Pressure	_____AIDS/HIV
____Allergies	_____Cancer
____Thyroid Disease	_____Kidney Disease
____Mental Illness	_____Arthritis

Please review the list of health problems listed below.   Place a check mark in the spaces provided to indicate if you are currently experiencing these symptoms/illnesses or if you have experienced them in the past.

Presently	In past		Presently	In past	
_____	_____	Frequent urination	_____	_____	Fever
_____	_____	Painful urination	_____	_____	Unexplained Weight Loss
_____	_____	Incontinence of urine	_____	_____	Unexplained Weight Gain
_____	_____	Urinary infection	_____	_____	Weakness/Fatigue
_____	_____	Nocturia (nighttime) urination ____X/ night	_____	_____	Rashes
_____	_____	Blood in urine	_____	_____	Skin discoloration/bruising

AIU001

PATIENT QUESTIONNAIRE (continued)

Presently	In past	
_____	_____	Changes in hair, nails
_____	_____	Headache
_____	_____	Vision problems Incl. catarracts, glaucoma
_____	_____	Pain or Tearing of Eyes
_____	_____	Hearing loss
_____	_____	Pain/discharge from Ears
_____	_____	Dizziness
_____	_____	Chronic Nasal Congestion
_____	_____	Nosebleeds
_____	_____	Sinus Pain
_____	_____	Dental ailments
_____	_____	Mouth sores
_____	_____	Hoarseness
_____	_____	Difficulty swallowing
_____	_____	Chest pain
_____	_____	Rheumatic Fever
_____	_____	Irregular Heart Beat
_____	_____	High Blood Pressure
_____	_____	Varicose Veins
_____	_____	Phlebitis
_____	_____	Wheezing/cough
_____	_____	Painful respiration
_____	_____	Coughing up blood
_____	_____	Asthma
_____	_____	Chronic lung disease
_____	_____	Fainting/Blackouts

Presently	In past	
_____	_____	Seizures
_____	_____	___ Paralysis/__numbness/ ___Tingling/___tremors
_____	_____	Joint Pain/Stiffness
_____	_____	Backache
_____	_____	Pain/swelling/redness of limbs
_____	_____	Varicose Veins
_____	_____	Phlebitis
_____	_____	Change in appetite
_____	_____	Nausea/vomiting
_____	_____	Vomiting blood
_____	_____	Rectal bleeding
_____	_____	Change in Bowel Habits ___ Diarrhea ___ Constipation
_____	_____	Indigestion
_____	_____	Gas
_____	_____	Hemorrhoids
_____	_____	Thyroid problems
_____	_____	Intolerance to heat/cold
_____	_____	Excessive sweating
_____	_____	Excessive thirst
_____	_____	Excessive urination
_____	_____	Anemia
_____	_____	Easy bruising/bleeding
_____	_____	Past transfusions
_____	_____	Change in mental status mood, nervousness

Exhibit 4-5 CPT GUIDED PROGRESS NOTE – SECOND OPINION

SECOND OPINION: Requires ALL of the following three items be completed at the indicated level: History, Review of Systems Exam, Specified Type of Decision Making.

History Elements: Location, Quality, Severity, Duration, Timing, Content, Modifying Factors, Signs & Symptoms. **Systems**: Constitutional, Eyes, ENMT, CardVasc, Resp., GI, GU, Musc.Skel., Skin, Neuro., Psych, Hemo. **Types of Decision Making:** Straightforward, Low , Moderate , High .

	History	Examination	Problem
99272	**Dec.Mak**: Straightforward HPI: Req. 1 - 3 Elements ROS: System related to problem	Limited exam of affected area + other symptomatic or related organ system	Low Severity
99273	**Dec. Mak**: Low Complexity HPI: Requires 4 or more elements ROS: Related system + ltd. other system PFSH: One pertinent item	Extended exam of affected area + other symptomatic or related organ system	Moderate Severity
99274	**Dec. Mak**: Moderate Complexity HPI: Complete, All elements ROS: Complete - all body systems PFSH: One item from each area.	General multisystem exam or complete exam of a single organ system.	High Severity

Date_____ ☐ Patient History Form Reviewed _____

_____

_____

_____

_____

_____

_____

_____

_____

_____

_____

_____

_____

_____

_____

_____

_____

_____

_____

_____

_____

_____

_____

_____

Exhibit 4-6 CPT GUIDED PROGRESS NOTE – ESTABLISHED PATIENT

ESTABLISHED PATIENT: Requires 2 of the following three items be completed at the indicated level: History, Review of Systems Exam, Specified Type of Decision Making.

History Elements: Location, Quality, Severity, Duration, Timing, Content, Modifying Factors, Signs & Symptoms.
Systems: Constitutional, Eyes, ENMT, CardVasc, Resp., GI, GU, Musc.Skel., Skin, Neuro., Psych, Hemo.
Types of Decision Making: Straightforward, Low Complexity, Moderate Complexity, High Complexity.

	History	**Examination**	**Time**
9 9 2 1 2	**Dec. Mak**: Straightforward HPI: Req. 1 - 3 Elements ☐ Patient History Form Reviewed_____	Limited exam of affected area.	10
9 9 2 1 3	**Dec. Mak**: Low Complexity HPI: Requires 1 to 3 Elements ROS: System related to Problem ☐ Patient History Form Reviewed_____	Ltd. Exam of affected area + other symptomatic or related organ system	15
9 9 2 1 4	**Dec. Mak:** Moderate Complexity HPI: Requires 4 or More Elements ROS: Related system + ltd other syst. PFSH: One pertinent item. ☐ Patient History Form Reviewed_____	Extended exam of affected system + other symptomatic or related organ systems	25

AIU006_

Exhibit 4-7 CPT GUIDE SHEET

NEW PATIENT: Requires **ALL 3** of the following items be completed at the indicated level: History, Review of Systems Exam, Specified Type of Decision Making.

	History	Examination	Time
99202	HPI: Requires 1 to 3 elements ROS: System related to problem **Dec. Mak.:** Straightforward	Ltd. exam of affected area + other symptomatic or related organ system	20
99203	HPI: Requires 4 or more elements ROS: Related syst. + ltd. other syst. PFSH: One pertinent item **Dec. Mak.:** Low complexity	Extended exam of affected system + other symptomatic or related organ systems	30
99204	HPI: Complete – all elements ROS: Complete – all body systems PFSH: At least one item from each area: Personal, Family or Social **Dec. Mak.:** Moderate complexity	General multisystem examination or complete examination of a single organ system	45
99204	HPI: Complete – all elements ROS: Complete – all body systems PFSH: At least one item from each area: Personal, Family or Social **Dec. Mak.:** High complexity	General multisystem examination or complete examination of a single organ system	60

CONFIRMATORY CONSULTATION (SECOND OPINION): Req. **ALL 3** of the following to be completed at the specified level: Hx, ROS Exam, & Type of Dec.

			Problem severity
99272	HPI: Requires 1 to 3 elements ROS: System related to problem **Dec. Mak.:** Straightforward	Ltd. exam of affected area + other symptomatic or related organ system	Low
99273	HPI: Requires 4 or more elements ROS: Related syst. + ltd. other syst. PFSH: One pertinent item. **Dec. Mak.:** Low complexity	Extended exam of affected system + other symptomatic or related organ systems	Mod
99274	HPI: Complete – all elements ROS: Complete – all body systems PFSH: At least one item from two areas: Personal, Family or Social **Dec. Mak.:** Moderate complexity	General multisystem examination or complete examination of a single organ system	High
99275	HPI: Complete – all elements ROS: Complete – all body systems PFSH: At least one item from two areas: Personal, Family or Social **Dec. Mak.:** High complexity	General multisystem examination or complete examination of a single organ system	High

History Elements: Location, Quality, Severity, Duration, Timing, Content, Modifying Factors, Signs & Symptoms.

Systems: Constitutional, Eyes, ENMT, CardVasc, Resp., GI, GU, Musc.Skel., Skin, Neuro., Psych, Hemo.

Types of Decision Making: Straightforward, Low complexity, Moderate complexity, High complexity.

AIU004

Exhibit 4-8 HEALTH INSURANCE CLAIM FORM (HCFA 1500)

PLEASE
DO NOT
STAPLE
IN THIS
AREA

HEALTH INSURANCE CLAIM FORM

| | PICA | | PICA | | |

| 1. MEDICARE | MEDICAID | CHAMPUS | CHAMPVA | GROUP HEALTH PLAN (SSN or ID) | FECA BLK LUNG (SSN) | OTHER (ID) | 1a. INSURED'S I.D. NUMBER | (FOR PROGRAM IN ITEM 1) |

☐ (Medicare #) ☐ (Medicaid #) ☐ (Sponsor's SSN) ☐ (VA File #) ☐ (SSN or ID) ☐ (SSN) ☐ (ID)

2. PATIENT'S NAME (Last Name, First Name, Middle Initial)

3. PATIENT'S BIRTH DATE MM | DD | YY   SEX   M ☐   F ☐

4. INSURED'S NAME (Last Name, First Name, Middle Initial)

5. PATIENT'S ADDRESS (No., Street)

6. PATIENT RELATIONSHIP TO INSURED   Self ☐ Spouse ☐ Child ☐ Other ☐

7. INSURED'S ADDRESS (No., Street)

CITY   STATE

8. PATIENT STATUS   Single ☐ Married ☐ Other ☐

CITY   STATE

ZIP CODE   TELEPHONE (Include Area Code) (   )

Employed ☐ Full-Time Student ☐ Part-Time Student ☐

ZIP CODE   TELEPHONE (INCLUDE AREA CODE) (   )

9. OTHER INSURED'S NAME (Last Name, First Name, Middle Initial)

10. IS PATIENT'S CONDITION RELATED TO:

11. INSURED'S POLICY GROUP OR FECA NUMBER

a. OTHER INSURED'S POLICY OR GROUP NUMBER

a. EMPLOYMENT? (CURRENT OR PREVIOUS)   ☐ YES   ☐ NO

a. INSURED'S DATE OF BIRTH MM | DD | YY   SEX   M ☐   F ☐

b. OTHER INSURED'S DATE OF BIRTH MM | DD | YY   SEX   M ☐   F ☐

b. AUTO ACCIDENT?   ☐ YES   ☐ NO   PLACE (State)

b. EMPLOYER'S NAME OR SCHOOL NAME

c. EMPLOYER'S NAME OR SCHOOL NAME

c. OTHER ACCIDENT?   ☐ YES   ☐ NO

c. INSURANCE PLAN NAME OR PROGRAM NAME

d. INSURANCE PLAN NAME OR PROGRAM NAME

10d. RESERVED FOR LOCAL USE

d. IS THERE ANOTHER HEALTH BENEFIT PLAN?   ☐ YES   ☐ NO   *If yes,* return to and complete item 9 a-d.

READ BACK OF FORM BEFORE COMPLETING & SIGNING THIS FORM.
12. PATIENT'S OR AUTHORIZED PERSON'S SIGNATURE I authorize the release of any medical or other information necessary to process this claim. I also request payment of government benefits either to myself or to the party who accepts assignment below.

SIGNED _____   DATE _____

13. INSURED'S OR AUTHORIZED PERSON'S SIGNATURE I authorize payment of medical benefits to the undersigned physician or supplier for services described below.

SIGNED _____

← PATIENT AND INSURED INFORMATION →

14. DATE OF CURRENT: MM | DD | YY   ◄ ILLNESS (First symptom) OR INJURY (Accident) OR PREGNANCY(LMP)

15. IF PATIENT HAS HAD SAME OR SIMILAR ILLNESS. GIVE FIRST DATE   MM | DD | YY

16. DATES PATIENT UNABLE TO WORK IN CURRENT OCCUPATION MM | DD | YY   MM | DD | YY   FROM   TO

17. NAME OF REFERRING PHYSICIAN OR OTHER SOURCE

17a. I.D. NUMBER OF REFERRING PHYSICIAN

18. HOSPITALIZATION DATES RELATED TO CURRENT SERVICES MM | DD | YY   MM | DD | YY   FROM   TO

19. RESERVED FOR LOCAL USE

20. OUTSIDE LAB?   ☐ YES   ☐ NO $ CHARGES

21. DIAGNOSIS OR NATURE OF ILLNESS OR INJURY. (RELATE ITEMS 1,2,3 OR 4 TO ITEM 24E BY LINE)

1. └___.__   3. └___.__

2. └___.__   4. └___.__

22. MEDICAID RESUBMISSION CODE   ORIGINAL REF. NO.

23. PRIOR AUTHORIZATION NUMBER

24. A DATE(S) OF SERVICE						B Place of Service	C Type of Service	D PROCEDURES, SERVICES, OR SUPPLIES (Explain Unusual Circumstances) CPT/HCPCS	MODIFIER	E DIAGNOSIS CODE	F $ CHARGES	G DAYS OR UNITS	H EPSDT Family Plan	I EMG	J COB	K RESERVED FOR LOCAL USE
From MM	DD	YY	To MM	DD	YY											
1																
2																
3																
4																
5																
6																

25. FEDERAL TAX I.D. NUMBER   SSN ☐ EIN ☐

26. PATIENT'S ACCOUNT NO.

27. ACCEPT ASSIGNMENT? (For govt. claims, see back)   ☐ YES   ☐ NO

28. TOTAL CHARGE $

29. AMOUNT PAID $

30. BALANCE DUE $

31. SIGNATURE OF PHYSICIAN OR SUPPLIER INCLUDING DEGREES OR CREDENTIALS (I certify that the statements on the reverse apply to this bill and are made a part thereof.)

SIGNED _____   DATE _____

32. NAME AND ADDRESS OF FACILITY WHERE SERVICES WERE RENDERED (If other than home or office)

33. PHYSICIAN'S, SUPPLIER'S BILLING NAME, ADDRESS, ZIP CODE & PHONE #

PIN#   GRP#

← PHYSICIAN OR SUPPLIER INFORMATION →

790-0115 (12/90) (OCR) 1 pt.

(APPROVED BY AMA COUNCIL ON MEDICAL SERVICE 8/88)   **PLEASE PRINT OR TYPE**

FORM HCFA-1500 (12-90)
FORM OWCP-1500   FORM RRB-1500

Exhibit 4-9 DIAGNOSTIC IMAGING SERVICES SHEET

DIAGNOSTIC IMAGING 2957

SERVICE SUMMARY (Check One In Each Column)

ENCOUNTER TYPE	SERVICE INFO	SCHEDULING
New Pt.	Screening	Routine (Scheduled)
Estab/ F/U	Symptomatic	Stat
ER Follow-up Exam	Follow-up Study	
Consult		

REASON FOR VISIT (Mark Primary As #1 And Each Additional Consecutively)

RADIOLOGY - ROUTINE	ABDOM.	ULTRASOUND	CARDIOVASC/OTHER	REFERRALS (Correlate to Reason for Visit #)		
		ABDOMINAL/SONO		IN	OUT	
Chest	KUB Flatplate					
Spine	Obstructus Series	Abdominal/Sono Other	2-D Echocardiogram			Allergy
Cervical		Adrenal	Cartoid Arteries			Cardiology
Lumber	UPPER EXTREM.	Aorta/Renal/Vessels	Colorflow Doppler			Chiropractics
Decubitus	Clavicle	Breast	FNA/Biopsy			Dermatology
Dorsal/Thorax	Elbow - Bilateral	Gallbladder	M-Mode			Diabetic Teaching
Lateral	Elbow - Unilateral	GI Tract				E N T
Oblique	Forearm - Bilateral	Pancreas				Endocrinology
Ribs - Unilateral	Forearm - Unilateral	Pelvic				Gastroenterology
Ribs - Bilateral	Hand - Bilateral	Popliteal				Hematology/Oncology
Routine	Hand - Unilateral	Renal				Infectious Disease
Sacrum	Humerius	Retroperitoneal				Nephrology
Coccyx	Scalpula	Spleen				Neurology
Scoliosis Series	Shoulder - Bilateral	Venous Doppler				Nutrition
	Shoulder - Unilateral					OB/GYN
SKULL	Wrist - Bilateral	OB/GYN				Ophthalmology
Facial Bones	Wrist - Unilateral	Amniotic Index				Optometry
Mandible Series		Biophysical				Orthopedics
Nasal Bones	Bone Age Studies	Pelvic				Physiatry
Orbits	Bone Survey	Routine OB				Physical Therapy
Skull Series		Transvaginal				Podiatry
Sinuses						Primary Care Provider
	RADIOLOGY - PREP	SMALL PARTS				Pulmonary
LOWER EXTREM.	I V P with Tomos	Head and Neck				Rheumatology
Ankle - Bilateral	Barium Enema	Subcutaneous				Surgery
Ankle - Unilateral	Barium Enema w/air cnt.	Testicle				Urology
Femur - Bilateral	Cystogram	Thyroid				
Femur - Unilateral	ERCP					
Foot - Bilateral	Esophagram					Cardiac Testing
Foot - Unilateral	Fluoro - 30 mins.					Hearing Test
Hips - Bilateral	GB Series					Laboratory Tests
Hips - Unilateral	GI Series Upper					Pulmonary Function Test
Knee - Bilateral	GI Series w/small bowel					Rx
Knee - Unilateral	Hysterosalpingogram					Stress Test
Pelvis - Bilateral	Intravenous Pyelogram					Vision Test
Pelvis - Unilateral	T M J Tomos					
Tibia/Fibula	VCUG					
Other (Specify):						

NUCLEAR MEDICINE			MAMMOGRAPHY			
Bone Scan			Bilateral			
Gallium Scan			Unilateral			
Liver Scan			Mag. Views			
Lung			Spot Compressor			
M U G A						
Renal						
Stress Thalium						
Thyroid						
Other(Specify):			Other (Specify):			

FOLLOW UP	FINANCIAL CLASS (Correlate to Dx#)		COMMENTS:
Days (#_____)	Workers Comp	Future Billable	
Weeks (#_____)	MVA	Post Op Care	
Months (#_____)	Pre-Existing Condition		
PRN			

5/23/95

Exhibit 4-10 SURGERY DEPARTMENT SERVICES SHEET

SURGERY		2970

ADDRESSOGRAPH/LABEL

SERVICE SUMMARY (Check One In Each Column)

ENCOUNTER TYPE		H&P		MEDICAL DECISION	
Procedure		Focused		Strtfwd	
Estab/ F/U		Exp. Focused		Low	
ER Follow-up Exam		Detailed		Moderate	
Consult		Comprehensive		High	
Pre-Operative					
Post-Operative					

DIAGNOSIS/REASON FOR VISIT (Mark Primary As #1 And Each Additional Consecutively)

							BODY SITE/SYSTEMS (Correlate to Dx#)	IN	OUT	REFERRALS (Correlate to Dx #)	
Abscess (indicate site)		Hemorrhoids		Neoplasm,Benign (indicate site)							
Abdominal Pain		Hepatitis		Neoplasm,Malig. (indicate site)							
Aneurysm		Hernia-Hiatal		Neoplasm, Unspecified (indicate site)							
Appendicitis		Hernia-Inguinal		Nevi			Abdomen			Allergy	
Billary Tract Disease		Hernia-Other		Normal Breast			Anus			Cardiology	
Cellulitis (indicate site)		Hernia-Umbilical/Ventral		Occult Blood			Arm			Dermatology	
Colitis		HIV		Pilonidal Cyst			Bladder			Diabetic Teaching	
Constipation		Infection		PVD-Arterial			Breast			ENT	
DVT/Phlebitis		Inflamm. Bowel Disease		PVD-Venous			Colon			Endocrinology	
Diverticular Disease		INJURY/TRAUMA (ind. site)		Rectal Bleeding			Ear			Gastroenterology	
Epiderm./Sebac. Cyst		Abrasion		Skin Lesion - Tumor			Face			Hematology/Oncology	
Fibrocystic Breasts		Burn		Skin Lesion - Epidermal CA			Foot			Infectious Disease	
Fistual/Fissure		Contusion		Soft Tissue Mass			Gallbladder			Mammography	
Foreign Body		Hematoma/Seroma		Statis Ulcer			Genital Organ (FEM)			Nephrology	
Ganglion Cyst		Laceration		Thyroid Nodule			Genital Organ (MALE)			Neurology	
Gangrene		Fracture		Vascular Insufficiency			Gland			Nutrition	
G.I. Bleed		Intestinal Obstruction		Wound Infection			Hand			OB/GYN	
		Lipoma					Head			Ophthalmology	
		Liver Disease					Hematopoetic			Optometry	
		Lymphadenopathy					Hepatic			Orthopedics	
		Mammography Follow-up					Intestine			Physiatry	
							Kidney			Physical Therapy	
							Leg			Podiatry	
							Lymphatic			Primary Care Provider	
							Musculoskeletal			Pulmonary	
							Neck			Radiation Oncology	
							Nose			Radiology/X-Ray	
							Pancreas			Rheumatology	
							Rectum			Urology	
							Reproductive System				
							Respiratory System			DME	
							Stomach/Small Intestine			Laboratory Tests	
							Throat			Cardiac Testing	
							Trunk			Hearing Test	
							Vascular			CT Scan	
										MRI	
				Health Maintenance						Pulmonary Function Test	
										Rx	
							Other (Specify):			Stress Test	
Other (Specify):										Ultra Sound	

SERVICES/TREATMENTS/PROCEDURES (Correlate To Dx #)

						IMMUNIZATIONS/INJECTIONS		HEALTH MAINT/PERIODIC SCREEN	
Exam W/Prob.		Endoscopy		Minor Surgery-Removal of Mass		Antibiotic Prophylaxis		Breast Exam	
Arterial Seg. Pessure		Endoscopy with Bx		Other Rectal Surgery		Tetanus		Sigmoidoscopy	
Aspiration		Excision		Placement of Vascular Line				Vascular Exam	
Aspiration Cyst of Breast		Hemorrhoid Banding		Proctoscopy/Anoscopy				Review of Radiographs	
Biopsy - Open		Hemorrhoidectomy		Removal of Hickman/Porta Cath.					
Biopsy -F N A		I&D		Suture/Staple Removal					
Biopsy Lymph Node		Insert/Removal-Central Line		Suturing/Stapling					
DSG Change (Wound Care)		Incis. Thrombosed Hemorrh.		Venous Outflow Study					
Debridement				Unna Boot Application					
Other(Specify):						**Other (Specify):**			

FOLLOW UP		FINANCIAL CLASS (Correlate to Dx#)				COMMENTS:	
Days (#____)		Workers Comp		Future Billable			
Weeks (#____)		MVA		Post Op Care			
Months (#____)		Pre-Existing Condition					
PRN							

5/23/95

Chapter 5

HOME-BASED HEALTH CARE

At the conclusion of this chapter you should be able to:

Discuss the impetus behind the growing trend toward home-care services

Identify a variety of services which are available to the patient at home

Identify the agencies which provide accreditation and reimbursement as well as their requirements for services and documentation

Discuss changes in the medical record media and how this will benefit home-care professionals

Discuss areas of concern to the health information management professional in this setting

INTRODUCTION AND OVERVIEW

Home care is a service to the recovering, disabled, or chronically ill person providing for treatment and/or effective functioning in the home environment. Although it may appear so, home health care is not a new concept. Organized home care was practiced in the United States as early as the 1790s in Boston. Local health departments have provided home care since the late 1800s, as well as the Visiting Nurse Associations (VNA), although the VNAs in this country were primarily instructive institutions. They taught hygiene, sanitation and disinfection in addition to care of the sick at home.

A major force in the development of home-care services was the implementation of Medicare in 1965. Medicare laws included reimbursement for services provided in the home. This created funding for home care for the first time. Because of this, the number of agencies increased greatly through many avenues including temporary personnel agencies, pharmaceutical firms and acute-care facilities as well as entrepreneurial health professionals.

The home-care industry is at least ten times larger than it was in 1983. This type of health care is rapidly expanding because of the growing elderly population wishing to remain at home and as a means of decreasing health-care costs. This may be due to governmental changes in payment procedures for acute-care facilities. Although home-care services had largely been provided by independent private or public non-profit visiting nurse associations, at least a third of these services are now provided by hospitals, while for-profit agencies serve an even larger population.

As facilities make the transition from offering primarily acute-care inpatient services to being part of, or at the center of, an integrated delivery system that involves physicians, long-term care, home care and acute care, home care is getting a lot more attention. In the future, care will be driven not from the institutional setting but from the ambulatory care and physician practice. Agencies will increasingly be required to provide managed-care organizations with data for case management[1].

TYPE OF CARE RENDERED

The care provided in the home setting is quite expansive. All of the following services can be provided in the home by qualified personnel working for an agency or being subcontracted for services:

- Nursing care
- Medical care
- Therapies: physical therapy, occupational therapy, speech therapy
- Social services
- Personal care, housekeeping, live-ins, companions
- Patient transportation
- Respite care
- Medical equipment
- Nutritional counseling
- Meals on wheels
- Hospice care
- Maternal/child care
- Home health aides to assist with activities of daily living (ADL)

Configuration of services greatly differs depending on the needs of the patient, and agency availability. All services must be ordered in writing by a physician although some states allow services to be ordered by a physician assistant (PA) or nurse practitioner (NP). Although some services may be contracted personally by the patient where allowed by law, most insurance plans do not cover services not ordered by a qualified health-care provider.

The federal government generally divides these services as into two categories: home health agencies whose services must include the provision of medical/nursing care and home-care agencies that provide non-medical care services, i.e. transport, supplies, personal care, etc.

In order for a home health-care agency to receive payment for services from Medicare, it must seek certification in accordance with the Conditions of Participation. Medicare certifies over 6000 agencies in the United States. Those agencies must have the following:

- Skilled nursing services (a registered nurse or licensed practical nurse who is under the supervision of a registered nurse, plus at least one other therapy, i.e. occupational therapy, physical therapy, speech therapy, social services, etc.
- The patient must be homebound: confined to the home most of the time
- The patient must require part-time or intermittent skilled nursing care or treatment under plans established by physicians

Home-care services are provided by many different types of facilities. These include but are not limited to:

- Hospitals
- Proprietary corporations
- Private non-profit groups
- Government agencies (state, local, federal programs)
- Voluntary non-profit organizations, i.e. VNA

Within these categories allied health professionals supply most of the care in accordance with physician orders. There is an office that coordinates the provided services. The physician orders are either phoned or faxed in. Many agencies will contract with various independent service organizations to provide requested services.

Administrators are usually required to have a masters-level degree as well as a clinical background.

PATIENT POPULATION

Candidates for home care must have a strong social support system, an adaptable home, i.e. wheelchair access, single level, etc., and probable private funds (although limited home-care services are provided by many insurance plans).

Referrals come from many sources. Most common are hospital referrals; however, they can also be referred directly from the physician, family members and patients themselves.

LEGAL AND REGULATORY ISSUES

Licensing

Home health agencies must be licensed in all states, usually by the state's Department of Health or equivalent agency. Home-care agency licensing requirements vary from state to state.

Accrediting agencies

Voluntary accreditation is available from several agencies. The National League of Nursing (NLN) has a subsidiary called the Community Health Accreditation Program (CHAP). The Joint Commission on Accreditation of Healthcare Organizations (JCAHO) also has a specific program of standards for home-care services; they accept the accreditation decision of CHAP in lieu of a survey. Furthermore, the Health Care Financing Administration (HCFA) recognized the accreditation decisions of both CHAP and JCAHO by granting 'deemed status' to agencies with accreditation. In addition to the above, the National Home Caring Council offers accreditation for homemaker services.

Both the JCAHO standards and HCFA spell out minimum qualifications for health-care professionals providing services to home-care patients, including training and licensure/certification. These providers include aides, occupational therapists, physical therapists, physicians, licensed practical nurses, public health nurses, registered nurses, social workers, speech therapists and audiologists as well as any assistants to the above.

Federal regulations

As stated earlier, Medicare certification is provided by HCFA under Conditions of Participation for home health-care agencies. Home agencies providing maternal and child care through programs paid for by federal grant monies must adhere to the regulations set forth in the specific grant.

RELEASE OF INFORMATION

When home health services are provided by a variety of health-care professionals who either work for the coordinating agency or are contracted as independent providers, securing health information can become more difficult. It is necessary to ensure that the medical information necessary for continuity of care be available to all health-care professionals providing care, but it is important to monitor the release of that same information to be certain that it is only made available to those within the network of care. As with any health-care facility, release of medical information to anyone outside of the agency requires a signed authorization by the patient or legal representative prior to release. It should be noted that some states provide for an implied consent when the patient consents to treatment or care by a new health-care provider.

DOCUMENTATION GUIDELINES

According to the Conditions of Participation the general requirements for documentation of care provided in the home include a care plan which must be developed and reviewed by a physician at least every 60 days and more often if warranted by the condition of the patient.

Compilation of all components from various health-care providers is also a challenge. Disciplines submit documentation from outside the agency. This must be correctly integrated into one record in chronological order of services provided. Various payers may also require specialized forms. The agency must also meet these needs.

Keeping all providers abreast of the up-to-the-minute patient care plan and status can also be a challenge. Providers used to carry the record with them when visiting the patient. It is now illegal to remove the record from the agency and therefore it is not unusual for providers to copy needed information onto log sheets or cards to carry with them. This can, however, lead to errors in copying information which may increase liability. Many home health-care providers now carry laptop computers which can be uploaded with patient information and downloaded to main record-keeping location.

Specific requirements for documenting care

In accordance with HCFA rules, when the patient is discharged from nursing-care services, all other therapies and services with the exception of physical therapy must also be discharged. COP will review the documentation to determine the necessity of services provided by nursing personnel and therapists and 'carve out' days from payment based on lack of documentation. They also require that all orders be signed by the physician within 14 days, that a written summary report be sent to the physician every 62 days and that the physician review the plan of care every 62 days.

General policies which should be maintained for adequate records as stated by the Joint Commission (JCAHO) include the following:

- Presence of a clinical record for every patient. (Some agencies use the family system although this is not recommended)
- Standard format and design for all forms within the agency
- The record must contain consents for treatment and receipt of patient rights information
- Documentation within 24 hours of provided services and filed within 7 days
- Documentation of outside services must be signed and included within 14 days
- Record must demonstrate coordination of service between all health-care providers
- Presence of good documentation practices, i.e. ink, legible, well written, standard abbreviations, etc.
- All entries must be signed and dated
- Record must be easily accessible when needed
- A master patient index and active patient census must be maintained
- Indices by diagnoses and procedure must be maintained
- Retention of records for 7 years after last encounter and 7 years after minor reaches majority unless statute of limitations for individual state require longer
- Release of information must be regulated in accordance with law

Record content

Information contained in the record includes demographic data, clinical data, historical data and socioeconomic data. These categories of information are the same as might be found in most other health records.

Many different individual forms may be used. The most common are the following:

- Referral forms
- Patient consent forms
- Assessment and database
- Orders
- Medications sheets
- Ongoing progress notes
- Summaries

There must be an appropriate initial assessment which will form a database for the patient. This should include:

- Demographics
- Current health status (diagnosis, problem, vital statistics, etc.)
- Activities of daily living – limitations
- Sociophysiological status
- Environmental and economic status
- Care-giver information
- Dietary or nutritional information
- Plans and interventions required

- Expected outcomes with time frames
- Presence of advanced directives

RETENTION AND STORAGE

The most appropriate format for these records would be the source-oriented record because the actual care-givers do not record their information in one common place.

As with any other health-care organization, the methods of filing will depend on the size of the facility. One facility uses alphabetical filing so that records are more easily accessible to all of their staff, including nursing, etc. Records are continuous to include all encounters between a patient's uninterrupted sequential visits.

As stated previously, retention requirements of agency records change from state to state; however, it is recommended that they be maintained for a minimum of 7 years.

As records are a compilation of the documentation of various health-care providers, the information must be sorted in a way that will make retrieval easiest.

- Chronologically by provider
- Chronologically by patient problem
- Strict chronological order with integration of all information

Storage is still recommended in open-ended shelving units as is recommended in acute care, as this is the most efficient method of filing and retrieval. Most agencies, because of their relatively small patient population, choose to file records alphabetically, as opposed to using a numerical system.

CHALLENGES OF HIM PROFESSIONALS

Approximately 90–95% of home-care agencies still have paper-based record systems. One vendor of home-care software finds that studies have shown that this industry is the most paperwork-intensive area of health care[1]. Because of the unsupervised nature of the job, payers require documented proof of every step in the care-giving process. For example, it is found that nurses spend 2 hours documenting for every 1 hour of patient contact. By the end of 1997, it was expected that about 15% of the agencies in the US would have some form of mobile computing. If nurses are provided with a modem by their agency, and can download a day's worth of charts from home, they can avoid excessive trips into the office many times per week. It will also enable them to reduce charting time and thereby be able to increase the amount of time they spend with patients.

Ultimately, the managed-care organization will want to manage the continuum of care for a given disease across ambulatory care, home care and acute care and they will want to manage diseases to a specific protocol[1].

The latest trend in home care is telemedicine[2] which allows the nurse to point a camera at the patient's wound, in order for it to be viewed by a physician for further diagnosis. It enables specialists at premier health-care centers to lend their expertise to physicians at great distances. Telemetry monitoring is also transmittable from remote locations. Certificate courses are available to nurses who specialize in certain areas, such as diabetes and wound care, on using these advanced methods. As managed care is driving some of these trends, it is expected that their use will continue to rise.

The question often arises of how the HIM professional fits into the home-care scenario. As the need increases for more accurate, comprehensive and computerized databases, many job opportunities have been created. Time spent doing HIM duties takes away from patient care for other health-care professionals. Concerned about whether or not providers are actually doing what they are supposed to do, payers must be assured that patients are being properly cared for and this will be accomplished through documentation. As home care becomes more computerized, the job market will expand. In addition, HIM professionals have an important role in auditing documentation services needed in reimbursements for JCAHO compliance, and as Medicare and Medicaid requirements as well as concern with being able to pull information together when needed[3].

Medical record department challenges

In the past, documentation issues were addressed by nursing personnel who were untrained in medical record and file-maintenance procedures. Now, medical record/ health information professionals are being utilized more often although still somewhat scarcely. More commonly, these agencies would contract with a HIM professional on a consultation basis.

Traditional record practices are impractical in this setting. One big difference is the setting itself. Patients are cared for in their home. The professionals providing care are usually removed from the agency, therefore making coordination and communication more difficult.

Software technology is now available which enables nurses and other professionals in the field to access records at the home office, update patient charts, report progress or problems and transmit the required billing information to the home office the same day[4].

Health information department staffing requirements

There are no regulatory requirements for credentialed HIM professionals in these settings or any other. Unless an agency is relatively large, they will most likely not have an organized medical record department. However, those that do find the need will benefit from the following positions:

- Director to develop goals and objectives, set priorities and ensure standards are met and that the facility meets the accreditation and regulatory needs
- Coordinator to implement and coordinate systems and objectives, supervise clerical functions, and interface with clinical personnel to maintain compliance and provide coding services
- Clerk to perform the routine file clerk functions, i.e. assembly, filing, retrieval
- Trackers are used to follow up on ordered services to ensure that documentation is received from any providers seeing the patient. They also follow up with phone calls to physicians and other providers for needed signatures within the allowable time limits
- Carriers or transporters are used by many agencies to actually hand-carry forms to and from the physicians' offices and other contracted providers to meet documentation

requirements. Contractors at one agency bring in paperwork once a week although it is required to be present on the record within 48 hours

- Unit secretaries at one agency work with the nursing staff to secure documentation. Their policy is for nurses to turn in the previous day's documentation before being permitted to go out in the field to see new patients

HIM issues

The following issues were stated as problematic areas by some home health agency HIM personnel:

- Administrators do not understand the HIM professional's ability to contribute to improved systems
- Communication of information among diverse providers is difficult. They are all visiting patients at differing times and days. The use of a portable notebook computer with a central database will alleviate many problems. It is also recommended that a basic medical record be left in the home of the patient for the duration of care so that the information is available to any health-care provider visiting the patient
- Analysis of incomplete records is often considered less important than it should be because it is often difficult to get various health-care providers to complete their portions after the fact
- Must update code assignments used for billing every 2 months or when medically indicated which mandates continually updated information from providers. (Coding schemes used include ICD-9-CM for diagnosis, HCPCS for drugs and CPT-4 for procedures and treatments)

PERFORMANCE IMPROVEMENT AND QUALITY ASSURANCE ACTIVITIES

Regulatory and accreditation agencies mandate the home health agencies perform quality review activities. This will provide meaningful information on the quality of care and utilization of services. It will also permit the agency to assess the satisfaction of its patients and provider as well as to assess its liability risks and to be proactive in avoiding any future problems.

All of these practices will result in cost savings, increased efficiency, improved patient care as well as a resolution of interagency departmental conflicts which are often present when providers from multiple agencies are used.

JCAHO has expanded the ORYX initiative to include accredited home-care organizations to begin integrating the use of outcomes measures into the accreditation process. This gives them new opportunities to examine their processes of care and will serve to focus performance improvement activities.

References

1.   Chidley E. Home healthcare prepares to automate. *For the Record* 1997;9:8–11
2.   Tellis-Nayak M. The postacute continuum of care: understanding your patient's options. *Am J Nurs* 1998;98:44–8
3.   Gennusa CR. There's no place like home...for health care. *Adv Health Inf Prof* 1996;6:no. 5, March 11

4.   FieldChart™ now available for Home Healthcare Professionals. *For The Record (Products and Services)* 1997;9:no. 12

Additional suggested reading

Abdelhak M, *et al. Health Information: Management of a Strategic Resource.* Philadelphia: W.B. Saunders, 1996

Joint Commission introduces ORYX requirements for behavioral health and home care organizations. *For the Record* 1998;September 7

Manual of Standards for Hospice and Home Care. Oakbrook, IL: Joint Commission on Accreditation of Health Care Organizations, 1998

Peden AH. *Comparative Records for Health Information Management.* Albany, NY: Delmar Publishers, 1998

Personal communication

McNaughton, Constance, RHIT, Director of Medical Records, Essex Valley Visiting Nurse Association, East Orange, NJ, November 1998

Chapter 6

HOSPICE CARE

At the conclusion of this chapter you should be able to:

Define 'hospice'

Discuss the interdisciplinary group process in this health-care setting

Identify the agencies which accredit and/or regulate hospice organizations and discuss their requirements

Identify and discuss services which are unique in this setting

INTRODUCTION AND OVERVIEW

Hospice programs, as they are known today, did not appear in the US until the 1970s. Initially, some were formal, institutionally sponsored programs which offered a full range of home-care and inpatient services. Others, which have emerged as the present concept of the hospice, were freestanding groups of volunteers who primarily offered emotional support to the terminally ill and bereaved.

TYPE OF CARE RENDERED

Emphasis is on care, not cure, and making the most of each hour and each remaining day by providing comfort and relief from stresses and pain.

Care is provided in the patient's place of residence, whether that be in the patient's home or in a nursing home with hospice staff on call 24 hours a day.

The interdisciplinary group process is an essential component of all hospice services. When a patient is being admitted to hospice care, the medical director, the nurse and the social worker *all agree* to admit the patient to the program. Federal regulations then require that they together develop an initial plan of care within 48 hours of the patient's admission to the program. Changes in the patient's conditions which may arise due to the crisis nature of the patient's care may warrant adjustments to the care plan or may require the development of an entirely new care plan.

Not all hospice care will be provided at the same level. Again, as the crisis nature of the patient's case has a tendency to require differing degrees of intervention, it is essential that the program be able to respond to these changes. It is required that the program support through documentation the needs for provision of services at varying levels.

Continuous care must be supported in the documentation in accordance with definitions specified in federal regulations which actually state what will constitute continuous care in the hospice setting. The definition is as follows: A brief period of crisis for which 8 or more hours (out of a 24-hour day) of home nursing care are required. During this period, 51% of care must be provided by an RN or LPN. Documentation is critical in justifying the need for such an intensified level of home care as well as for determining the actual number of hours. The documentation may, however, reflect that there was initially no crisis, but that there was a precipitated potential crisis (see Exhibit 6-1).

Contract Services, as stated earlier, are required to document all services rendered. They may use forms generated by the hospice or forms designed by their own agencies as long as they provide all of the necessary information. Problems arise in securing this information in a timely fashion. One hospice has included in its contracts with services that payment will not be made for services rendered until complete documentation is received.

PATIENT POPULATION

Hospice patients are of all ages and are in the final stages of a terminal disease, usually with a prognosis of less than 6 months. With the increase in AIDS patients, the number of hospice organizations has mushroomed over the last decade.

The National Hospice Organization (NHO) states that there are approximately 1400 hospice programs. Only 200 of these are certified to provide care to Medicare patients.

LEGAL AND REGULATORY ISSUES

Licensing

Less than 20 states require that hospice programs be licensed or certified. This, however, is changing with the increased focus on health-care services.

Accrediting agencies

The National Hospice Organization publishes standards but has no survey process and does not require accreditation. The Joint Commission on Accreditation of Healthcare Organizations offers accreditation with its standards published in its manual for home care and hospice organizations. It is very uncommon, however, for freestanding agencies to seek accreditation.

Federal regulations

In order for any agency to seek reimbursement from Medicare, a federal program, it is necessary to comply with the Conditions of Participation, which are the guidelines for health-care services set forth by the Health Care Financing Administration. In meeting all of the conditions of participation and standards for certification to provide hospice care, a program is required to provide the following services to terminally ill persons who elect hospice care:

- Medical services
- Nursing care
- Psychosocial and pastoral counseling
- Pharmacy services
- Equipment and supplies
- Therapies, including physical therapy, occupational therapy, speech therapy

- Volunteer supportive services
- Lab services
- Nutritional services
- Transportation
- Inpatient respite care
- Short-term inpatient care
- Bereavement services

DOCUMENTATION GUIDELINES

Documentation serves several purposes:

- To make a record of the services provided to both the patient and family
- To reflect the processes by which needs were identified, services were rendered and subsequent problems were addressed
- As a vehicle through which the program demonstrates compliance with federal and state agencies and accrediting bodies
- As a means by which services rendered can be reimbursed from third-party payers

The patient/family record

The hospice record has many parts which are similar to parts discussed for other facilities/services. As with many organizations there are difficulties in maintaining the record which stem from services being provided by multiple disciplines which are part of the organization itself, as well as contracted services which are not formally a part of the organization. Many services for hospice patients are provided in the home and therefore have all the similar problems as discussed in the previous chapter.

Sections of the record include the following:

Application In order for a patient to be accepted into the hospice program, an application must be made by the referring physician. The medical physician of the hospice must certify that the patient is terminally ill and therefore eligible to receive hospice services. Also included in this section is the consent signed by the patient that he/she wants these services and a statement of participation by the family.

Assessments These include initial comprehensive nursing assessment, initial nursing visit report, initial comprehensive health history and examination, and psychosocial assessment (see Exhibit 6-2).

Care plan This includes anticipated services and is often broken down to address the planned action by different members of the team to address different needs of the patient, i.e. symptom management plan, medication record and home health aide plan of care (see Exhibits 6-3 and 6-4).

Progress notes and orders These are similar to what we have discussed before. They include the day-to-day notations made by all interdisciplinary group members and contract personnel regarding patient and family visits, phone contacts, service coordination and case management. Orders are requests by the physician and the nursing staff for treatment or interventions (and where law permits, requests of physician assistants and nurse practitioners). Verbal orders must be signed within 48 hours (*see* Exhibit 6-5).

Summary sheet/face sheet   As in most facilities, this contains demographic information about the patient and family.

Volunteer reports   These are unique to this setting. Hospice services are most often supplemented by volunteers who provide support and companionship to the patient and their families. A record of these services is required to be maintained.

Bereavement services   These are also unique to this setting. Information in this section will include adult and child pre-bereavement assessment as well as a bereavement follow-up plan. This demonstrates the importance of the role of all members of the patient support system, family and friends, who will play an active role in the hospice plan.

CHALLENGES OF HIM PROFESSIONALS

As the records in hospice agencies have similar problems to those in the home-care agencies, the challenges faced by HIM personnel are also quite similar.

PERFORMANCE IMPROVEMENT AND QUALITY ASSURANCE ACTIVITIES

Like most health-care organizations, hospices are required to collect information necessary for regulatory agencies, accreditation agencies as well as for sound business decisions to be made internally or by the parent organization.

Information collected and generated most often includes the following:

- Patient care days generated at levels of care
- Patient/family contacts
- Patients served, with fiscal data
- Volunteer visits by type of service

From this information, the following reports or information might be generated weekly, monthly, semiannually or annually:

- Projections of cost savings due to volunteer usage
- Projections of service caseload and service visits for future time frames

Suggested reading

Abdelhak M, *et al. Health Information: Management of a Strategic Resource.* Philadelphia: W.B. Saunders, 1996
Burnham R. Hospice care: making an informed choice. *USA Today Magazine* 1999;127:Issue 2646, March
Friedrich MJ. Hospice care in the United States: a conversation with Florence S. Wald. *J Am Med Assoc* 1999;281:Issue 18, May
Manual of Standards for Hospice and Home Care. Oakbrook Terrace, IL: Joint Commission on Accreditation of Health Care Organizations, 1998
Peden AH. *Comparative Records for Health Information Management.* Albany, NY: Delmar Publishers, 1998

SAMPLE FORMS IN HOSPICE CARE

Exhibit 6-1 HOSPICE NURSING VISIT NOTE

Pt. NAME _____MR# _____DATE _____TIME _____
Patient/Family Reports: _____
T: _____P: _____R: _____BP: _____Last BM: _____/_____
EENT: _____Respiratory _____M/S _____
                                                ☐ See wound
Neuro: _____GI _____Skin _____ flow sheet
C/V _____ GU _____Activity _____
Psychosocial _____

PAIN FOLLOW-UP ASSESSMENT

LOCATION/INTENSITY (Scale Used)   Quality MANNER OF EXPRESSING PAIN: Relieved by: PLAN:

New problem addressed this visit _____
On-going problems addressed _____
_____

Resolved problems _____
Goals _____
_____
_____

Interventions/teaching to   ☐ Pt   ☐ Family
_____
_____

Patient/family response   ☐ Pt   ☐ Family   ☐ verbalizes   ☐ returned
                                                       understanding   demonstration
                                                       of instructions
                              ☐ Pt   ☐ Family   ☐ needs further instruction on:
_____

Other comments: _____
☐ Conference/TC   ☐ Dr. ☐ SW   ☐ PC ☐ VC ☐ SNF ☐ Family _____
           RE: ☐ New orders   ☐ Change in condition   ☐ Other _____
Regarding: _____
☐ Supervisory visit   ☐ LPN   ☐ HHA   HHA care plan   ☐ reviewed   ☐ updated
                    ☐ LPN   ☐ HHA instructed in _____

Additional
comments: _____

Revisit plan _____   _____
                                                                    Signature/title

Exhibit 6-2 HOSPICE PSYCHOSOCIAL ASSESSMENT

Pt. Name _____MR# _____Date _____

Diagnosis _____Date of diagnosis _____

Family Structure: (Use narrative or genogram. Include number and length of marriages, quality of current relationship with spouse or significant other, number of children and quality of relationships, culture, religion, ethnicity, extended family or support system.)

Present Housing Situation: _____

Safety Risk   ☐ Yes   ☐ No   If yes, due to _____

Significant Dates in Family (Birthdays, Anniversaries, Deaths, Marriages, etc.)

_____

_____

Family Development: (Lifecycle issues – new marriage, infants or children or teens living at home, middle aged or retired, other alterations such as separated, divorced, gay, etc.)

_____

_____

_____

Family Function:

Communication style: ☐ Open ☐ Direct ☐ Clear ☐ Closed ☐ Indirect ☐ Masked

Role flexibility: _____

Alcohol or substance abuse: _____

Mental health history: _____

Patient Assessment:

Comprehension and acceptance of terminal illness: _____

_____

_____

Work/career history and level of satisfaction: _____

Leisure/social activity: _____

History of previous losses:_____

_____

HOSPICE PSYCHOSOCIAL ASSESSMENT (continued)

Coping style: _____

'What is important to you now?' _____

_____

Issues of Advance Directives and Funeral Planning _____

_____

Expectations of Hospice _____

_____

Caregiver Assessment:
For Patient Without Caregivers – Identify plan for future caregiving needs:

_____

_____

_____

Who is identified as the primary caregiver? _____

Ability and willingness to deliver care: _____

_____

Other persons involved in care and availability _____

_____

Other agencies involved _____

Areas of greatest concern _____

_____

Past losses and coping styles _____

_____

'What is important to you at this time?' _____

_____

Expectations of Hospice _____

_____

PATIENT–FAMILY STRENGTHS: _____

_____

PATIENT–FAMILY PROBLEMS	Patient	Caregiver
Anger related to:		
Coping		
Depression/helplessness/hopelessness		
Powerlessness		
Altered self-esteem/self-worth		

HOSPICE PSYCHOSOCIAL ASSESSMENT (continued)

PATIENT–FAMILY PROBLEMS	Patient	Caregiver
Body image disturbance		
Fear		
Financial concerns		
Impaired home maintenance		
Role stress		
Legal issues		
Social isolation		
Family conflict		
Anticipatory grief		
Funeral planning		
Communication difficulty		

GOALS:

☐ Develop effective coping strategies ☐ Establish trusting relationship
☐ Identify and cope with feelings ☐ Express feelings appropriately
☐ Mobilize resources ☐ Participate in grief work
☐ Effective communication ☐ Develop/improve problem solving skills
☐ Other _____

_____

INTERVENTIONS:
☐ Referral to _____

☐ Plan family meeting to _____

☐ Long-range planning for _____

☐ Counseling re: _____

☐ Obtain community resource _____

☐ Instruct patient/family in:

    ☐ Coping   ☐ Relaxation techniques   ☐ Fear reduction
    ☐ Stress management   ☐ Guided imagery   ☐ Diversional activities
    ☐ Communication techniques   ☐ Conflict resolution strategies
    ☐ How to access resources   ☐ Other _____

Crisis intervention   ☐ Assist with decision making
Evaluate support systems   ☐ Facilitate family communication
Encourage verbalization of feelings   ☐ Engage in live review
Arrange for admission of patient to _____

☐ Other _____

Anticipated visit pattern _____

_____
SIGNATURE/TITLE

Exhibit 6-3 INTERDISCIPLINARY CARE PLAN

HOSPICE PROGRAM
INTERDISCIPLINARY CARE PLAN

PATIENT NAME: _____ MR #: _____

DIAGNOSIS(ES):

ATTENDING PHYSICIAN: _____

PROGNOSIS: < 6 MONTHS

MEDICATIONS: As per med sheet ADMINISTERED BY: _____

Identified Problems (see reverse side)

1	5	9	13	17	21	25	29	33	37
2	6	10	14	18	22	26	30	34	38
3	7	11	15	19	23	27	31	35	39
4	8	12	16	20	24	28	32	36	

Person participating in care plan development/relationship: Patient care coordinator, Medical Director, Chaplain, Volunteer Coordinator, MSW, RN, Attending Physician.

Initial Assessment

Frequency of Visits/By Discipline: Nursing _____

MSW: Evaluation Visit   Home Health Aide _____

Volunteer: Evaluation Visit   Clergy: Evaluation Visit

Date of Next Review: _____

_____

_____   _____   _____
Primary Nurse/Date   Social Worker/Date   Counselor/Date

                                        _____
                                        Medical Director/Date

INTERDISCIPLINARY CARE PLAN (continued)

INTERDISCIPLINARY PATIENT/FAMILY PROBLEM LIST

1. Knowledge deficit
2. Altered bowel habits
3. Altered respiratory status
4. Cardiac output alteration
5. Urinary elimination alteration
6. Potential for injury
7. Comfort, alteration in pain
8. Mobility impaired
9. Nutrition, alteration in
10. Skin integrity, impairment or actual
11. Sleep pattern, disturbance
12. Knowledge deficit re: infusion device
13. Alteration in mental status
14. Alteration in fluid volume
15. ADL deficit
16. Communication, impairment of
17. General patient care management
18. Knowledge deficit re: Diabetes Mellitus
19. Injury potential related to chemotherapy
20. Anxiety, patient/family
21. Knowledge deficit 2nd to dying process or terminal illness
22. Home maintenance management impaired
23. Coping ineffective individual/family
24. Anticipatory grieving patient/family
25. Spiritual distress
26. Self-concept disturbance
27. Lack of social support
28. Non-compliance with plan of care
29. Social isolation and loneliness
30. Estate plan, funeral and burial plan, lack of
31. Health-care insurance, lack of
32. Income insufficient
33. Housing unsafe
34. Living arrangements insufficient
35. Lack of transportation
36. Emotional distress
37. Long-term planning
38. Altered quality of life re: terminal illness
39. Suicide risk

Exhibit 6-4 HOME HEALTH AIDE CARE PLAN

Hospice Center
Home Health Aide Care Plan

Patient Name _____ Medical Record # _____

DNR Signed ☐ Yes ☐ No

PERSONAL CARE	HOME MANAGEMENT
Bed Bath _____ Tub Bath _____ Shower _____ Oral Hygiene _____ Shampoo _____ Shave _____ Skin Care _____ Lotion/Massage _____ Dressing Activity _____ Other _____	☐ Kitchen _____ ☐ Linen Change _____ ☐ Laundry _____ ☐ Equipment _____ ☐ Bathroom _____ ☐ Grocery Shopping _____ ☐ Transport Client _____ ☐ Precautions _____ ☐ Other _____

ACTIVITIES	VITAL SIGNS
Ambulate _____times/day _____ad lib _____cane _____walker _____crutch _____restricted to _____ _____ Wheelchair Activity _____ Transfer Bed to Chair _____ Up in Chair _____ ROM Exercises _____times/day Site _____ Bedrest _____ Turn _____ Other _____	☐ Pulse _____ ☐ Respirations _____ ☐ Blood Pressure _____ ☐ Temperature _____ ☐ Weight _____ ☐ Precautions _____

ELIMINATION	SAFETY PRECAUTIONS

SAFETY PRECAUTIONS

Client	Caregiver	
☐	☐	_____
☐	☐	_____
☐	☐	_____
☐	☐	_____

ELIMINATION	UNIVERSAL PRECAUTIONS ☐ YES
Toilet _____ Bedside Commode _____ Bedpan _____ Urinal _____ Empty Catheter Drainage Bag at _____ Change Ostomy Appliance PRN or at _____ Other _____	Call Hospice Nurse for _____ _____ _____ _____ _____

NUTRITION	SPECIAL INSTRUCTIONS:
Prepare Breakfast _____ Prepare Lunch _____ Prepare Dinner _____ Prepare Snack _____ at _____o'clock Force fluids _____glasses/day Special diet (as follows) _____ _____ Other _____	

Hospice RN _____ Date _____

White – Medical Record Copy   Yellow – Pt. Home Copy   Pink – Home Health Aide Copy

Exhibit 6-5 HOSPICE INTERDISCIPLINARY PROGRESS NOTE

Type of contact	Discipline	Patient _____
☐ Home Visit ☐ Hospital Visit ☐ SNF Visit ☐ Telephone Consult	☐ Nurse ☐ Med. Soc. Worker ☐ Spiritual ☐ Bereavement ☐ Physician ☐ Other ☐ Volunteer	Medical Record # _____ Primary Caregiver _____ Date & Time Contact _____

NARRATIVE

Signature/Title

HOSPICE INTERDISCIPLINARY PROGRESS NOTE

Type of contact	Discipline	Patient _____
☐ Home Visit ☐ Hospital Visit ☐ SNF Visit ☐ Telephone Consult	☐ Nurse ☐ Med. Soc. Worker ☐ Spiritual ☐ Bereavement ☐ Physician ☐ Other ☐ Volunteer	Medical Record # _____ Primary Caregiver _____ Date & Time Contact _____

NARRATIVE

Signature/Title

Exhibit 6-6 DNR/DNI REQUEST FORM

HQSPICE PROGRAM

DNR/DNI REQUEST FORM

These directives are the expressed wishes of the patient and/or patient proxy, are medically appropriate, and are documented in the patient's permanent medical record.

Do Not Resuscitate (DNR): In the event of an acute cardiac or respiratory arrest, no cardiopulmonary resuscitation will be initiated.

Do Not Intubate (DNI): In the event of acute or impending respiratory failure, endotracheal intubation to provide sustained assisted ventilation will not be performed. (DNI does not prohibit emergency management to prevent or reverse acute airway obstruction with oral, nasal, or esophageal obturator airways or treatment of transient respiratory insufficiency with oxygen or short trials of assisted ventilation with positive pressure ventilation equipment or ambu-bags.)

_____   _____
Physician Signature   Date

_____
Address

_____   _____
Nurse/Organization Patient Representative   Date

White copy: Medical Record
Yellow Copy: Patient

Exhibit 6-7 DNR/DNI AUTHORIZATION FORM

Hospice Program
DNR/DNI Authorization Form

(An advanced request by the patient to limit the
scope of emergency medical care)

I, _____, request limited emergency medical care as herein described.

I understand DNR means that if my heart stops beating or if I stop breathing, no medical treatment will be started or continued.

I understand DNI means that if I stop breathing I will not be placed on an artificial breathing machine.

I understand either or both of these decisions will not prevent me from obtaining medical care by paramedics and other medical care prior to my death at the direction of my physician.

I understand I may revoke these directives at any time.

I give permission for this information to be given to paramedics, doctors, nurses, or other health personnel as necessary to implement these directives.

I hereby agree to the 'Do Not Resuscitate' (DNR) Order _____ (initial)

I hereby agree to the 'Do Not Intubate' (DNI) Order _____ (initial)

_____   _____
Patient/proxy signature   Date

_____   _____
Responsible Party   Date

White – Medical records
Yellow – Patient/Facility
Pink – MD

Chapter 7

CORRECTIONAL HEALTH CARE

At the conclusion of this chapter you should be able to:

> State several terms used throughout the United States to identify facilities of confinement

> Identify the federal agency responsible for the coordination of health-care services in federal facilities

> Name and describe the three primary sections of health programs of the US Bureau of Prisons

> Name the agencies which offer accreditation and guidance of these facilities and discuss the services they provide

> Discuss the benefits of accreditation to these organizations and how this differs from other health-care settings

> Differentiate between 'essential' standards and 'important' standards giving examples of each

INTRODUCTION AND OVERVIEW

Correctional facilities, prisons, jails and detention centers exist at all levels of our government. Facilities at city and county levels are often referred to as 'jails' while state and federal facilities are referred to as 'prisons'. The term 'detention center' is usually reserved for juvenile offenders, and is also used by the Department of Immigration and Naturalization. Additionally, there are separate facilities maintained for military personnel serving in the armed forces of the United States.

At all of these institutional settings, it is necessary to provide health services to those in residence. How these services are offered, whether by on-site personnel employed by the system or through contracted services varies throughout the nation. This chapter deals with these health services.

The Bureau of Prisons/Health Programs Section coordinates medical, dental and mental health services of federal inmates[1]. The Health Program Section has three primary sections:

- Chief health professionals serve as a liaison to professional staff in the field institutions and provide recruitment assistance
- Health promotion/disease prevention provides assistance to staff and inmates to increase awareness of, and compliance with, methods and practices currently used to control the spread of infectious diseases

- Health programs for the efficient and effective plan of health-care delivery in the Federal Bureau of Prisons.

Table 7-1 Population of correctional facilities[2]

No. of persons in correctional facilities	1998 midyear statistics
Prison inmates (state & federal)	1,277,866
Jails (local)	592,462

PATIENT POPULATION

These places of incarceration have no shortage of residents as seen in the figures displayed in Table 7-1. In 1997, one out of every 155 US residents was behind bars. For that same period of time it was reported that local jails were responsible for approximately 640,000 offenders[3].

TYPE OF CARE RENDERED

The purpose of these facilities is not to offer a particular type of health care but to house an incarcerated population for a specific period of time. This population must be provided with basic health services as well as specialized evaluation and treatment as necessary. Therefore, the type of care available is as varied as those services available to the general public. The providers of care may include physicians, nursing personnel, physician assistants as well as any other health-care professional employed directly or through contracted services.

LEGAL AND REGULATORY ISSUES

Licensing

Licensure is granted by the government level which operates a particular facility. Therefore, the licensing requirements can vary greatly. Although it is not required that all correctional facilities and jails have on-premise medical facilities, prisoners must have access to health care whether provided by the prison and jail, or through local health-care organizations with these agencies.

Accrediting agencies

The National Commission on Correctional Health Care (NCCHC) is an organization that offers accreditation to correctional facilities. This not-for-profit organization works toward improving the quality of health care in confinement facilities at all levels of government.

The services of the NCCHC include the following:

- Health services administration
- Educational conferences and seminars
- Quality assurance reviews
- Technical assistance and consultation
- Professional certification
- Publications

They are supported by 37 organizations representing health, law and corrections, all of which have representation on the NCCHC Board of Directors.

As with other accreditation processes, the external peer review is voluntary and is done through on-site surveys much like that of other accreditation organizations, thereby rendering a professional judgement on the quality of the facility health services. In order to ensure no bias by the Accreditation Committee of the NCCHC, the survey information collected at the on-site review is submitted in a blind report for accreditation determination.

Accreditation is based on national standards that cover the following areas:

- Facility governance and administration
- Environmental health and safety
- Personnel and training
- Health-care services support
- Inmate care and treatment
- Health promotion
- Disease prevention
- Special needs and services
- Health records
- Medical legal issues

One might wonder what the benefits of accreditation might be to a facility that operates outside of the financial restrictions imposed on other health-care organizations. According to the NCCHC, accreditation promotes efficiency as well as increasing facility prestige, staff morale, efforts to recruit personnel, community support and justification for budgetary requests. In addition, it is helpful in minimizing adverse events, reducing liability premiums, and protecting the facility from lawsuits related to health care.

Standards are classified as being either 'essential' or 'important'. A facility seeking accreditation must meet 100% of essential standards and 85% of important standards. The facility health service may be deficient in no more than two of the essential standards to be considered for accreditation. Detailed information on these standards is discussed later in this chapter.

Other organizations

American Correctional Health Services Association (ACHSA) is a membership organization for all correctional health-care professionals. It serves as an effective forum for current issues and needs confronting correctional health care.

The American Correctional Association publishes standards which are developed by correctional professionals which mainly focus on prison administration and operation.

The American Public Health Association has developed health-care standards which provide some guidance to correctional health-care programs but offer no accreditation process.

RELEASE OF INFORMATION

It is important to understand that an incarcerated person has two separate records. One is their administrative record maintained by facility personnel and the other is the health record maintained by medical personnel. The two must be maintained separately. These health records should not be stored in the same location as inmate confinement records. Confidentiality must be maintained by securing health records from unauthorized access by non-medical personnel. The relationship of doctor/patient still extends to inmates and their clinicians.

They are subject to the same state and federal regulations concerning release of information as general medical records. As drug/alcohol use and HIV/AIDS is very predominant in this population, it is important to remember that records of inmates with these documented conditions are protected by specific laws that still apply.

Upon transfer, the medical record should accompany or precede the inmate in order to maintain continuity of care. When appropriate, the record must be flagged to alert the receiver of the information of the inmate needs for immediate or rapid treatment or attention.

An acceptable method of maintaining privacy of records in transport is to place them in a locked bag to be opened only by medical personnel at the receiving facility. This is carried by the correctional officer who has responsibility for making the transfer.

A large percentage of requests for information come from the inmates themselves, their attorneys or public defenders filing suit on behalf of the inmates, sometimes against the correctional system.

DOCUMENTATION GUIDELINES

Medical record format and content

The NCCHC[4] recommends that the medical record be maintained as a problem-oriented medical record (POMR). Regardless of the system in use, the record should be standardized and uniform in its content and forms. All clinical encounters must be documented with date, time and authentication.

At a minimum the record should contain the following:

- Identifying information
- Problem list (including allergies)
- Initial screening
- Health assessment forms
- All findings, diagnoses, treatments and dispositions
- Medications
- Laboratory reports and other diagnostic studies
- Progress notes
- Consent and refusal forms
- Discharge summary from hospitalizations
- Release of information forms

- Report of consultations including dental and psychiatric evaluations
- Special treatment plan if appropriate
- Immunization records
- Place, date, time of each medical encounter
- Signature and title of writer

Essential standards (required 100% of time)

Receiving screening This should include:

- Inquiry into the current illness and health problems of the person
- Observation of behavior
- Deformities
- Skin condition
- Disposition of person, i.e. referral

The purpose is to prevent inmates with health or behavior risks from entering the general facility population. This process may be carried out by a trained correctional staff member but, when available, medical personnel should be used.

Access to treatment This must be communicated to inmates verbally and in writing. This will allow the patient to utilize the services that are available.

Full health assessment Physical examination must be conducted within 14 days of arrival to include recording of vital signs and appropriate laboratory testing.

Non-emergency medical requests There must be a mechanism in place for the daily handling of these requests to the general population as well as those in segregation.

Sick call provisions i.e. clinic set-up must be available to address the needs of ambulatory inmates, although it is not essential that this service be offered on a daily basis. The size of the facility, the volume of services needed and availability of personnel will determine the frequency of sick calls from once a week to 5 times per week.

Medical orders These must comply with state law (or federal law for federal facilities). The laws will define who may write orders and what limitations exist. Medication administration training is required for all personnel who are to administer medicinal substances.

Emergency services These must be available 24 hours per day for emergency medical and dental care.

Important standards (required 85% of time)

Mental health evaluation This must be conducted within 14 days of confinement with treatment needs addressed as soon as possible, to prevent further deterioration and exploitation.

Treatment philosophy Inmates must be treated with respect and dignity; for example, appropriate consents must be obtained from the patient for invasive exams/treatments.

Treatment protocols Protocols must be established which specify the steps to be taken in appraising the patient's physical status. (These differ from standing orders that specify the same course of treatment for each patient suspected of the same condition.)

Grievance mechanism This must be in place to address complaints about health services. It must also be evident that the policy is in use and must state the time frame for response to the grievance and the process for appeal.

Infection control program A program should include concurrent surveillance of patients and staff, prevention techniques, treatment and reporting of infections in accordance with applicable laws. These would most likely include control programs and treatment of tuberculosis, HIV, sexually transmitted diseases, as well as other communicable diseases that are prevalent in confined situations.

Health promotion and disease prevention This requires health education, training in self-care and inoculations for immunization.

Continuity of care This will include securing and utilizing information on previous care as well as sharing information in accordance with law when inmates are transferred. It is also necessary upon discharge or release from the facility into the community to provide referral and information as required to continue health care.

Not every inmate will have a comprehensive medical record or need medical services other than the initial screening. However, once services are rendered a record must be established.

RETENTION AND STORAGE

Retention of records is in accordance with the statute of limitations for the jurisdiction in which the facility is operating. Facilities which use contracted health management services may have policies for retention which exceed the legal requirements.

As with any other type of facility, there are both active and inactive medical records. Active records are those which are most often accessed or used and are usually stored in an area which is convenient to their use. Inactive records are usually those of inmates who are no longer confined in the correctional system.

The storage options in these facilities will be similar to those in any other type of health-care setting. Depending on the size of the population, filing options might include terminal or middle digit, color coding and other schemes which will increase efficiency.

Numbering schemes may be developed by the individual facility where each new inmate receives the next sequential number or utilizes an available number such as the prisoner number assigned by the system. An accession number is also often used which would indicate when the person entered the system.

CHALLENGES OF HIM PROFESSIONALS

There is currently no requirement for a credentialled HIM professional despite an effort by AHIMA in 1992 to force the issue with a letter writing campaign. Despite this, many correctional facilities or systems employ health information professionals to manage the health record processes. This requires an understanding of the public health and legal considerations of providing health care in a unique environment.

One issue stated by a practicing HIM professional is the problem with employee retention. It is difficult to assess an employment candidate's ability to withstand the restriction of the strictly secure environment. Although many state that working in this confined setting will not be a problem, many last only a short time.

HIM professionals who wish to remain in this type of setting may choose to become a Certified Correctional Health Professional (CCHP) which recognizes an individual's knowledge of the national standards for health care established by the NCCHC.

PERFORMANCE IMPROVEMENT AND QUALITY ASSURANCE ACTIVITIES

Statistical data is collected on a Uniform Record and Reprint System Form and is submitted to the Bureau of Justice and National Prisoner Statistics Organization. It is then forwarded to the Department of Criminal Justice and the Federal Bureau of Prisons.

Forms used for Quality Improvement Review to assess the completeness and timeliness of the health record are included (see Exhibits 7-1 and 7-2).

References

1. United States Bureau of Prisons. http://www.bop.gov. 1998;November
2. United States Bureau of Justice. http://www.ojp.usdoj.gov/bjs. 1999;May
3. *CorrectCare.* National Commission of Correctional Health Care, 1998;12:Issue 1
4. *Manual of Standards.* National Commission of Correctional Health Care, 1998

Personal communication

Pichinson, Lisa, RHIA, Prison Health Services, Philadelphia, PA, March 1997

SAMPLE FORMS IN CORRECTIONAL HEALTH CARE

Exhibit 7-1 QUALITY IMPROVEMENT DOCUMENT

Timeliness & Completeness of Medical Records   Effective Date 01-01-xx

Date _____

Reviewer's Signature _____

Site _____

Key Code: Y = Present   N = Absent   N/A = Not Applicable

1.	The periodic physical examination form is complete with vital signs, weight, time, date & signature of examiner									
2.	Examination included all body systems									
3.	Laboratory, X-rays & other diagnostic studies were obtained									
4.	Problem list reflects the patient's medical health problems & is congruent with the medical record									
5.	The medical record is in the approved order									
6.	Entries of encounters are made in the 'SOAP' format									
7.	All entries are legible and include the date, time & signature of writer									
8.	Telephone and verbal orders are signed by the physician giving the order within 48 hours									
9.	All orders are noted & implemented & include date, time, signature & title of the nurse noting the order									
10.	All laboratory, X-ray, diagnostic tests & results of consultation are noted with the physician's initial and date noted									
11.	The results for all labs, tests, etc. ordered are filed in the patient medical record									

Exhibit 7-2 MEDICAL RECORDS AUDIT

Correctional Health Care

OUT-OF-CUSTODY MEDICAL RECORDS AUDIT
Facility: _____ **OOC Charts from** ___ / ___ **to** ___ /

Policy: All out-of-custody medical records must be in compliance with company policies and procedures.

Procedure: A random sample of _____ medical records were chosen and evaluated to meet the following criteria:

Criteria	Met standard	Did not meet standard
1. Correct numbering labels were used to represent the PP#		
2. All dividers were removed		
3. All documents were filed in the correct location		
4. All documents were filed in reverse chronological order		
5. All documents were fastened onto the chart prongs		
6. All carbon copies were removed		
7. All lab slips were on horizontal lab mount sheets		
8. Vertical line of 'X' was written after the last entry on every page		
9. Left side of chart was placed on top of right side of chart		
10. Medical records filed in continuous terminal digit order from box to box		
TOTALS		

Audit performed by: _____ Date performed: _____

Records accepted into the Regional MRD: Met Criteria   YES   NO
                                                          (circle one)

Chapter 8

POST-ACUTE (SUBACUTE) CARE

At the conclusion of this chapter you should be able to:

Define post-acute and subacute care and describe the health-care settings most often associated with this period of care

Describe the impetus behind the increase in the utilization of post-acute services

Describe the requirements of documentation in this health-care setting

Describe various quality assurance measures currently utilized in post-acute and subacute care

INTRODUCTION AND OVERVIEW

According to the Joint Commission on Accreditation of Health Care Organizations, 'subacute care programs are those which are separate and distinct inpatient programs providing highly skilled rehabilitative care or medical intensive care for patients following an acute event or significant change in condition'; 'goal-oriented, comprehensive, inpatient care designed for an individual who has had an acute illness, injury, or exacerbation of a disease process'[1]. It is rendered in place of inpatient hospitalization in the acute-care setting or immediately following a hospital stay to patients who require less intensive care than provided in the hospital yet more intensive care than they would receive in a skilled nursing facility.

More accurately the definition of subacute care describes programs rather than sites at which a patient receives health care. They have been referred to as the new halfway houses for the recovering patients[2]. They are often located in long-term care facilities, which may not be equipped to handle this level of care, or in underutilized units of hospitals. There are more than 45,000 subacute care beds in the US, and non-elderly patients occupy a third of them according to the American Subacute Care Association and it is one of the fastest growing levels of care in the industry[2]. In 1995, there was a projected growth from $1 billion at that time to $10 billion by the year 2000[3]. One significant reason for this trend is that hospital stays are getting shorter due to the pressures of managed-care organizations. Controversies arise, and are evidenced in the news, of patients being discharged too soon and suffering avoidable consequences. Hospital stays have decreased significantly as is somewhat obvious by the number of hospitals being downsized and closed. Patients also leave sooner due to advances in medical technology and the fact that the longer you remain in the hospital the more likely it is you might develop a complication from infection. Sometimes the result of this abbreviated hospital stay is that the patient will have to recover from his or her medical or surgical episode elsewhere. As there are fewer family members available or capable of fulfilling this role, these alternative sites have been established (Table 8-1).

The cost expended for care in subacute settings is 40–60% lower than in acute-care hospitals even though the subacute program offerings are clinically and therapeutically comparable to those offered in the medical, surgical or rehabilitation units of acute-care facilities[4].

Subacute care is a cross between traditional long-term care and the med/surg and stepdown nursing of 10 years ago. It was created for those patients who need complex medical treatment or rehab but do not require high-tech monitoring or complex diagnostic procedures. Driven by a growth in Medicare Risk plans and other third-party payers searching for cost-effective alternatives to acute care, the specialty was born in skilled nursing facilities[5].

Subacute care requires coordination of services from multiple disciplines, such as physician, nursing and various therapies to manage specific patient problems which hinder the patient's return to the community. Subacute care can be provided in many settings. Many hospitals and long-term care facilities have established subacute care units to address this growing need. The length of stay at this level is usually between 14 and 21 days.

Table 8-1 Categories of subacute care[6]

Category	Average length of stay	Nursing care/day	Usual setting
Transitional	5–30 days	5.5–8.0 hours	Hospital HMO based
General	10–40 days	3.5–5.0 hours	Nursing home
Chronic	60–90 days	3.0–5.0 hours	Nursing home
Long-term transitional	25+ days	6.5–9.0 hours	Hospital

Other sources state that transitional facilities are one step down from ICUs, providing long-term care for patients with acute yet stable conditions who have either chronic or ICU-type needs. These sources state the average minimum stay is 25 days with nursing care provided from 9 to 12 hours per day[7].

Another type of facility not mentioned above is the Assisted Living Facility[7]. These facilities, which are being built as new facilities or being opened in structures which were formerly other types of health-care centers, such as hospitals, deliver many levels of care. They have been created to fill the gap in services between independent living and nursing-home care, and facilities are regulated by the state rather than federal government. Some provide little more than group meals, others offer services resembling skilled nursing homes.

The Assisted Living Federation of America (ALFA) defines assisted living as special accommodation for housing, personalized support services and health care designed to meet the needs, both scheduled and unscheduled, of those who require help with their activities of daily living (ADL). Through waivers some states allow residents to use Medicaid dollars to pay for care provided at these facilities. Residents in assisted living are older and frailer, in greater need of help at varying degrees. As their needs increase, the services provided can also be increased without the resident having to change facilities. It is not surprising that the level of professional nursing services at these facilities is on the rise as the there is a high occupancy in specialized units. There is also an increasing demand for care of patients with Alzheimer's disease in this setting.

Adult day care[7], another type of post-acute care, provides assisted living, subacute care and skilled care. Patients who live in their own homes or with family members come to an adult day-care facility to gain the benefits of social interaction. Clients who live alone in their homes are provided with a social outlet even if they have no medical needs. For adults who require intensive supervision, it affords care-givers the opportunity to go to work, do the grocery shopping or run errands. The National Adult Day Services Association is developing accreditation criteria for member facilities. There are currently three levels of care:

- Core which is described as unskilled assisted living
- Enhanced which encompasses skilled nursing that requires little supervision and support, i.e. changing dressings, monitoring serum drug levels
- Intensive which is for people who need maximum care and generally includes skilled nursing care as well as therapies that require a great deal of supervision and support

TYPE OF CARE RENDERED

Care for patients in various stages of illness and injury, usually after, but sometimes in place of, hospitalization for acute episodes. To control costs, alternatives are sought for low-risk patients to bypass hospitals.

Following is a list identifying the types of care offered by subacute settings:

- Cardiac recovery
- Oncology recovery including chemotherapy and radiation treatments
- Dialysis
- Subacute rehabilitation
- Intravenous therapy
- Ventilator maintenance
- Neurological impairment, i.e. post cerebrovascular accident
- Orthopedic aftercare
- Complex medical conditions requiring close monitoring, i.e. coronary artery bypass graft (CABG), congestive heart failure (CHF), etc.

Patients receive the coordinated services of various health professionals aimed at returning the patient to their home, often with a visiting nurse or other home-care services which include:

- Continuing treatment of partially resolved acute conditions
- Management of coexisting problems and illnesses
- Delivery of rehabilitative and restorative care

- Uncomplicated care, i.e. antibiotics or basic physical therapy for patients not requiring acute care
- Management of the ethical and psychosocial consequences of illness[8]

Subacute care can be specialized or generalized and can include an overlap of various types of services rendered in other settings such as rehab and SNF care.

According to Levenson[8], subacute care should neither be a downsizing of acute care nor an upscaling of nursing home care. As each patient is quite unique in his/her needs, the care needs to be patient-specific. The frequency of physician visits must be determined by the patient diagnosis, co-morbidities and complications. Once-a-month visits required in LTC are insufficient to most patients. Subacute settings must be able to anticipate, identify and prevent or manage intermediate-level complications, such as UTI, without having to transfer patients back into the acute-care setting as this would be highly inefficient and costly. The attention to the patient problems should be based on the functional and physical status, prognosis and wishes of the patient.

Nurse practitioners and physician assistants play an important role in subacute care. Nurse practitioners are trained in medical models of diagnosis and treatment and physician assistants can perform basic diagnosis and treatment tasks and perform technical procedures consistent with their skills. Some physicians employ them in their practices to assist in the care of subacute patients.

PATIENT POPULATION

As stated previously, patients in subacute care are recovering from treatment or surgery at a more intense level such as inpatient hospitalization. Although they have now reached the point of not requiring inpatient hospital care, they are not ready to return to their previous life circumstances

LEGAL AND REGULATORY ISSUES

Licensing

Licensing in most states is required under the same criteria as long-term care facilities. This function is often under the direction of the state's Department of Health.

Accrediting agencies

Up until 1995, the Joint Commission on Accreditation of Health Care Organizations (JCAHO) had been applying the standards from the *Accreditation Manual for Long Term Care*. The JCAHO now has an accreditation protocol for subacute programs which has been written to interpret already existing standards in acute care and skilled care and to apply them to subacute care. The established protocol applies to facilities with services not as intensive as acute care yet at a higher level than skilled nursing care.

The standards provide requirements concerning time frames, staff qualifications, organizational structure, leadership, safety and equipment management. All of these must be tailored to the subacute patient. In regard to patient care, the standards address the following:

- Care management
- Care planning
- Care of the dying patient
- Patient/family education
- Medical care
- Nursing care
- Oral health
- Nutritional care
- Therapeutic activities
- Rehabilitation
- Respiratory services
- Pharmaceutical services
- Social services
- Spiritual services
- Diagnostic services

The Commission on Accreditation of Rehabilitation Facilities (CARF) has been applying its standards for rehabilitation medicine to subacute care facilities as well.

Federal regulations

These must comply with the Omnibus Budget Reconciliation Act of 1987.

DOCUMENTATION GUIDELINES

Subacute facilities have regulations for documentation which are similar to long-term care facilities. Documentation requirements may be more demanding than at hospitals. These facilities must abide by long-term care rules and regulations. Paperwork is generated for each patient as if he were a long-term resident, although the stay may only be 5–14 days[7].

Specific requirements for documenting care

The documentation standards of the JCAHO were adapted for subacute care facilities using the *Accreditation Manual for Long Term Care*. The following items are required:

- Resident medical assessment
- Post-procedure status
- Identification information
- Diagnosis support and justification

Specific items for documentation are often mandated by the state licensing agency and may include the following:

- History and physical examination performed by a physician, nurse practitioner, clinical nursing specialist or physician assistant. The professional permitted to perform these duties is specified in the regulations of the licensing agency
- Documentation of prior care to include signs and symptoms, treatment and/or medications, resident responses to previous therapies and medications, changes in physical or emotional condition

- Documentation of a plan of care which must be reviewed every 2 weeks for the first quarter, each month of the second quarter and quarterly thereafter or as indicated by the patient's condition (see Exhibit 8-1)
- Physician orders. Telephone orders must be countersigned in accordance with licensing agency regulations
- Documentation of existence or non-existence of an advanced directive
- A progress report to be documented within 10 days after initiation of a rehabilitation plan
- Discharge plan (see Exhibit 8-2)
- Discharge note written on the day of discharge which includes the diagnosis, prognosis, psychosocial and physical condition of the resident
- Discharge summary containing appropriate information from each service completed by the resident (see Exhibit 8-3)

RETENTION AND STORAGE

The issues which relate to this section on retaining health information and the methods of storage of that information are similar to those in other segments of health care, particularly long-term care.

CHALLENGES OF HIM PROFESSIONALS

The complex nature of regulations, accreditation standards and reimbursement systems makes information management in subacute care quite challenging. Emphasis is placed on providers to maintain a high level of quality of outcome as in other settings while caring for patients in this cost-effective setting. Because of the need to continually monitor current costs and care needs, quality data management on a concurrent basis is mandatory[9].

PERFORMANCE IMPROVEMENT AND QUALITY ASSURANCE ACTIVITIES

The explosive growth in this industry has gone beyond efforts to regulate its quality. Not all subacute care facilities have lower quality of care. Many are quite good but it is up to the individual patient or family to assess this.

According to the JCAHO the scope of care of the subacute program is specifically reflected in monitoring and evaluation activities. They have cited this level of care as a major emergence in health care today.

A case management system involving clinical pathways is an essential step forward in efficient restructuring of resources to reduce wasted time, energy and materials, and to promote a well-coordinated continuity of care through collaborative practice patterns[4].

Within a subacute setting a clinical pathway is defined as a treatment regimen that includes all elements of care enabling patients with a specified DRG to move toward desirable outcomes. It differs from an acute-care clinical pathway in that it focuses on a specific target population in an advanced phase of the recovery period. Patients admitted to subacute care are assigned to a clinical pathway designed to meet their individual care needs. It is written in outline the typical course of recovery within the prescribed time period, thus achieving the desired outcomes. Essential elements of the clinical pathway are:

- Duration: time it takes for patient to reach a predetermined point
- Human functional health pattern: basic areas of assessment for the S.A. pt.
- Intensity or level of care: patient's functional capacity and extent of care required to maximize their capabilities. Measures what the patient can actually do at the time of admission
- Interdisciplinary team involvement
- Clinical treatment plan
- Allowance for deviations/variances from the norm

In the past years many subacute care providers have acquired software for clinical outcomes measurements to attract managed-care business. The patient care delivery system should include care maps/critical pathways, quality management and utilization management, disease management, health assessment and wellness/prevention/health promotion as well as external report capabilities. Managed-care organizations soon will require proof of quality outcomes generated by information systems as a means of market differentiation for contracting purposes[10].

In terms of quality-based competition, hallmarks for a managed-care company to contract with a subacute care provider will be price, access, quality outcomes and accreditation. Being price competitive will not be easy if the subacute care provider cannot track its costs and utilization. Access to services can best be achieved with a case management system in place. Quality outcomes are valuable only if they are trended against a benchmark. Accreditation is a measure of quality that managed-care companies mandate[11].

A case management system involving clinical pathways is an essential step forward[4] in efficient restructuring of resources to reduce wasted time, energy and materials and to promote a well-coordinated continuity of care through collaborative practice patterns. A clinical pathway is defined as a treatment regimen that includes all elements of care enabling patients to move toward desirable outcomes. A subacute clinical pathway differs from an acute-care clinical pathway as it focuses on a specific target population in an advanced phase of the recovery period.

The essential elements of subacute clinical pathways are as follows:

- Duration: the time it takes a patient's condition to stabilize or a predetermined treatment course to be completed, enabling the patient to re-enter the community
- Human functional health pattern: these patterns represent a composite of the patient's profile and delineate the basic areas of assessment for the subacute patient. The information is provided through patient information obtained through observation and documentation
- Intensity or level of service: the patient's functional capacity and the extent of care required to maximize their capabilities
- Interdisciplinary team involvement: requires coordination of all team members working together to determine the patient's case type (or DRG) and the appropriate clinical pathway

- Clinical treatment plan: reflects all disciplines' roles in patient care. The critical interventions listed in the pathway must ensure that the patient receives the care necessary to make certain that the expected outcome and discharge occur within the determined time frame. The plan must delineate crucial incidents with proper progressive sequencing of medical and nursing interventions
- Deviation/variances from the norm: occur when patient care or outcomes differ from the original projection. These deviations must be monitored to identify and document specific factors that affect a change in outcome or length of stay
- Expected outcomes: are evaluated to ascertain whether or not they were achieved. The outcome criteria initially projected must be written in measurable, behavioral and realistic terms

References

1. Joint Commission on Accreditation of Health Care Organizations. http://www.jcaho.org/acr_orgs/help_frm.htm. 1999
2. Ruben D. No place to heal. *Health* 1998;12:Issue 1, Jan/Feb, 102
3. Stahl DA. Maximizing reimbursement for subacute care. *Nurs Manage* 1995;April
4. Colucciello ML, Mangles LM. Clinical pathways in subacute care settings. *Nurs Manage* 1997;June
5. Davis SM. Subacute care: yesterday's med/surg. *RN* 1997;November
6. Griffin K. *Handbook of Subacute Health Care.* Gaithersburg, MD: Aspen Publications, 1995
7. Tellis-Nayak M. The postacute continuum of care: understanding your patient's options. *Am J Nurs* 1998;98:44–8
8. Levenson SA. *Subacute and Transitional Care Handbook.* St. Louis: Beverly-Cracorn, 1996
9. Peden AH. *Comparative Records for Health Information Management.* Albany, NY: Delmar Publishers, 1998
10. Stahl DA. Business strategies in subacute care. *Nurs Manage* 1997;February
11. Stahl DA. Managed care trends: the effect on subacute care. *Nurs Manage* 1997;March

Additional suggested reading

Stahl DA. Balanced Budget Act of 1997: what it means to subacute care. *Nurs Manage* 1997;November

SAMPLE FORMS IN POST-ACUTE (SUBACUTE) CARE

Exhibit 8-1 PHYSICIAN PLAN OF CARE AND DISCHARGE PLAN

DIAGNOSIS:

LEVEL OF CARE: ☐ SNF ☐ S/A ☐ A

TREATMENT:
1. Specific treatment and medication orders (see order sheets)
2. Special therapies: PT, OT, ST, etc. (see order sheets)

SHORT-TERM GOALS:
☐ Improve acute condition   ☐ reality orientation
☐ Re-establish continence   ☐ stabilize physical and mental status
☐ Other _____
Time estimate _____☐ days ☐ weeks ☐ months

LONG-TERM GOALS:
☐ Minimal assistance in ADL   ☐ develop maximum potential
☐ Maintain status quo   ☐ function independently
Time estimate _____☐ days ☐ weeks ☐ months

PROGNOSIS:
Long Term: ☐ Good   ☐ Fair   ☐ Poor
Short Term: ☐ Good   ☐ Fair   ☐ Poor   ☐ Terminal

STATUS OF MAJOR IMPAIRMENT

☐ Improving   ☐ Stable   ☐ Degenerating

DISCHARGE PLAN
PROBABLE LENGTH OF STAY

_____ months _____ weeks   ☐ Permanent NH placement

ANTICIPATION OF AFTERCARE

☐ Permanent NH placement
☐ Sheltered boarding home (minimal assistance)
☐ Return to independent living

REHABILITATION POTENTIAL

☐ Lower level of care
☐ Minimal assistance in ADL in supervised or institutional setting
☐ Limited employment and/or activities
☐ Return to former employment and/or activities
☐ Maintain status quo
       ☐ Good   ☐ Fair   ☐ Poor   ☐ None

_____   _____
Signature   Date

Exhibit 8-2 DISCHARGE PLAN

SUBACUTE CARE FACILITY
DISCHARGE PLAN

PATIENT NAME _____ ADMISSION DATE _____

In developing the discharge plan, each department should specifically include the following, if applicable:

    A.   Short-term goal/projected level of care with time estimate
    B.   Treatment/teaching required prior to discharge
    C.   Resources needed and available for post-care (home health, boarding, etc.)

NURSING

	SIGNATURE	DATE

SOCIAL SERVICE

	SIGNATURE	DATE

DIETARY

	SIGNATURE	DATE

PATIENT ACTIVITES

	SIGNATURE	DATE

PHYSICAL THERAPY

	SIGNATURE	DATE

OCCUPATIONAL THERAPY

	SIGNATURE	DATE

MEDICINE – refer to MD plan of care

	PHYSICIAN SIGNATURE	DATE

SUMMARY

MEDICAL DIRECTOR SIGNATURE	DATE

Exhibit 8-3 DISCHARGE SUMMARIES

SUBACUTE CARE FACILITY
DISCHARGE SUMMARIES

PATIENT NAME _____ DISCHARGE DATE _____

In developing the discharge summary, each department should specifically include the following, if applicable:

A. Treatment provided and results	C. Preparation for discharge
B. Reason for discharge	D. Recommendation for post-care

NURSING

_____
                                          SIGNATURE   DATE

SOCIAL SERVICE

_____
                                          SIGNATURE   DATE

DIETARY

_____
                                          SIGNATURE   DATE

PATIENT ACTIVITIES

_____
                                          SIGNATURE   DATE

PHYSICAL THERAPY

_____
                                          SIGNATURE   DATE

OCCUPATIONAL THERAPY

_____
                                          SIGNATURE   DATE

MEDICINE

_____
                             PHYSICIAN SIGNATURE   DATE

MEDICAL DIRECTOR SIGNATURE   DATE
_____

Chapter 9

LONG-TERM CARE

At the conclusion of this chapter you should be able to:

Describe the type of care generally rendered in long-term care facilities

Describe the requirements for documentation in this health-care setting

Identify the assessments required for long-term care patients

Describe the overall content of the minimum data set (MDS) and the uses of the data collected

INTRODUCTION AND OVERVIEW

Long-term health care is needed by individuals who are no longer able to cope with their activities of daily living for any length of time and have no alternate care providers or who need the services beyond what the care provider is able to offer. Long-term care facilities have an average length of stay of 30 or more days. This is a critical issue facing our nation because of the aging of our population. Due to the changing demographics in our society, the number of long-term care facilities and the proportion of health care provided in this arena have grown to great proportions. Advances in medicine now permit people to live longer while there are fewer non-working family, friends and neighbors available to care for their elders at home[1].

Nursing homes (long-term care facilities) have long been the subject of repeated scandals for poor care, patient abuse and patient neglect. As there is such a shortage of long-term care beds with a high demand, state governments may have been reluctant to close facilities because the problem of care would shift to being their responsibility.

There continues to be a problem of bed availability, especially for patients receiving public assistance.

TYPE OF CARE RENDERED

Long-term care is residential, overnight care that is provided at a variety of levels. As determined by the needs of the patient, care rendered may be at one of the following levels:

- Skilled nursing care
- Intermediate care
- Respite care
- Assisted living centers
- Independent living facilities

There is new emphasis in skilled nursing care. Forty-seven per cent of all people over the age of 85 have a diagnosis of dementia[2]. There needs to be communication between nursing home and hospital nurses to understand the patient which will save time and frustration. Patients who have had a particular routine in their lives and in the nursing home will benefit from efforts to continue that routine, e.g. elderly patient who always worked at night will look for something to do with their time in the late evening rather than be ready to retire to bed.

Most facilities offer more than one level of care. Should the patient's condition change during their stay, the level of care would be adjusted accordingly.

PATIENT POPULATION

The majority of patients, referred to as residents in these facilities, are elderly (90% are over 65[1]), with the balance including patients who need extensive care due to debilitating disease, trauma and spinal cord injuries, birth defects and mental illness.

The users of long-term care represent a mosaic of sub-segments of the population including:

- The elderly, as well as those with chronic illness and functional disabilities. Of persons 65+, 80% have at least one chronic health problem while the majority have multiple health problems. About 15% of persons aged 65–69 years experience activities of daily living disabilities which occurs in over half of those 85 years and older[3]
- Veterans who are disabled (by 2000 37% or 8.9 million veterans will be seniors)
- The terminally ill, e.g. those with AIDS
- Young disabled: 75% of the chronically ill are under 65 years and 42% with functional disabilities are under 65
- Mentally ill: one-quarter of the population suffers some sort of mental illness

LEGAL AND REGULATORY ISSUES

Licensing

As with any other type of facility, licensing is required in accordance with the state laws applicable to the area. When a facility is licensed to operate it must follow the laws and regulations of that state concerning the care and treatment of patients.

Accrediting agencies

JCAHO accreditation is required to be eligible for Medicare reimbursement as well as to negotiate any managed-care contracts.

Federal regulations

The Health Care Finance Administration established the Nursing Home Reform Act in 1987 which set guidelines for long-term care services.

Within the last year the federal government has instituted Resource Utilization Groups (RUGS) which is a prospective payment system for long-term care facilities. This payment system is discussed in the reimbursement chapter later in this text.

RELEASE OF INFORMATION

Medicare reviews a large portion of medical records in the long-term care setting. There are problems with them requesting copies of records in bulk. Other requests are from lawyers (who often have power of attorney), disability, and insurance carriers other than Medicare.

Long-term care facilities are now being requested to re-disclose information that was originally provided to them by the hospital which transferred the patient to them. Although HIM professionals have believed that re-disclosure is not legally correct, it is now felt by some institutions that since this information is incorporated as part of the patient's permanent record at the facility in lieu of a history and physical, it may be forwarded to the fiscal intermediary. Others continue to refer requests for hospital information back to the hospital.

In accordance with HCFA section 483.10(d)(3), the release or refusal of information is at the discretion of the patient except in cases of transfer to another facility or as required by law.

DOCUMENTATION GUIDELINES

Record content is governed, for the most part, by federal regulations, for those facilities accepting Medicare and Medicaid reimbursement, and by state licensing regulations. These mandates will direct a facility as to which information must be recorded and at what intervals. The facility may choose the method of recording this information as well as the design of forms or computer screens to be used for data collection.

Patients in the long-term care setting progress at a substantially slower rate in comparison to an acute-care patient. Because of this it takes a longer time for these patients to achieve goals set toward maximum functional levels. It is important that accurate and complete documentation be maintained which demonstrates the patient's progress.

As in any other facility, a separate medical record must be maintained for each resident.

Specific requirements for documenting care

Information collection is begun prior to admission as the patient is assessed by the receiving facility to determine if he or she will be accepted for admission. If the patient, or representative, has consented to the admission to a long-term care facility, they are implying consent for the release of basic health information necessary to establish a continuum of care and to insure that the patient's immediate health-care needs are addressed upon arrival.

The admission record or face sheet should contain sufficient information to:

- Identify the patient: name, address, phone, record number, date of birth, age, sex
- Determine the responsible party: next of kin or legal representative and information necessary to contact that person
- Physician's name, address and phone
- Third-party payer: name, identification number, phone/contact
- Other information such as referral source, patient's marital status and religion

Additional information which should be available upon admission includes:

- Certification of level of care upon admission (federally reimbursed)
- Evidence that patient/responsible party was informed of patient rights
- Advanced directive/health-care proxy
- Initial orders for medication and treatment as determined by the responsible physician
- Consents for treatment
- Inventory of personnel effects brought in by patient
- A care plan by the health-care team is required by most licensing agencies within a specified number of days after admission to the long-term care facility. HCFA section 483.20(d)(2) requires development within 7 days of completion of the comprehensive assessment. The JCAHO requires that this be reviewed every 90 days (Standard TX 3.1). A team consisting of nursing personnel, therapists, social services and nutritional services would evaluate and prioritize the needs of the patient and determine appropriate goals (see Exhibit 9-1)

Within 24 hours of admission the record must contain the following:

- Nursing care plan

Within 48 hours of admission the record must contain the following:

- History and physical
- Initial assessment in subacute to include assessment by nursing personnel, therapists, social services and nutritional services
- Recreation plan in subacute
- RAPS (Resident Assessment Protocol Summary), which identifies potential problems and existing problems to develop care plan (Medicare)

Within 5 days of admission there must be the following:

- Minimum data set (MDS) (then quarterly and annually) (see Exhibit 9-2)

Additional forms and data which will be included in the patient record:

- Physician orders: because the physician is not present for long periods of time, changes and renewals in medications and care regimens are made via the telephone. These telephone orders must be signed within 48 hours
- Progress records contain narrative documentation of the patient's status, including responses to therapies and medications. The physician must document periodically that the patient has been examined as well as certifying the need for continued care as outlined by the patient's insurer. The JCAHO and HCFA require that the

physician visit every 30 days for the first 3 months and then every 60 days. The progress notes should reflect these visits

- Nurses' notes are crucial in the long-term care facility since the majority of care provided to the patient is by nursing personnel. The notes contain continued documentation of the patient's health status (including symptoms, behavior, appetite, weight, skin condition), nursing care rendered and the patient's response to that care. In addition, nursing personnel will document efforts to contact other medical personnel as well as unusual incidents which occur
- Restraint orders must be present including the reason and time limit, with incorporation into the care plan and acknowledgement by the family (JCAHO TX 8.1)

Discharge plan and documentation

As many patients aim to return to the community, it is necessary to include in the patient record a discharge plan which will state what goals the patient needs to achieve to accomplish this (see Exhibits 9-3 and 9-4).

As the patient approaches these goals, a plan must be in place to provide the patient with the appropriate education and referral to make their return to the community a success. The patient or caretaker would also be given written discharge instructions to ensure proper care outside of the facility.

Patients permanently discharged must have a discharge order written by the physician (whether for discharge home or transfer to another facility).

Nursing personnel must also write a discharge note stating the time and method of discharge and the condition of the patient. If the patient expires, the nurse's documentation will also include the time and circumstances of death, as well as notification to the physician and next of kin, and disposition of the body.

A discharge summary must be completed by the physician to summarize important information related to the patient's stay.

RETENTION AND STORAGE

The time required for retention of medical records is determined by state/licensing regulations. It is recommended that information be maintained for 10 years by AHIMA. Storage is often a problem because of the volume of information collected on patients who are confined for years. An adequate system of thinning the record and storing inactive components is required (see Exhibit 9-5).

CHALLENGES OF HIM PROFESSIONALS

Responsibilities in long-term care include traditional management functions, facilitating JCAHO committees within the facility, and fulfilling the roles of Quality Improvement Coordinator, Statistician and Medical Staff Liaison. HIM professionals have the responsibility for coding the appropriate diagnoses for each resident's stay. This is required reporting on the medical data set (MDS). As part of the MDS team the health information professional works to make sure that the facility is reimbursed properly under the RUGS system.

Other responsibilities of the HIM in long-term care are:

- To create and maintain a filing system that provides for efficient filing and retrieval of records, while assuring confidentiality, security, and safety of records
- Chart audits for documentation compliance; QA reports; forms
- Administrative rounds; meal monitoring; family tours
- Making new charts; ordering forms; thinning records; filing loose reports; coding diagnosis
- Assembly and analysis of discharge records; chart completion procedures, correspondence processing
- Ensure record completion within the allowable time

The prospective payment system is going to change the role of the HIM in skilled facilities. Our expertise in data collection, analysis, assessing for quality/accurate data will be needed and better used. There will be an even closer tie-in with billing. It will be essential for the HIM professional to learn much more about Medicare billing rules, Fiscal Intermediaries coding expectations, etc. Coding knowledge will be better used.

AHIMA has a long-term care section which focuses on the special education and information needs of those who are working in this environment.

PERFORMANCE IMPROVEMENT AND QUALITY ASSURANCE ACTIVITIES

Long-term care facilities are required to complete all the required elements of the medical data set (MDS) which is mandated by HCFA. MDS will contain information on admission, significant changes, and assessments annually, quarterly, re-entry and discharge subsets[1]. The goal for MDS automation is to implement a more efficient and effective process for evaluating and assuring quality, which reduces the burden on providers. The data will be used for utilization review, Medicaid certification, and quality monitoring by the state survey agency as well as to determine the survey focus using quality indicators, as a resource for standards of care, clinical practice, research, analysis and policy information. The data will not be individually identified. AHIMA has been involved in development of confidentiality measures.

Clinical pertinence (Medical Record Review) must be completed quarterly for long-term care facilities (*see* Exhibits 9-6 and 9-7).

JCAHO has established the ORYX initiative to integrate performance measures into the accreditation process. Approved by the JCAHO board in January 1997, this initiative changes from a standards-based static assessment of health-care organizations to a continuous and dynamic assessment that includes performance measures and outcomes. Facilities were required to select a performance measurement system which included 2–5 clinical performance indicators relating to 20% of the patient population by early 1998. It was also planned that enrollment with a performance measurement system would be required by June 1998 with submission of data by June 1999.

References

1. Raffle MW, Raffle NK. *US Health Care System: Origins and Functions*, 4th edn. Albany, NY: Delmar Publishers, 1994
2. Tellis-Nayak M. The postacute continuum of care: understanding your patient's options. *Am J Nurs* 1998;98:44–8
3. Williams SJ, Torrens PR. *Introduction to Health Services*, 5th edn. Albany, NY: Delmar Publishers, 1999

Additional suggested reading

Abdelhak M, *et al. Health Information: Management of a Strategic Resource.* Philadelphia: W.B. Saunders, 1996

Anderson R. Long-term care facilities prepare for HCFAs MDS pilot project. *Adv Health Inf Prof* 1996;6: no. 23

Cofer J. *Health Information Management*, 10th edn. Berwyn, IL: Physician Record Co., 1994

Comprehensive Accreditation Manual for Long Term Care. Oakbrook Terrace, IL: Joint Commission on Accreditation of Healthcare Organizations, 1998

Peden AH. *Comparative Records for Health Information Management.* Albany, NY: Delmar Publishers, 1998

Personal communications

Juliano, Donna, RHIA, Director of Medical Records, King James Care Center, Somerset, NJ, April 1997

Tolbert, Antoinette, RHIA, Director of Medical Records, Willow Creek Rehabilitation and Care Center, Somerset, NJ, February 1999

SAMPLE FORMS IN LONG-TERM CARE

Exhibit 9-1 PATIENT PLAN

LONG-TERM CARE PATIENT PLAN

DEPARTMENT CODES A ACTIVITIES N NURSING D DIETARY S SOCIAL SERVICES PT PHYSICAL THERAPY OT OCCUPATIONAL THERAPY RT RESPIRATORY THERAPY ST SPEECH THERAPY	Diagnosis _____ _____ Resident's identified strength _____ _____ Discharge plan _____ Diet _____ Rehab potential _____ Overall goal _____

Date	Problem	Goal	Time span	Approach or plan	Dept code	Date resolved

Resident	Resident no.	Physician	Room no.

PATIENT PLAN (continued)

RE-EVALUATION

Change in Diagnosis _____

_____

Current Level of Care _____

Medical Reason for Placement

_____

_____

_____

Coordinator _____

Date _____

- -

Re-evaluation of Discharge Plan

Change in Diagnosis _____

_____

Current Level of Care _____

Medical Reason for Placement

_____

_____

_____

Coordinator _____

Date _____

- -

Re-evaluation of Discharge Plan

Change in Diagnosis _____

_____

Current Level of Care _____

Medical Reason for Placement

_____

_____

_____

Coordinator _____

Date _____

Exhibit 9-2 MINIMUM DATA SET FORM

MINIMUM DATA SET (MDS) — *VERSION 2.0*
FOR NURSING HOME RESIDENT ASSESSMENT AND CARE SCREENING
BASIC ASSESSMENT TRACKING FORM

SECTION AA. IDENTIFICATION INFORMATION	

GENERAL INSTRUCTIONS

Complete this information for submission with all full and quarterly assessments (Admission, Annual, Significant Change, State or Medicare required assessments, or Quarterly Reviews, etc.).

1. **RESIDENT NAME** ⊙
   a. (First)   b. (Middle Initial)   c. (Last)   d. (Jr./Sr.)

2. **GENDER** ⊙
   1. Male   2. Female

3. **BIRTHDATE** ⊙
   Month   Day   Year

4. **RACE/ ETHNICITY** ⊙
   1. American Indian/Alaskan Native   4. Hispanic
   2. Asian/Pacific Islander   5. White, not of
   3. Black, not of Hispanic origin   Hispanic origin

5. **SOCIAL SECURITY ⊙ AND ⊙ MEDICARE NUMBERS** [C in 1st box if non Med. no.]
   a. Social Security Number
   b. Medicare number (or comparable railroad insurance number)

6. **FACILITY PROVIDER NO.** ⊙
   a. State No.
   b. Federal No.

7. **MEDICAID NO.** ["+" if pending, "N" if not a Medicaid ⊙ recipient]

8. **REASONS FOR ASSESS-MENT**
   [Note—Other codes do not apply to this form]
   a. Primary reason for assessment
      1. Admission assessment (required by day 14)
      2. Annual assessment
      3. Significant change in status assessment
      4. Significant correction of prior full assessment
      5. Quarterly review assessment
      10. Significant correction of prior quarterly assessment
      0. *NONE OF ABOVE*
   b. Codes for assessments required for Medicare PPS or the State
      1. Medicare 5 day assessment
      2. Medicare 30 day assessment
      3. Medicare 60 day assessment
      4. Medicare 90 day assessment
      5. Medicare readmission/return assessment
      6. Other state required assessment
      7. Medicare 14 day assessment
      8. Other Medicare required assessment

9. **SIGNATURES OF PERSONS COMPLETING THESE ITEMS:**

a. Signatures   Title   Date

b.   Date

⊙ = Key items for computerized resident tracking

☐ = When box blank, must enter number or letter

☐a = When letter in box, check if condition applies

Code "−" if information unavailable or unknown

TRIGGER LEGEND

1 - Delirium	10A - Activities (Revise)
2 - Cognitive Loss/Dementia	10B - Activities (Review)
3 - Visual Function	11 - Falls
4 - Communication	12 - Nutritional Status
5A - ADL-Rehabilitation	13 - Feeding Tubes
5B - ADL-Maintenance	14 - Dehydration/Fluid Maintenance
6 - Urinary Incontinence and Indwelling Catheter	15 - Dental Care
7 - Psychosocial Well-Being	16 - Pressure Ulcers
8 - Mood State	17 - Psychotropic Drug Use
9 - Behavioral Symptoms	17* - For this to trigger, O4a, b, or c must = 1-7
	18 - Physical Restraints

MINIMUM DATA SET FORM (continued)

Resident _____   Numeric Identifier _____

MINIMUM DATA SET (MDS) — *VERSION 2.0*
FOR NURSING HOME RESIDENT ASSESSMENT AND CARE SCREENING
BACKGROUND (FACE SHEET) INFORMATION AT ADMISSION

SECTION AB. DEMOGRAPHIC INFORMATION

1.	DATE OF ENTRY	Date the stay began. Note — Does not include readmission if record was closed at time of temporary discharge to hospital, etc. In such cases, use prior admission date.

☐☐ — ☐☐ — ☐☐☐☐
Month   Day   Year

2.	ADMITTED FROM (AT ENTRY)	1. Private home/apt. with no home health services 2. Private home/apt. with home health services 3. Board and care/assisted living/group home 4. Nursing home 5. Acute care hospital 6. Psychiatric hospital, MR/DD facility 7. Rehabilitation hospital 8. Other
3.	LIVED ALONE (PRIOR TO ENTRY)	0. No 1. Yes 2. In other facility
4.	ZIP CODE OF PRIOR PRIMARY RESIDENCE	☐☐☐☐☐
5.	RESIDENTIAL HISTORY 5 YEARS PRIOR TO ENTRY	*(Check all settings resident lived in during 5 years prior to date of entry given in item AB1 above.)* Prior stay at this nursing home — a. Stay in other nursing home — b. Other residential facility — board and care home, assisted living, group home — c. MH/psychiatric setting — d. MR/DD setting — e. *NONE OF ABOVE* — f.
6.	LIFETIME OCCUPA-TION(S) (Put "/" between two occupations)	
7.	EDUCATION *(Highest level completed)*	1. No schooling 5. Technical or trade school 2. 8th grade/less 6. Some college 3. 9-11 grades 7. Bachelor's degree 4. High school 8. Graduate degree
8.	LANGUAGE	*(Code for correct response)* a. Primary Language 0. English 1. Spanish 2. French 3. Other b. If other, specify ☐☐☐☐☐☐☐☐☐☐
9.	MENTAL HEALTH HISTORY	Does resident's RECORD indicate any history of mental retardation, mental illness, or developmental disability problem? 0. No 1. Yes
10.	CONDITIONS RELATED TO MR/DD STATUS	*(Check all conditions that are related to MR/DD status that were manifested before age 22, and are likely to continue indefinitely)* Not applicable — no MR/DD (Skip to AB11) — a. MR/DD with organic condition Down's syndrome — b. Autism — c. Epilepsy — d. Other organic condition related to MR/DD — e. MR/DD with no organic condition — f.
11.	DATE BACKGROUND INFORMATION COMPLETED	☐☐ — ☐☐ — ☐☐☐☐ Month Day Year

SECTION AC. CUSTOMARY ROUTINE

1.	CUSTOMARY ROUTINE	*(Check all that apply. If all information UNKNOWN, check last box only)*

(In year prior to DATE OF ENTRY to this nursing home, or year last in community if now being admitted from another nursing home)

CYCLE OF DAILY EVENTS

Stays up late at night (e.g., after 9 pm)	a.
Naps regularly during day (at least 1 hour)	b.
Goes out 1+ days a week	c.
Stays busy with hobbies, reading, or fixed daily routine	d.
Spends most of time alone or watching TV	e.
Moves independently indoors (with appliances, if used)	f.
Use of tobacco products at least daily	g.
NONE OF ABOVE	h.

EATING PATTERNS

Distinct food preferences	i.
Eats between meals all or most days	j.
Use of alcoholic beverage(s) at least weekly	k.
NONE OF ABOVE	l.

ADL PATTERNS

In bedclothes much of day	m.
Wakens to toilet all or most nights	n.
Has irregular bowel movement pattern	o.
Showers for bathing	p.
Bathing in PM	q.
NONE OF ABOVE	r.

INVOLVEMENT PATTERNS

Daily contact with relatives/close friends	s.
Usually attends church, temple, synagogue (etc.)	t.
Finds strength in faith	u.
Daily animal companion/presence	v.
Involved in group activities	w.
NONE OF ABOVE	x.
UNKNOWN — Resident/family unable to provide information	y.

END

SECTION AD. FACE SHEET SIGNATURES

SIGNATURES OF PERSONS COMPLETING FACE SHEET:

a. Signature of RN Assessment Coordinator			Date
b. Signatures	Title	Sections	Date
c.			Date
d.			Date
e.			Date
f.			Date
g.			Date

☐ = When box blank, must enter number or letter

☐a. = When letter in box, check if condition applies

Code "—" if information unavailable or unknown

NOTE: Normally, the MDS Face Sheet is completed once, when an individual first enters the facility. However, the face sheet is also required if the person is reentering this facility after a discharge where return had not previously been expected. It is **not** completed following temporary discharges to hospitals or after therapeutic leaves/home visits.

Form 1728RHH   © 1997 Briggs Corporation, Des Moines, IA 50306 (800) 247-2343 PRINTED IN U.S.A.
Copyright limited to addition of trigger system.

MDS 2.0   1/30/98

MINIMUM DATA SET FORM (continued)

Resident _____ Numeric Identifier_____

MINIMUM DATA SET (MDS) — *VERSION 2.0*
FOR NURSING HOME RESIDENT ASSESSMENT AND CARE SCREENING
FULL ASSESSMENT FORM
(Status in last 7 days, unless other time frame indicated)

SECTION A. IDENTIFICATION AND BACKGROUND INFORMATION

1. RESIDENT NAME

a. (First)   b. (Middle Initial)   c. (Last)   d. (Jr./Sr.)

2. ROOM NUMBER

3. ASSESSMENT REFERENCE DATE
a. Last day of MDS observation period

Month   Day   Year

b. Original (0) or corrected copy of form (enter number of correction)

4a. DATE OF REENTRY
Date of reentry from most recent temporary discharge to a hospital in last 90 days (or since last assessment or admission if less than 90 days)

Month   Day   Year

5. MARITAL STATUS
1. Never married   3. Widowed   5. Divorced
2. Married   4. Separated

6. MEDICAL RECORD NO.

7. CURRENT PAYMENT SOURCES FOR N.H. STAY
(Billing Office to indicate; **check all that apply in last 30 days**)
Medicaid per diem	a.
Medicare per diem	b.
Medicare ancillary part A	c.
Medicare ancillary part B	d.
CHAMPUS per diem	e.
VA per diem	f.
Self or family pays for full per diem	g.
Medicaid resident liability or Medicare co-payment	h.
Private insurance per diem (including co-payment)	i.
Other per diem	j.

8. REASONS FOR ASSESSMENT
[Note—If this is a discharge or reentry assessment, only a limited subset of MDS items need be completed]

a. Primary reason for assessment
1. Admission assessment (required by day 14)
2. Annual assessment
3. Significant change in status assessment
4. Significant correction of prior full assessment
5. Quarterly review assessment
6. Discharged—return not anticipated
7. Discharged—return anticipated
8. Discharged prior to completing initial assessment
9. Reentry
10. Significant correction of prior quarterly assessment
0. NONE OF ABOVE

b. Codes for assessments required for Medicare PPS or the State
1. Medicare 5 day assessment
2. Medicare 30 day assessment
3. Medicare 60 day assessment
4. Medicare 90 day assessment
5. Medicare readmission/return assessment
6. Other state required assessment
7. Medicare 14 day assessment
8. Other Medicare required assessment

9. RESPONSIBILITY/ LEGAL GUARDIAN
(Check all that apply)
Legal guardian	a.
Other legal oversight	b.
Durable power of attorney/health care	c.
Durable power of attorney/financial	d.
Family member responsible	e.
Patient responsible for self	f.
NONE OF ABOVE	g.

10. ADVANCED DIRECTIVES
(For those items with supporting documentation in the medical record, **check all that apply**)
Living will	a.
Do not resuscitate	b.
Do not hospitalize	c.
Organ donation	d.
Autopsy request	e.
Feeding restrictions	f.
Medication restrictions	g.
Other treatment restrictions	h.
NONE OF ABOVE	i.

SECTION B. COGNITIVE PATTERNS

1. COMATOSE
(Persistent vegetative state/no discernible consciousness)
0. No   1. Yes (*If yes, skip to Section G*)

2. MEMORY
(Recall of what was learned or known)
a. Short-term memory OK—seems/appears to recall after 5 minutes
0. Memory OK   1. Memory problem **2**

b. Long-term memory OK—seems/appears to recall long past
0. Memory OK   1. Memory problem **2**

☐ = When box blank, must enter number or letter.

[a.] = When letter in box, check if condition applies

Code "—" if information unavailable or unknown

---

3. MEMORY/ RECALL ABILITY
(Check all that resident was *normally* able to recall during *last 7 days*)
Current season	a.	That he/she is in a nursing home	d.
Location of own room	b.	NONE OF ABOVE	e.
Staff names/faces	c.	are recalled	

4. COGNITIVE SKILLS FOR DAILY DECISION-MAKING
(Made decisions regarding tasks of daily life)
0. INDEPENDENT—decisions consistent/reasonable
1. MODIFIED INDEPENDENCE—some difficulty in new situations only **2**
2. MODERATELY IMPAIRED—decisions poor; cues/supervision required **2**
3. SEVERELY IMPAIRED—never/rarely made decisions **2, 5B**

5. INDICATORS OF DELIRIUM— PERIODIC DISORDERED THINKING/ AWARENESS
(Code for behavior in the *last 7 days.*) [Note: Accurate assessment requires conversations with staff and family who have direct knowledge of resident's behavior over this time.]
0. Behavior not present
1. Behavior present, not of recent onset
2. Behavior present, over last 7 days appears different from resident's usual functioning (e.g., new onset or worsening)

a. EASILY DISTRACTED—(e.g., difficulty paying attention; gets sidetracked) 2 = **1, 17***

b. PERIODS OF ALTERED PERCEPTION OR AWARENESS OF SURROUNDINGS—(e.g., moves lips or talks to someone not present; believes he/she is somewhere else; confuses night and day) 2 = **1, 17***

c. EPISODES OF DISORGANIZED SPEECH—(e.g., speech is incoherent, nonsensical, irrelevant, or rambling from subject to subject; loses train of thought) 2 = **1, 17***

d. PERIODS OF RESTLESSNESS—(e.g., fidgeting or picking at skin, clothing, napkins, etc.; frequent position changes; repetitive physical movements or calling out) 2 = **1, 17***

e. PERIODS OF LETHARGY—(e.g., sluggishness; staring into space; difficult to arouse; little body movement) 2 = **1, 17***

f. MENTAL FUNCTION VARIES OVER THE COURSE OF THE DAY—(e.g., sometimes better, sometimes worse; behaviors sometimes present, sometimes not) 2 = **1, 17***

6. CHANGE IN COGNITIVE STATUS
Resident's cognitive status, skills, or abilities have changed as compared to status of 90 days ago (or since last assessment if less than 90 days)
0. No change   1. Improved   2. Deteriorated **1, 17***

SECTION C. COMMUNICATION/HEARING PATTERNS

1. HEARING
(With hearing appliance, if used)
0. HEARS ADEQUATELY—normal talk, TV, phone
1. MINIMAL DIFFICULTY when not in quiet setting **4**
2. HEARS IN SPECIAL SITUATIONS ONLY—speaker has to adjust tonal quality and speak distinctly **4**
3. HIGHLY IMPAIRED/absence of useful hearing **4**

2. COMMUNICATION DEVICES/ TECHNIQUES
(Check all that apply during last 7 days)
Hearing aid, present and used	a.
Hearing aid, present and not used regularly	b.
Other receptive comm. techniques used (e.g., lip reading)	c.
NONE OF ABOVE	d.

3. MODES OF EXPRESSION
(Check all used by resident to make needs known)
Speech	a.	Signs/gestures/sounds	d.
Writing messages to express or clarify needs	b.	Communication board	e.
American sign language or Braille	c.	Other	f.
		NONE OF ABOVE	g.

4. MAKING SELF UNDERSTOOD
(Expressing information content—however able)
0. UNDERSTOOD
1. USUALLY UNDERSTOOD—difficulty finding words or finishing thoughts **4**
2. SOMETIMES UNDERSTOOD—ability is limited to making concrete requests **4**
3. RARELY/NEVER UNDERSTOOD **4**

5. SPEECH CLARITY
(Code for speech in the last 7 days)
0. CLEAR SPEECH—distinct, intelligible words
1. UNCLEAR SPEECH—slurred, mumbled words
2. NO SPEECH—absence of spoken words

6. ABILITY TO UNDERSTAND OTHERS
(Understanding verbal information content—however able)
0. UNDERSTANDS
1. USUALLY UNDERSTANDS—may miss some part/intent of message **2, 4**
2. SOMETIMES UNDERSTANDS—responds adequately to simple, direct communication **2, 4**
3. RARELY/NEVER UNDERSTANDS **2, 4**

7. CHANGE IN COMMUNICATION/ HEARING
Resident's ability to express, understand, or hear information has changed as compared to status of *90 days ago* (or since last assessment if less than 90 days)
0. No change   1. Improved   2. Deteriorated **17***

TRIGGER LEGEND
1 - Delirium
2 - Cognitive Loss/Dementia
4 - Communication
5B - ADL Maintenance
17* - Psychotropic Drugs
   (For this to trigger, O4a, b, or c must = 1-7)

MDS 2.0 1/30/98

MINIMUM DATA SET FORM (continued)

SECTION D. VISION PATTERNS

1.	VISION	(Ability to see in adequate light and with glasses if used) 0. ADEQUATE—sees fine detail, including regular print in newspapers/books 1. IMPAIRED—sees large print, but not regular print in news-papers/books **3** 2. MODERATELY IMPAIRED—limited vision; not able to see newspaper headlines, but can identify objects **3** 3. HIGHLY IMPAIRED—object identification in question, but eyes appear to follow objects **3** 4. SEVERELY IMPAIRED—no vision or sees only light, colors, or shapes; eyes do not appear to follow objects	
2.	VISUAL LIMITATIONS/ DIFFICULTIES	Side vision problems—decreased peripheral vision (e.g., leaves food on one side of tray, difficulty traveling, bumps into people and objects, misjudges placement of chair when seating self) **3**	a.
		Experiences any of following: sees halos or rings around lights; sees flashes of light; sees "curtains" over eyes	b.
		NONE OF ABOVE	c.
3.	VISUAL APPLIANCES	Glasses; contact lenses; magnifying glass 0. No 1. Yes	

SECTION E. MOOD AND BEHAVIOR PATTERNS

1.	INDICATORS OF DEPRES- SION, ANXIETY, SAD MOOD	*(Code for indicators observed in last 30 days, irrespective of the assumed cause)* 0. Indicator not exhibited in last 30 days 1. Indicator of this type exhibited up to five days a week 2. Indicator of this type exhibited daily or almost daily (6, 7 days a week)

VERBAL EXPRESSIONS OF DISTRESS	h. Repetitive health complaints—e.g., persistently seeks medical attention, obsessive concern with body functions 1 or 2 = **8**	
a. Resident made negative statements—e.g., "Nothing matters; Would rather be dead; What's the use; Regrets having lived so long; Let me die" 1 or 2 = **8**	i. Repetitive anxious complaints/concerns (non-health related) e.g., persistently seeks attention/reassurance regarding schedules, meals, laundry/clothing, relationship issues 1 or 2 = **8**	
b. Repetitive questions—e.g., "Where do I go; What do I do?" 1 or 2 = **8**	SLEEP-CYCLE ISSUES	
c. Repetitive verbal-izations—e.g., calling out for help ("God help me") 1 or 2 = **8**	j. Unpleasant mood in morning 1 or 2 = **8**	
	k. Insomnia/change in usual sleep pattern 1 or 2 = **8**	
d. Persistent anger with self or others—e.g., easily annoyed, anger at placement in nursing home; anger at care received 1 or 2 = **8**	SAD, APATHETIC, ANXIOUS APPEARANCE	
	l. Sad, pained, worried facial expressions—e.g., furrowed brows 1 or 2 = **8**	
e. Self deprecation—e.g., "I am nothing; I am of no use to anyone" 1 or 2 = **8**	m. Crying, tearfulness 1 or 2 = **8**	
f. Expressions of what appear to be unreal-istic fears—e.g., fear of being abandoned, left alone, being with others 1 or 2 = **8**	n. Repetitive physical movements—e.g., pacing, hand wringing, restless-ness, fidgeting, picking 1 or 2 = **8, 17***	
	LOSS OF INTEREST	
g. Recurrent statements that something terrible is about to happen—e.g., believes he or she is about to die, have a heart attack 1 or 2 = **7, 8**	o. Withdrawal from activities of interest—e.g., no interest in longstanding activities or being with family/friends 1 or 2 = **8**	
	p. Reduced social inter-action 1 or 2 = **8**	

2.	MOOD PERSIS- TENCE	One or more indicators of depressed, sad or anxious mood were not easily altered by attempts to "cheer up", console, or reassure the resident over last 7 days 0. No mood 1. Indicators present, 2. Indicators present, indicators easily altered **8** not easily altered **8**	
3.	CHANGE IN MOOD	Resident's mood status has changed as compared to status of 90 days ago (or since last assessment if less than 90 days) 0. No change 1. Improved 2. Deteriorated **1, 17***	
4.	BEHAVIORAL SYMPTOMS	*(A) Behavioral symptom frequency in last 7 days* 0. Behavior not exhibited in last 7 days 1. Behavior of this type occurred 1 to 3 days in last 7 days 2. Behavior of this type occurred 4 to 6 days, but less than daily 3. Behavior of this type occurred daily	

(B) Behavioral symptom alterability in last 7 days
0. Behavior not present OR behavior was easily altered
1. Behavior was not easily altered

	(A)	(B)
a. WANDERING (moved with no rational purpose, seemingly oblivious to needs or safety) A = 1, 2, or 3 = **9, 11**		
b. VERBALLY ABUSIVE BEHAVIORAL SYMPTOMS (others were threatened, screamed at, cursed at) A = 1, 2, or 3 = **9**		
c. PHYSICALLY ABUSIVE BEHAVIORAL SYMPTOMS (others were hit, shoved, scratched, sexually abused) A = 1, 2, or 3 = **9**		
d. SOCIALLY INAPPROPRIATE/DISRUPTIVE BEHAVIORAL SYMPTOMS (made disruptive sounds, noisiness, screaming, self-abusive acts, sexual behavior or disrobing in public, smeared/threw food/feces, hoarding, rummaged through others' belongings) A = 1, 2, or 3 = **9**		
e. RESISTS CARE (resisted taking medications/injections, ADL assistance, or eating) A = 1, 2, or 3 = **9**		

5.	CHANGE IN BEHAVIORAL SYMPTOMS	Resident's behavior status has changed as compared to status of 90 days ago (or since last assessment if less than 90 days) 0. No change 1. Improved **9** 2. Deteriorated **1, 17***	

SECTION F. PSYCHOSOCIAL WELL-BEING

1.	SENSE OF INITIATIVE/ INVOLVE- MENT	At ease interacting with others	a.
		At ease doing planned or structured activities	b.
		At ease doing self-initiated activities	c.
		Establishes own goals **7**	d.
		Pursues involvement in life of facility (e.g., makes/keeps friends; involved in group activities; responds positively to new activities; assists at religious services)	e.
		Accepts invitations into most group activities	f.
		NONE OF ABOVE	g.
2.	UNSETTLED RELATION- SHIPS	Covert/open conflict with or repeated criticism of staff **7**	a.
		Unhappy with roommate **7**	b.
		Unhappy with residents other than roommate **7**	c.
		Openly expresses conflict/anger with family/friends **7**	d.
		Absence of personal contact with family/friends	e.
		Recent loss of close family member/friend	f.
		Does not adjust easily to change in routines	g.
		NONE OF ABOVE	h.
3.	PAST ROLES	Strong identification with past roles and life status **7**	a.
		Expresses sadness/anger/empty feeling over lost roles/status **7**	b.
		Resident perceives that daily routine (customary routine, activities) is very different from prior pattern in the community **7**	c.
		NONE OF ABOVE	d.

SECTION G. PHYSICAL FUNCTIONING AND STRUCTURAL PROBLEMS

1. (A) ADL SELF-PERFORMANCE—*(Code for resident's PERFORMANCE OVER ALL SHIFTS during last 7 days—Not including setup)*
0. INDEPENDENT—No help or oversight—OR—Help/oversight provided only 1 or 2 times during last 7 days
1. SUPERVISION—Oversight, encouragement or cueing provided 3 or more times during last 7 days—OR—Supervision (3 or more times) plus physical assistance provided only 1 or 2 times during last 7 days
2. LIMITED ASSISTANCE—Resident highly involved in activity; received physical help in guided maneuvering of limbs or other nonweight bearing assistance 3 or more times—OR—More help provided only 1 or 2 times during last 7 days
3. EXTENSIVE ASSISTANCE—While resident performed part of activity, over last 7-day period, help of following type(s) provided 3 or more times:
—Weight-bearing support
—Full staff performance of activity during part (but not all) of last 7 days
4. TOTAL DEPENDENCE—Full staff performance of activity during entire 7 days
8. ACTIVITY DID NOT OCCUR during entire 7 days

(B) ADL SUPPORT PROVIDED—*(Code for MOST SUPPORT PROVIDED OVER ALL SHIFTS during last 7 days; code regardless of resident's self-performance classification)*
0. No setup or physical help from staff
1. Setup help only
2. One person physical assist
3. Two+ persons physical assist
8. ADL activity itself did not occur during entire 7 days

			(A) SELF-PERF	(B) SUPPORT
a.	BED MOBILITY	How resident moves to and from lying position, turns side to side, and positions body while in bed A = 1 = **5A**; A = 2, 3, or 4 = **5A, 16**; A = 8 = **16**		
b.	TRANSFER	How resident moves between surfaces—to/from: bed, chair, wheelchair, standing position (EXCLUDE to/from bath/toilet) A = 1, 2, 3, or 4 = **5A**		
c.	WALK IN ROOM	How resident walks between locations in his/her room A = 1, 2, 3, or 4 = **5A**		
d.	WALK IN CORRIDOR	How resident walks in corridor on unit A = 1, 2, 3, or 4 = **5A**		
e.	LOCOMO- TION ON UNIT	How resident moves between locations in his/her room and adjacent corridor on same floor. If in wheelchair, self-sufficiency once in chair A = 1, 2, 3, or 4 = **5A**		
f.	LOCOMO- TION OFF UNIT	How resident moves to and returns from off unit locations (e.g., areas set aside for dining, activities, or treatments). If facility has only one floor, how resident moves to and from distant areas on the floor. If in wheelchair, self-sufficiency once in chair A = 1, 2, 3, or 4 = **5A**		
g.	DRESSING	How resident puts on, fastens, and takes off all items of street clothing, including donning/removing prosthesis A = 1, 2, 3, or 4 = **5A**		
h.	EATING	How resident eats and drinks (regardless of skill). Includes intake of nourishment by other means (e.g., tube feeding, total parenteral nutrition) A = 1, 2, 3, or 4 = **5A**		
i.	TOILET USE	How resident uses the toilet room (or commode, bedpan, urinal); transfers on/off toilet, cleanses, changes pad, manages ostomy or catheter, adjusts clothes A = 1, 2, 3, or 4 = **5A**		
j.	PERSONAL HYGIENE	How resident maintains personal hygiene, including combing hair, brushing teeth, shaving, applying makeup, washing/drying face, hands, and perineum (EXCLUDE baths and showers) A = 1, 2, 3, or 4 = **5A**		

TRIGGER LEGEND

1 - Delirium	8 - Mood State
3 - Visual Function	9 - Behavior Symptoms
5A - ADL Rehabilitation	11 - Falls
7 - Psychosocial Well-Being	17* - Psychotropic Drugs
	(*For this to trigger, O4a, b, or c must = 1-7)

MINIMUM DATA SET FORM (continued)

2.	BATHING	How resident takes full-body bath/shower, sponge bath, and transfers in/out of tub/shower (EXCLUDE washing of back and hair). **Code for most dependent** in self-performance and support. A = 1, 2, 3 or 4 = **5A** (A) BATHING SELF-PERFORMANCE codes appear below.		
		0. Independent—No help provided	(A)	(B)
		1. Supervision—Oversight help only		
		2. Physical help limited to transfer only		
		3. Physical help in part of bathing activity		
		4. Total dependence		
		8. Activity itself did not occur during entire 7 days		
		(Bathing support codes are as defined in **Item 1**, code B above)		

3.	TEST FOR BALANCE (See training manual)	(Code for ability during test in the **last 7 days**) 0. Maintained position as required in test 1. Unsteady, but able to rebalance self without physical support 2. Partial physical support during test; or stands (sits) but does not follow directions for test 3. Not able to attempt test without physical help		
		a. Balance while standing		
		b. Balance while sitting—position, trunk control 1, 2 or 3 = **17***		

4.	FUNCTIONAL LIMITATION IN RANGE OF MOTION (see training manual)	(Code for limitations during **last 7 days** that interfered with daily functions or placed resident at risk of injury)		
		(A) RANGE OF MOTION (B) VOLUNTARY MOVEMENT 0. No limitation 0. No loss 1. Limitation on one side 1. Partial loss 2. Limitation on both sides 2. Full loss	(A)	(B)
		a. Neck		
		b. Arm—Including shoulder or elbow		
		c. Hand—Including wrist or fingers		
		d. Leg—Including hip or knee		
		e. Foot—Including ankle or toes		
		f. Other limitation or loss		

5.	MODES OF LOCOMOTION	(Check all that apply during last 7 days)		
		Cane/walker/crutch	a.	
		Wheeled self	b.	Wheelchair primary mode of locomotion	d.
		Other person wheeled	c.	NONE OF ABOVE	e.

6.	MODES OF TRANSFER	(Check all that apply during last 7 days)		
		Bedfast all or most of time **16**	a.	Lifted mechanically	d.
		Bed rails used for bed mobility or transfer	b.	Transfer aid (e.g., slide board, trapeze, cane, walker, brace)	e.
		Lifted manually	c.	NONE OF ABOVE	f.

7.	TASK SEGMENTATION	Some or all of ADL activities were broken into subtasks during last 7 days so that resident could perform them 0. No 1. Yes	

8.	ADL FUNCTIONAL REHABILITATION POTENTIAL	Resident believes he/she is capable of increased independence in at least some ADLs **5A**	a.
		Direct care staff believe resident is capable of increased independence in at least some ADLs **5A**	b.
		Resident able to perform tasks/activity but is very slow	c.
		Difference in ADL Self-Performance or ADL Support, comparing mornings to evenings	d.
		NONE OF ABOVE	e.

9.	CHANGE IN ADL FUNCTION	Resident's ADL self-performance status has changed as compared to status of **90 days ago** (or since last assessment if less than 90 days) 0. No change 1. Improved 2. Deteriorated	

SECTION H. CONTINENCE IN LAST 14 DAYS

1.	CONTINENCE SELF-CONTROL CATEGORIES (Code for resident's **PERFORMANCE OVER ALL SHIFTS**)
	0. CONTINENT—Complete control (includes use of indwelling urinary catheter or ostomy device that does not leak urine or stool)
	1. USUALLY CONTINENT—BLADDER, incontinent episodes once a week or less; BOWEL, less than weekly
	2. OCCASIONALLY INCONTINENT—BLADDER, 2 or more times a week but not daily; BOWEL, once a week
	3. FREQUENTLY INCONTINENT—BLADDER, tended to be incontinent daily, but some control present (e.g., on day shift); BOWEL, 2-3 times a week
	4. INCONTINENT—Had inadequate control. BLADDER, multiple daily episodes; BOWEL, all (or almost all) of the time

a.	BOWEL CONTINENCE	Control of bowel movement, with appliance or bowel continence programs, if employed 1, 2, 3 or 4 = **16**	
b.	BLADDER CONTINENCE	Control of urinary bladder function (if dribbles, volume insufficient to soak through underpants), with appliances (e.g., foley) or continence programs, if employed 2, 3 or 4 = **6**	

2.	BOWEL ELIMINATION PATTERN	Bowel elimination pattern regular—at least one movement every three days	a.	Diarrhea	c.
				Fecal impaction **17***	d.
		Constipation **17***	b.	NONE OF ABOVE	e.

3.	APPLIANCES AND PROGRAMS	Any scheduled toileting plan	a.	Did not use toilet room/ commode/urinal	f.
		Bladder retraining program	b.	Pads/briefs used **6**	g.
		External (condom) catheter **6**	c.	Enemas/irrigation	h.
		Indwelling catheter **6**	d.	Ostomy present	i.
		Intermittent catheter **6**	e.	NONE OF ABOVE	j.

4.	CHANGE IN URINARY CONTINENCE	Resident's urinary continence has changed as compared to status of **90 days ago** (or since last assessment if less than 90 days) 0. No change 1. Improved 2. Deteriorated	

SECTION I. DISEASE DIAGNOSES

Check only **those diseases that have a relationship** to current ADL status, cognitive status, mood and behavior status, medical treatments, nursing monitoring, or risk of death. (Do not list inactive diagnoses)

1.	DISEASES	(If none apply, CHECK the NONE OF ABOVE box)			
		ENDOCRINE/METABOLIC/NUTRITIONAL		Hemiplegia/Hemiparesis	v.
		Diabetes mellitus	a.	Multiple sclerosis	w.
		Hyperthyroidism	b.	Paraplegia	x.
		Hypothyroidism	c.	Parkinson's disease	y.
		HEART/CIRCULATION		Quadriplegia	z.
		Arteriosclerotic heart disease (ASHD)	d.	Seizure disorder	aa.
		Cardiac dysrhythmias	e.	Transient ischemic attack (TIA)	bb.
		Congestive heart failure	f.	Traumatic brain injury	cc.
		Deep vein thrombosis	g.	**PSYCHIATRIC/MOOD**	
		Hypertension	h.	Anxiety disorder	dd.
		Hypotension **17***	i.	Depression **17***	ee.
		Peripheral vascular disease **16**	j.	Manic depression (bipolar disease)	ff.
		Other cardiovascular disease	k.	Schizophrenia	gg.
		MUSCULOSKELETAL		**PULMONARY**	
		Arthritis	l.	Asthma	hh.
		Hip fracture	m.	Emphysema/COPD	ii.
		Missing limb (e.g., amputation)	n.	**SENSORY**	
		Osteoporosis	o.	Cataracts **3**	jj.
		Pathological bone fracture	p.	Diabetic retinopathy	kk.
		NEUROLOGICAL		Glaucoma **3**	ll.
		Alzheimer's disease	q.	Macular degeneration	mm.
		Aphasia	r.	**OTHER**	
		Cerebral palsy	s.	Allergies	nn.
		Cerebrovascular accident (stroke)	t.	Anemia	oo.
		Dementia other than Alzheimer's disease	u.	Cancer	pp.
				Renal failure	qq.
				NONE OF ABOVE	rr.

2.	INFECTIONS	(If none apply, CHECK the NONE OF ABOVE box)			
		Antibiotic resistant infection (e.g., Methicillin resistant staph)	a.	Septicemia	g.
		Clostridium difficile (c. diff.)	b.	Sexually transmitted diseases	h.
		Conjunctivitis	c.	Tuberculosis	i.
		HIV infection	d.	Urinary tract infection in last 30 days **14**	j.
		Pneumonia	e.	Viral hepatitis	k.
		Respiratory infection	f.	Wound infection	l.
				NONE OF ABOVE	m.

3.	OTHER CURRENT OR MORE DETAILED DIAGNOSES AND ICD-9 CODES	Dehydration 276.5 · **14**		
		a. _____		•
		b. _____		•
		c. _____		•
		d. _____		•
		e. _____		•

SECTION J. HEALTH CONDITIONS

1.	PROBLEM CONDITIONS	(Check all problems present in last 7 days unless other time frame is indicated)			
		INDICATORS OF FLUID STATUS		Dizziness/Vertigo **11, 17***	f.
		Weight gain or loss of 3 or more pounds within a 7 day period **14**	a.	Edema	g.
		Inability to lie flat due to shortness of breath	b.	Fever **14**	h.
				Hallucinations **17***	i.
		Dehydrated; output exceeds input **14**	c.	Internal bleeding **14**	j.
		Insufficient fluid; did NOT consume all/almost all liquids provided during last 3 days **14**	d.	Recurrent lung aspirations in last 90 days **17***	k.
				Shortness of breath	l.
				Syncope (fainting) **17***	m.
		OTHER		Unsteady gait **17***	n.
		Delusions	e.	Vomiting	o.
				NONE OF ABOVE	p.

TRIGGER LEGEND
3 - Visual Function
5A - ADL Rehabilitation
6 - Urinary Incontinence/Indwelling Catheter
11 - Falls
14 - Dehydration/Fluid Maintenance
16 - Pressure Ulcers
17* - Psychotropic Drugs
(*For this to trigger, O4a, b. or c must = 1-7)

Form 1728RHH   ©1997 Briggs Corporation, Des Moines, IA 50306 (800) 247-2343 PRINTED IN U.S.A. Copyright limited to addition of trigger system.

MDS 2.0 1/30/98

Resident _____ Numeric Identifier _____

2.	PAIN SYMPTOMS	*(Code the highest level of pain present in the last 7 days)* a. **FREQUENCY** with which resident complains or shows evidence of pain 0. No pain *(skip to J4)* 1. Pain less than daily 2. Pain daily	b. **INTENSITY** of pain 1. Mild pain 2. Moderate pain 3. Times when pain is horrible or excruciating		
3.	PAIN SITE	*(If pain present, check all sites that apply in last 7 days)*			
		Back pain	a.	Incisional pain	f.
		Bone pain	b.	Joint pain (other than hip)	g.
		Chest pain while doing usual activities	c.	Soft tissue pain (e.g., lesion, muscle)	h.
		Headache	d.	Stomach pain	i.
		Hip pain	e.	Other	j.
4.	ACCIDENTS	*(Check all that apply)*		Hip fracture in last 180 days **17***	c.
		Fell in past 30 days **11, 17***	a.	Other fracture in last 180 days	d.
		Fell in past 31-180 days **11, 17***	b.	NONE OF ABOVE	e.
5.	STABILITY OF CONDITIONS	Conditions/diseases make resident's cognitive, ADL, mood or behavior patterns unstable—(fluctuating, precarious, or deteriorating)			a.
		Resident experiencing an acute episode or a flare-up of a recurrent or chronic problem			b.
		End-stage disease, 6 or fewer months to live			c.
		NONE OF ABOVE			d.

SECTION K. ORAL/NUTRITIONAL STATUS

1.	ORAL PROBLEMS	Chewing problem			a.
		Swallowing problem **17***			b.
		Mouth pain **15**			c.
		NONE OF ABOVE			d.
2.	HEIGHT AND WEIGHT	Record (a.) height in inches and (b.) weight in pounds. Base weight on most recent measure in last 30 days; measure weight consistently in accord with standard facility practice—e.g., in a.m. after voiding, before meal, with shoes off, and in nightclothes.			
		a. HT (in.)		**b. WT (lb.)**	
3.	WEIGHT CHANGE	a. Weight loss—5% or more in last 30 days; or 10% or more in last 180 days 0. No 1. Yes **12**			
		b. Weight gain—5% or more in last 30 days; or 10% or more in last 180 days 0. No 1. Yes			
4.	NUTRITIONAL PROBLEMS	Complains about the taste of many foods **12**	a.	Leaves 25% or more of food uneaten at most meals **12**	c.
		Regular or repetitive complaints of hunger	b.	NONE OF ABOVE	d.
5.	NUTRITIONAL APPROACHES	*(Check all that apply in last 7 days)*			
		Parenteral/IV **12, 14**	a.	Dietary supplement between meals	f.
		Feeding tube **13, 14**	b.	Plate guard, stabilized built-up utensil, etc.	g.
		Mechanically altered diet **12**	c.	On a planned weight change program	h.
		Syringe (oral feeding) **12**	d.	NONE OF ABOVE	i.
		Therapeutic diet **12**	e.		
6.	PARENTERAL OR ENTERAL INTAKE	*(Skip to Section L if neither 5a nor 5b is checked)* a. Code the proportion of total calories the resident received through parenteral or tube feedings in the last 7 days 0. None 3. 51% to 75% 1. 1% to 25% 4. 76% to 100% 2. 26% to 50%			
		b. Code the average fluid intake per day by IV or tube in last 7 days 0. None 3. 1001 to 1500 cc/day 1. 1 to 500 cc/day 4. 1501 to 2000 cc/day 2. 501 to 1000 cc/day 5. 2001 or more cc/day			

SECTION L. ORAL/DENTAL STATUS

1.	ORAL STATUS AND DISEASE PREVENTION	Debris (soft, easily movable substances) present in mouth prior to going to bed at night **15**	a.
		Has dentures or removable bridge	b.
		Some/all natural teeth lost—does not have or does not use dentures (or partial plates) **15**	c.
		Broken, loose, or carious teeth **15**	d.
		Inflamed gums (gingiva); swollen or bleeding gums; oral abscesses; ulcers or rashes **15**	e.
		Daily cleaning of teeth/dentures or daily mouth care—by resident or staff **15**	f.
		NONE OF ABOVE	g.

SECTION M. SKIN CONDITION

1.	ULCERS (Due to any cause)	*(Record the number of ulcers at each ulcer stage—regardless of cause. If none present at a stage, record "0" (zero). Code all that apply during last 7 days. Code 9 = 9 or more.)* *[Requires full body exam.]*	Number at Stage
		a. Stage 1. A persistent area of skin redness (without a break in the skin) that does not disappear when pressure is relieved.	
		b. Stage 2. A partial thickness loss of skin layers that presents clinically as an abrasion, blister, or shallow crater.	
		c. Stage 3. A full thickness of skin is lost, exposing the subcutaneous tissues—presents as a deep crater with or without undermining adjacent tissue.	
		d. Stage 4. A full thickness of skin and subcutaneous tissue is lost, exposing muscle or bone.	
2.	TYPE OF ULCER	*(For each type of ulcer, code for the highest stage in the last 7 days using scale in item M1—i.e., 0=none; stages 1, 2, 3, 4)*	
		a. Pressure ulcer—any lesion caused by pressure resulting in damage of underlying tissue **16** **12, 1**	
		b. Stasis ulcer—open lesion caused by poor circulation in the lower extremities	
3.	HISTORY OF RESOLVED ULCERS	Resident had an ulcer that was resolved or cured in **LAST 90 DAYS** 0. No 1. Yes **16**	
4.	OTHER SKIN PROBLEMS OR LESIONS PRESENT	*(Check all that apply during last 7 days)*	
		Abrasions, bruises	a.
		Burns (second or third degree)	b.
		Open lesions other than ulcers, rashes, cuts (e.g., cancer lesions)	c.
		Rashes—e.g., intertrigo, eczema, drug rash, heat rash, herpes zoster	d.
		Skin desensitized to pain or pressure **15**	e.
		Skin tears or cuts (other than surgery)	f.
		Surgical wounds	g.
		NONE OF ABOVE	h.
5.	SKIN TREATMENTS	*(Check all that apply during last 7 days)*	
		Pressure relieving device(s) for chair	a.
		Pressure relieving device(s) for bed	b.
		Turning/repositioning program	c.
		Nutrition or hydration intervention to manage skin problems	d.
		Ulcer care	e.
		Surgical wound care	f.
		Application of dressings (with or without topical medications) other than to feet	g.
		Application of ointments/medications (other than to feet)	h.
		Other preventative or protective skin care (other than to feet)	i.
		NONE OF ABOVE	j.
6.	FOOT PROBLEMS AND CARE	*(Check all that apply during last 7 days)*	
		Resident has one or more foot problems—e.g., corns, calluses, bunions, hammer toes, overlapping toes, pain, structural problems	a.
		Infection of the foot—e.g., cellulitis, purulent drainage	b.
		Open lesions on the foot	c.
		Nails/calluses trimmed during **last 90 days**	d.
		Received preventative or protective foot care (e.g., used special shoes, inserts, pads, toe separators)	e.
		Application of dressings (with or without topical medications)	f.
		NONE OF ABOVE	g.

SECTION N. ACTIVITY PURSUIT PATTERNS

1.	TIME AWAKE	*(Check appropriate time periods over last 7 days)* Resident awake all or most of time (i.e., naps no more than one hour per time period) in:			
	10B only if BOTH N1a = and N2 = 0	Morning **10B**	a.	Evening	c.
		Afternoon	b.	NONE OF ABOVE	d.
		(IF RESIDENT IS COMATOSE, SKIP TO SECTION O)			
2.	AVERAGE TIME INVOLVED IN ACTIVITIES	*(When awake and not receiving treatments or ADL care)* 0. Most—more than 2/3 of time **10B** 1. Some—from 1/3 to 2/3 of time		2. Little—less than 1/3 of time **10A** 3. None **10A**	
3.	PREFERRED ACTIVITY SETTINGS	*(Check all settings in which activities are preferred)*			
		Own room	a.		
		Day/activity room	b.	Outside facility	d.
		Inside NH/off unit	c.	NONE OF ABOVE	e.
4.	GENERAL ACTIVITY PREFERENCES (Adapted to resident's current abilities)	*(Check all PREFERENCES whether or not activity is currently available to resident)*			
		Cards/other games	a.	Trips/shopping	g.
		Crafts/arts	b.	Walking/wheeling outdoors	h.
		Exercise/sports	c.	Watching TV	i.
		Music	d.	Gardening or plants	j.
		Reading/writing	e.	Talking or conversing	k.
		Spiritual/religious activities	f.	Helping others	l.
				NONE OF ABOVE	m.

TRIGGER LEGEND
10A - Activities (Revise)   13 - Feeding Tubes
10B - Activities (Review)   14 - Dehydration/Fluid Maintenance
11 - Falls   15 - Dental Care
12 - Nutritional Status   16 - Pressure Ulcers

17* - Psychotropic Drugs
(*For this to trigger, J4a, b, or c must 1 7.)

Form 1728RHH   © 1997 Briggs Corporation, Des Moines, IA 50306 (800) 247-2343 PRINTED IN U.S.A.
Copyright limited to addition of trigger system.

MDS 2.0   1/30/98

MINIMUM DATA SET FORM (continued)

Resident _____   Numeric Identifier _____

5.	PREFERS CHANGE IN DAILY ROUTINE	Code for resident preferences in daily routines
		0. No change 1. Slight change 2. Major change
		a. Type of activities in which resident is currently involved 1 or 2 = **10A**	
		b. Extent of resident involvement in activities 1 or 2 = **10A**	

SECTION O. MEDICATIONS

1.	NUMBER OF MEDICATIONS	(*Record the number of different medications used in the last 7 days; enter "0" if none used*)	
2.	NEW MEDICA-TIONS	(*Resident currently receiving medications that were initiated during the last 90 days*) 0. No 1. Yes	
3.	INJECTIONS	(*Record the number of DAYS injections of any type received during the last 7 days; enter "0" if none used*)	
4.	DAYS RECEIVED THE FOLLOWING MEDICATION	(*Record the number of DAYS during last 7 days; enter "0" if not used. Note—enter "1" for long-acting meds used less than weekly*) (NOTE: For **17** to actually be triggered, O4a, b, or c MUST = 1-7 AND at least one additional item marked **17** must be indicated. See sections B, C, E, G, H, I, J, and K.)	

a. Antipsychotic 1-7 = **17**	d. Hypnotic	
b. Antianxiety 1-7 = **11, 17**	e. Diuretic 1-7 = **14**	
c. Antidepressant 1-7 = **11, 17**		

SECTION P. SPECIAL TREATMENTS AND PROCEDURES

1.	SPECIAL TREAT-MENTS, PROCE-DURES, AND PROGRAMS	a. SPECIAL CARE—*Check treatments or programs received during the last 14 days*

TREATMENTS		PROGRAMS	
Chemotherapy	a.	Ventilator or respirator	l.
Dialysis	b.	Alcohol/drug treatment program	m.
IV medication	c.	Alzheimer's/dementia special care unit	n.
Intake/output	d.	Hospice care	o.
Monitoring acute medical condition	e.	Pediatric unit	p.
Ostomy care	f.	Respite care	q.
Oxygen therapy	g.	Training in skills required to return to the community (e.g., taking medications, house work, shopping, transportation, ADLs)	r.
Radiation	h.		
Suctioning	i.		
Tracheostomy care	j.		
Transfusions	k.	NONE OF ABOVE	s.

b. THERAPIES—*Record the number of days and total minutes each of the following therapies was administered (for at least 15 minutes a day) in the last 7 calendar days (Enter 0 if none or less than 15 min. daily)* [Note—count only post admission therapies]

(A) = # of days administered for 15 minutes or more	DAYS (A)	MIN (B)
(B) = total # of minutes provided in last 7 days		
a. Speech-language pathology and audiology services		
b. Occupational therapy		
c. Physical therapy		
d. Respiratory therapy		
e. Psychological therapy (by any licensed mental health professional)		

2.	INTERVEN-TION PROGRAMS FOR MOOD, BEHAVIOR, COGNITIVE LOSS	(Check all interventions or strategies used in last 7 days—no matter where received)	
		Special behavior symptom evaluation program	a.
		Evaluation by a licensed mental health specialist in last 90 days	b.
		Group therapy	c.
		Resident-specific deliberate changes in the environment to address mood/behavior patterns—e.g., providing bureau in which to rummage	d.
		Reorientation—e.g., cueing	e.
		NONE OF ABOVE	f.

3.	NURSING REHABILI-TATION/ RESTOR-ATIVE CARE	*Record the NUMBER OF DAYS each of the following rehabilitation or restorative techniques or practices was provided to the resident for more than or equal to 15 minutes per day in the last 7 days (Enter 0 if none or less than 15 min. daily.)*

a. Range of motion (passive)		f. Walking	
b. Range of motion (active)		g. Dressing or grooming	
c. Splint or brace assistance		h. Eating or swallowing	
TRAINING AND SKILL PRACTICE IN:		i. Amputation/prosthesis care	
d. Bed mobility		j. Communication	
e. Transfer		k. Other	

4.	DEVICES AND RESTRAINTS	(Use the following codes for last 7 days:) 0. Not used 1. Used less than daily 2. Used daily

Bed rails	
a. —Full bed rails on all open sides of bed	
b. —Other types of side rails used (e.g., half rail, one side)	
c. Trunk restraint 1 = **11, 18**; 2 = **11, 16, 18**	
d. Limb restraint 1 or 2 = **18**	
e. Chair prevents rising 1 or 2 = **18**	

5.	HOSPITAL STAY(S)	Record number of times resident was admitted to hospital with an overnight stay in last 90 days (or since last assessment if less than 90 days). (Enter 0 if no hospital admissions)	
6.	EMERGENCY ROOM (ER) VISIT(S)	Record number of times resident visited ER without an overnight stay in last 90 days (or since last assessment if less than 90 days). (Enter 0 if no ER visits)	
7.	PHYSICIAN VISITS	In the LAST 14 DAYS (or since admission if less than 14 days in facility) how many days has the physician (or authorized assistant or practitioner) examined the resident? (Enter 0 if none)	
8.	PHYSICIAN ORDERS	In the LAST 14 DAYS (or since admission if less than 14 days in facility) how many days has the physician (or authorized assistant or practitioner) changed the resident's orders? Do not include order renewals without change. (Enter 0 if none)	
9.	ABNORMAL LAB VALUES	Has the resident had any abnormal lab values during the last 90 days (or since admission)? 0. No 1. Yes	

SECTION Q. DISCHARGE POTENTIAL AND OVERALL STATUS

1.	DISCHARGE POTENTIAL	a. Resident expresses/indicates preference to return to the community 0. No 1. Yes	
		b. Resident has a support person who is positive toward discharge 0. No 1. Yes	
		c. Stay projected to be of a short duration—discharge projected within 90 days (do not include expected discharge due to death)	
		0. No 2. Within 31-90 days 1. Within 30 days 3. Discharge status uncertain	
2.	OVERALL CHANGE IN CARE NEEDS	Resident's overall self sufficiency has changed significantly as compared to status of 90 days ago (or since last assessment if less than 90 days) 0. No change 1. Improved—receives fewer supports, needs less restrictive level of care 2. Deteriorated—receives more support	

SECTION R. ASSESSMENT INFORMATION

1.	PARTICI-PATION IN ASSESSMENT	a. Resident:	0. No	1. Yes	
		b. Family:	0. No	1. Yes	2. No family
		c. Significant other:	0. No	1. Yes	2. None

2. SIGNATURES OF PERSONS COMPLETING THE ASSESSMENT:

a. Signature of RN Assessment Coordinator (sign on above line)

b. Date RN Assessment Coordinator signed as complete

	Month	Day	Year

c. Other Signatures	Title	Sections	Date
d.			Date
e.			Date
f.			Date
g.			Date
h.			Date

TRIGGER LEGEND
10A - Activities (Revise)
11 - Falls
14 - Dehydration/Fluid Maintenance
16 - Pressure Ulcers
17 - Psychotropic Drugs
17* - For this to trigger, O4a, b, or c must = 1-7
18 - Physical Restraints

Form 1728RHH   © 1997 Briggs Corporation, Des Moines, IA 50306 (800) 247-2343   PRINTED IN U.S.A. Copyright limited to addition of trigger system.

MDS 2.0   1/30/98

MINIMUM DATA SET FORM (continued)

Resident _____ Numeric Identifier _____

SECTION T. THERAPY SUPPLEMENT FOR MEDICARE PPS		
1.	SPECIAL TREAT-MENTS AND PROCE-DURES	**a. RECREATION THERAPY**—*Enter number of days and total minutes of recreation therapy administered **(for at least 15 minutes a day)** in the last 7 days (Enter 0 if none)*

		DAYS	MIN
		(A)	(B)
(A) = **# of days** administered for 15 minutes or more			
(B) = **total # of minutes** provided in last 7 days			

Skip unless this is a Medicare 5 day or Medicare readmission/return assessment.

b. ORDERED THERAPIES—*Has physician ordered any of following therapies to begin in FIRST 14 days of stay—physical therapy, occupational therapy, or speech pathology service?*

0. No   1. Yes

If not ordered, skip to item 2

c. Through day 15, provide an estimate of the number of days when at least 1 therapy service can be expected to have been delivered.

d. Through day 15, provide an estimate of the number of therapy minutes (across the therapies) than can be expected to be delivered.

2.	WALKING WHEN MOST SELF SUFFICIENT	*Complete item 2 if ADL self-performance score for TRANSFER (G.1.b.A) is 0, 1, 2, or 3 AND at least one of the following are present:*

- Resident received physical therapy involving gait training **(P.1.b.c)**
- Physical therapy was ordered for the resident involving gait training **(T.1.b)**
- Resident received nursing rehabilitation for walking **(P.3.f)**
- Physical therapy involving walking has been discontinued within the past 180 days

Skip to item 3 if resident did not walk in last 7 days

FOR FOLLOWING FIVE ITEMS, BASE CODING ON THE EPISODE WHEN THE RESIDENT WALKED THE FARTHEST WITHOUT SITTING DOWN. INCLUDE WALKING DURING RE-HABILITATION SESSIONS.)

a. Furthest distance walked without sitting down during this episode.

0. 150+ feet	3. 10-25 feet
1. 51-149 feet	4. Less than 10 feet
2. 26-50 feet	

b. Time walked without sitting down during this episode.

0. 1-2 minutes	3. 11-15 minutes
1. 3-4 minutes	4. 16-30 minutes
2. 5-10 minutes	5. 31+ minutes

c. Self-Performance in walking during this episode.

0. *INDEPENDENT*—No help or oversight
1. *SUPERVISION*—Oversight, encouragement or cueing provided
2. *LIMITED ASSISTANCE*—Resident highly involved in walking; received physical help in guided maneuvering of limbs or other nonweight bearing assistance
3. *EXTENSIVE ASSISTANCE*—Resident received weight bearing assistance while walking

d. Walking support provided associated with this episode (code regardless of resident's self-performance classification).

0. No setup or physical help from staff
1. Setup help only
2. One person physical assist
3. Two+ persons physical assist

e. Parallel bars used by resident in association with this episode.

0. No   1. Yes

3.	CASE MIX GROUP	Medicare					State				

Form 1728RHH   © 1997 Briggs Corporation, Des Moines, IA 50306 (800) 247-2343 PRINTED IN U.S.A.
Copyright limited to addition of trigger system.

MDS 2.0   1/30/98

Exhibit 9-3 DISCHARGE PLAN

LONG-TERM CARE FACILITY
DISCHARGE PLAN

Age _____ Sex _____ Marital Status _____ Admission Date _____

Admitted from _____

Diagnosis _____

_____

_____

Rehabilitation Potential _____

Medical reason for placement (Reason should coincide with U.R.)

_____

_____

_____

What must occur (physically, emotionally, psychosocially) before discharge/transfer to another level of care?

_____

_____

Where is patient going (ICF-SNF-Home) when current level is no longer applicable?

_____

_____

If no discharge is anticipated from current level of care, what is medical reason for stay?(Diagnosis alone is not enough)

_____

_____

If patient is being discharged to home or out of facility, what is being accomplished by staff to effect transfer?

_____

_____

Outside agencies contacted:

_____

_____

Discharge Coordinator _____ Date _____

Resident	Case No.	Physician	Room #

DISCHARGE PLAN (continued)

Date	Problem	Goal	Time span	Approach or plan	Dept code	Date resolved

Review date	Reviewer initials	Res./sponsor participation?	Review date	Reviewer initials	Res./sponsor participation?

Initials	Signature	Initials	Signature

Exhibit 9-4 DISCHARGE SUMMARY

DISCHARGE SUMMARY

INSTRUCTIONS: Discharges to home or a facility other than acute- Complete entire form
Expirations- Complete top box and narrative note at bottom
Discharges to hospital- Do not complete this form at discharge. If the patient does not return in 30 days, Medical Records will instruct nurse to complete entire form with the exception of activity, current medications, and appointment/referral.

Patient Name_____ MR#_____ Physician_____
Admission Date_____ Discharge Date_____ Time:_____
Discharge Disposition (Home or Name of Facility) _____
Rehab Potential/Prognosis: ___Good ___Fair ___Guarded   Advance Directives: ___Yes ___No
Admitting Diagnoses:_____

CONDITION ON DISCHARGE
Mode: ___Ambulatory ___Wheelchair ___Stretcher ___Other(specify)_____
Name of Ambulance Service:_____ Accompanied by:_____

GENERAL CONDITION
Temp_____   BP_____
Mental Status: ___Alert   ___Other(specify)_____
Invasive Device: ___None   ___Present(specify)_____
Bowels: ___Continent   ___Incontinent   ___Ostomy
Bladder: ___Continent   ___Incontinent   ___Ostomy   ___Indwelling Catheter   ___External Catheter

SKIN STATUS (include location and appearance of pressure ulcer, condition of incision, treatments & results)
_____
_____

ACTIVITY
___No limitations   ___Stairs_____
___Specific Instructions   ___Lifting_____
___Ambulation_____   ___Driving_____
___Bathing_____   ___Sexual Activity_____
___Dressing_____   ___Check with Doctor_____

CURRENT MEDICATIONS (Check box if Medication Instruction Sheet provided)
List:_____ ☐   _____ ☐
_____ ☐   _____ ☐
_____ ☐   _____ ☐
_____ ☐   _____ ☐

NARRATIVE NOTE / INSTRUCTIONS
_____
_____
_____
_____
_____

APPOINTMENT / REFERRAL
___None   ___Private MD (Name)_____ ___Ambulatory Services ___Social Service
Therapies: ___PT ___OT ___Speech ___VNA ___Other_____

____A copy of DISCHARGE SUMMARY was sent with the ambulance person.
____DISCHARGE SUMMARY was explained to the patient and/or family and a copy was given.

Signature of Patient or Patient's Representative_____

RN Signature_____   Date_____
(over)

DISCHARGE SUMMARY (continued)

Patient Name_____ MR#_____

INTERDISCIPLINARY SUMMARY OF CARE

SOCIAL SERVICES:

Signature_____ Date_____

THERAPEUTIC RECREATION:

Signature_____ Date_____

DIETARY: Diet_____ ; Copy of diet given ___Yes ___No ; Supplement_____

Signature_____ Date_____

PHYSICAL THERAPY:

Signature_____ Date_____

OCCUPATIONAL THERAPY:

Signature_____ Date_____

SPEECH THERAPY:

Signature_____ Date_____

I have reviewed both sides of this discharge summary. My signature below indicates that I agree with the statements regarding the prognosis, psychosocial and physical condition of this patient.

Discharge Diagnoses:_____

MD Signature_____Date_____

Rev. 02/99sch.dj

Exhibit 9-5 CHART THINNING GUIDE

1. Prepare a folder: Write PATIENT NAME, MR#, DATE THINNED

2. Place a "Chart Thinned" sticker on the face sheet plastic protector.

3. Take the following out of the chart in order:

   a) Thin out all old LOA sheets, Admission Application and old original nursing assessments (e.g. fall assessment, skin assessment) in < > on the inhouse chart order sheet.

   b) MDS and Care plans: _____ and older (keep last 15 months on chart and Background Face Sheet)

   c) History and Physical: _____ and older (keep 2 years on chart)

   d) Physician Orders: _____ and older (keep last 3 months on chart)
   (Thin out all Rx pad sheets provided they have been transcribed on P.O.S)
   (Thin out telephone orders as long as they are signed on the P.O.S)

   e) Progress Notes: _____ and older (keep last 3 months on chart)

   f) Pharma-Care recommend: _____ and older (keep last 3 months on chart)

   g) Pharmacist's Review: _____ and older (keep last 3 months on chart)

   h) Nutrition Notes: _____ and older (keep last 3 months on chart)

   i) Nurse's Notes: _____ and older (keep last 3 months on chart)

   j) Med & Tx sheets: _____ and older (keep last 3 months on chart)

   k) Labs/Radiology: _____ and older (keep last 6 months on chart)

   l) PT, OT, ST, TR Notes: _____ and older (keep last 3 months on chart)

   m) Consultations: _____ and older (keep last 6 months on chart)

   n) Social Service*: _____ and older (keep last 3 months on chart)
   (*Keep history and initial eval on chart)
   (*Keep last inquiry to pt./family regarding advance directives and pt. rights)

   o) Transfer forms: _____ and older (keep last 3 months on chart)

4. Keep all consents and advance directives always.

5. Destroy side effect sheets accompanying the Med/Tx sheets as long as no documentation is on the opposite side.

6. 12 months of the chart should stay at unit in the drawer if space permits. After 12 months they can be moved to Health Information Services.

thin.dj

Exhibit 9-6 CLINICAL PERTINENCE REVIEW

MEDICAL RECORDS DEPARTMENT

CLINICAL PERTINENCE REVIEW

Medical Record #:_____   Physician ID#:_____

Admission Date:_____
Discharge Date:_____

Type of Patient (circle one): LongTerm   NeuroMed

Today's Date:_____

Principal Diagnosis:_____

CRITERIA	Y	N	N/A
1. Death Certificate present & complete			
2. Face Sheet a) Complete with all pt. information			
b) Admitting diagnoses listed without abbreviations			
c) Discharge date and disposition			
d) Discharge diagnoses listed without abbreviations			
e) Physician's signature and date			
f) Mortuary information completed and signed			
3. Indication of Advance Directives			
4. Physician's discharge summary a) Complete			
b) Signed and dated			
5. Interdisciplinary discharge summary completed in 30 days of discharge by: a) Nursing			
b) Social Service			
c) Recreation			
d) Dietary			
e) Physical Therapy			
f) Speech Therapy			
g) Occupational Therapy			
h) If planned discharge, copy given to patient / family at time of discharge			
6. Initial MDS: Subacute - initiated within 24hrs. and complete&signed within 48hrs / LTC - complete within 14 days of admission			

CRITERIA	Y	N	N/A
7. Care plan: a) Interim within 24hrs			
b) Initial complete & signed by the IDCP team within 7 days after the MDS is done (subacute and LTC)			
8. History and Physical a) Chief Complaint			
b) Past History			
c) Mental Status			
d) Review each body system			
e) Diagnoses			
f) Treatment Plan			
g) Signed and dated by MD			
h) Completed within 48hrs of admission (or up to 5 days before)			
9. Monthly progress notes			
10. Physician's Medical Plan of Care completed and signed			
11. Initial & quarterly documentation by: a) Social Services			
b) Recreation			
c) Dietary			
12. Consents present and signed a) Admission			
b) Podiatry			
c) Dental			
13. Record is legible			
14. Medical record is complete within 30 days of discharge.			

cprvw.doc

Exhibit 9-7 LONG-TERM CARE RECORD REVIEW

Long Term Care Record Review

FORM	GUIDELINES	3RD DAY YES	3RD DAY NO	15TH DAY YES	15TH DAY NO	24TH & DAY QUAR YES	24TH & DAY QUAR NO	COMMENTS
MDS/Comprehensive Assessment, RAP, Trigger Legend	Within 14 days of admission							
MDS/Comprehensive Assessment Updated	Quarterly or as upon significant change							
Interdisciplinary Care Plan	Within 7 days after completion of MDS/Comprehensive Assessment but no later than 21 days after admission							
Interdisciplinary Care Plan Update	Quarterly. Must include RAPS to be care planned; problems and strengths; measurable goals for resident's needs; time frames to achieve, approaches to meet goals; IDCP member responsible.							
Medication Administration Record	Diagnosis for each medication. All boxes completed and initialed or notation made. Resident picture.							
Treatment Administration Record	All boxes filled in and initialed. Weekly skin assessment.							
Wound Care	Documented; addressed in PRN notes; bi-weekly pictures							
Activities of Daily Living (ADL) Flow Sheet	CAN must chart for each shift and a nurse should review and initial.							
Laboratory Reports	Verify that MD has been notified within 24 hours; reviewed and initialed by MD. All test ordered are charted.							
Consultations	Reason for consult given; ordered; legible; signed							
Pharmacist consultation	Monthly and signed by MD							
Social Service Assessment	Within 14 days of admission and progress notes every six months at minimum							
Nutrition Assessment	Within 14 days of admission and progress notes quarterly at minimum. A 5% change in weight should trigger a nutrition consult.							
Activity Assessment	Within 14 days of admission and progress notes every six months at minimum.							
Rehab Screen: PT, OT, ST if admitted from hospital (48 hrs.) otherwise(within 7 days)	If therapy begins, MD order must indicate type, frequency, duration and modality.							
Inventory Sheet	Completed and signed by patient/next of kin and facility representative							
Error Correction	No entries scribbled out/obliterated, whited out, pencilled, etc.							

Patient Name _____ MR# _____ DR. _____ ROOM _____ ADMIT _____ RE-ADMIT _____

CHART REVIEW DATES/REVIEWER INITIALS 1. _____ 2. _____

FORM	GUIDELINES	3RD (/ /) DAY YES	NO	15TH (/ /) DAY YES	NO	24TH & DAY QUAR (/ /) YES	NO	COMMENTS
Updated Face Sheet (4 hrs. post adm)	Must include name, date & time of admission, room #, record #, alternate physician, mortician and diagnosis							
Advanced Directives	Compare with MDS. If form states DNR, check for MD order							
Consents	Admission; ROI; Resident Rights, Restraint (if appl.); Dental; Podiatrist. On admission, check for patient/next of kin signatures and facility representative signatures							
Medicare Certification	If resident is in a Medicare certified bed, certification must be done on day 1,14,44,74							
Transfer form upon admission	Check for presence							
Allergies noted on chart cover	Any allergies noted in assessments should be written on chart cover							
Physician H & P	5 days prior or 2 days post admission							
Physician Orders – Day one	Must include diet, medication (if applicable), and routine care to maintain/improve resident's functional abilities until comprehensive assessment and IDCP is complete. Compare orders to MAR and TAR.							
Physician Orders	Signed and dated within 48 hours. Verified and carried out by nursing – ongoing.							
Physician Progress Notes	Monthly at minimum							
Nursing Admission Assessment	Within 4 hours of admission all sections should be completed and signed							
Vital Signs and Weight	On admission an monthly at minimum. If weight > or < by 5% nutritional consult must be done							
Restorative Assessment	Within 7 days of admission							
Pressure Sore; Fall Risk; Side rail; and Pain Assessment if indicated	Within 14 days of admission. If the resident is high risk in any area, the care plan must address the issue							
Nurses Notes	1st 5 days – all shifts, then quarterly at minimum. Inlude time of admission, where from, who accompanied, method of transportation; vitals and weight; condition; and time MD verified orders.							

Chapter 10

BEHAVIORAL HEALTH CARE

At the conclusion of this chapter you should be able to:

List multiple settings at which behavioral health care is rendered

List the agencies which offer accreditation to these facilities

Differentiate between the three types of programs accredited by the Commission on Accreditation of Rehabilitation Facilities (CARF)

Describe the documentation requirements for records in inpatient facilities

Describe how computerization is enhancing the assessment of patients in this setting

INTRODUCTION AND OVERVIEW

'The shortcomings of the mental health services in the United States are brought forcefully to the attention of Americans by the number of mentally ill homeless people who are seen on the streets'[1]. It is estimated that approximately one-third of the homeless are mentally ill.

Mental illnesses are complex disorders involving our capacities to think, feel and act[2]. Mental illness is an illness that affects or is manifested in a person's brain. It may impact on the way a person thinks, behaves and interacts with other people. The term 'mental illness' actually encompasses numerous psychiatric disorders, and just like illnesses that affect other parts of the body, they can vary in severity. Many people suffering from mental illness may look as though they are ill or that something is wrong, while others may appear to be confused, agitated or withdrawn.

It is a myth that mental illness is a weakness or defect in character. It is a real illness, as real as heart disease or cancer. The term 'mental illness' is an unfortunate one because it implies a distinction between 'mental' disorders and 'physical' disorders. Research has shown that there is much 'physical' in 'mental' disorders and vice versa such as a difference in brain chemistry in depression which can be corrected with medication.

In the past 20 years, especially, psychiatric research has made great strides in the precise diagnosis and successful treatment of many mental illnesses. This success, along with significant problems associated with financing and responsibility, has led to a change in the setting for treatment of patients.

TYPE OF CARE RENDERED

Types of facilities would include:

- Inpatient (institutional) care
  - Private
  - State
  - County
- Federal facilities (mostly Veterans Administration)
- Community mental health centers (established through federal legislation, 1963)
- Outpatient ambulatory-care centers
- Half-way houses
- Residential home setting

PATIENT POPULATION

One per cent of the adult population of the US has chronic mental illness making self-care impossible. Consider if the current population of the United States was about 260 million in 1997 and that 1% of that is 2,600,000. Furthermore, 20% (46 million) of all Americans are considered to be clinically depressed.

There is no cure or means of prevention known, but it is known that the mentally ill must be provided with a stable lifestyle with housing, and meaningful activities and socialization to avoid relapse.

LEGAL AND REGULATORY ISSUES

Licensing

Any inpatient or outpatient mental health-care facility is regulated by the state in which it operates unless it is a federal facility.

If part of a larger organization, the mental health unit or department is covered under the facility license. They do not have to be licensed separately.

Accrediting agencies

JCAHO offers accreditation for all types of facilities including mental health. The JCAHO now uses the *Accreditation Manual for Mental Health* which has standards specifically addressing care in this setting.

CARF also provides accreditation to behavioral health facilities by providing standards that promote quality care and continuous outcome evaluation for mental health programs. CARF accreditation is recognized by 80% of the states, 90% of the largest managed-care organizations, the National Committee on Quality Assurance (NCQA), the Veterans Administration and CHAMPUS.

Accreditation through CARF is available to different types of behavioral health-care facilities which include:

- Mental health programs that are organized to provide care primarily to persons with or who are at risk for psychiatric or other disabilities or disorders

156

- Psychosocial rehabilitation programs that are organized to develop, support and optimize the quality of life and functional abilities of persons with psychiatric disabilities or disorders
- Behavioral health-care programs which are within other larger broad-based programs. These organizations may seek accreditation for a care program as follows:
  - Assessment and referral
  - Prevention
  - Case management
  - Crisis management
  - Detoxification
  - Addictions pharmacotherapy
  - Outpatient treatment
  - Partial hospitalization/day treatment
  - Community-based rehabilitation
  - Crisis stabilization
  - Inpatient treatment
  - Residential treatment
  - Community housing
  - Employee assistance
  - Criminal justice
  - Children and adolescent services

RELEASE OF INFORMATION

There is an increased focus on patient rights in all types of facilities but especially in mental health facilities because patients cannot always speak for themselves and are therefore more vulnerable to abuse.

Release of information by the accrediting agency can occur when they discover adverse conditions at a facility. They are obligated to report:

- Situations present which endanger the safety of individuals and patients
- Problems required by organizations who consider accreditation as the basis of licensure or certification

(see Exhibit 10-1).

DOCUMENTATION GUIDELINES

Outlined below are the documentation requirements for patient records in behavioral health-care inpatient facilities:

- Initial screening must include:
  - Physical status (including identification of any life-threatening mental health problems)
  - Psychological status
  - Social functioning level
- Clinical assessment to include emotional and behavioral assessment (including substance abuse issues)

- Psychological assessment (more extensive than above) to include:
    - Environment/home
    - Leisure/recreation
    - Religion
    Childhood
    - Military history
    - Financial status
    - Sexual orientation
    - Family/social situation
- History and physical examination must be on record within 1 week of admission. The facility may use a previous history and/or physical which is not over 30 days old (see Exhibit 10-2)
- Comprehensive assessment must be charted within 30 days of admission. This is an assessment of presenting problems, disabilities, needs, causes, etc.
- A treatment plan is the heart of the mental health record and therefore very closely monitored by regulatory agencies. In fact, most mental health personnel state that their biggest problem is complying with the JCAHO standards regarding treatment plans (see Exhibits 10-3, 10-4, 10-5 and 10-6)

Special issues and treatment modalities which are monitored very closely and therefore require meticulous documentation include the following:

- Restraints and seclusion: the JCAHO requires the use of the least restrictive method of control to be tried first when feasible, i.e. seclusion before restraint, and therefore the record must reflect this effort. Restraints and seclusion may only be used to protect from harm the patient, other individuals and the facility. When they are used, the record must include thorough documentation which indicates justification, implementation and monitoring. The record must have a physician order within 1 hour of use which cannot be for greater than 24 hours and the patient must be monitored every 15 minutes (see Exhibit 10-7)
- ECT or other therapy with painful stimuli also requires meticulous documentation. For these therapies to be administered it is required that an informed consent be signed by the patient and/or guardian

When a patient is a minor there must be a mechanism in place designed to coordinate and facilitate the involvement of the family and/or the guardian. There must also be educational services which are appropriate to the mental and/or chronological age of the minor.

For patients with mental retardation and/or developmental disabilities, there must be an interdisciplinary approach with an interdisciplinary team plan for individualized programs documented within 30 days.

All inpatient records must be complete within 30 days of discharge unless more stringent requirements are mandated at a state level or by the individual organization.

When appropriate, a separate record is to be maintained on every family member involved in the care of the patients.

The JCAHO requires that there be evidence of continuity and coordination of care not only during the patient stay but at discharge. It is therefore required that the discharge process include referrals to all appropriate services required by the patient.

With mental health you often have continuing partial hospitalization and/or outpatient care. As with other types of ambulatory services, there must be a problem list with diagnoses, conditions, procedures, drug allergies and medications by the third visit.

Computerization   In an effort to streamline assessment, it is possible to computerize this entire process using a medical decision-making package. In this type of program, the provider selects from broad problem areas and from there can select from an extensive list of specific objectives. Each objective is a pre-formulated goal with measurement criteria and discharge planning criteria. The treatment team, which includes a psychiatrist/ psychologist, nurse, social worker and various therapists, can choose as many or as few as appropriate for the individual patient. After selection of appropriate objectives, a list is printed which states the patient's problems and objectives. Each problem is numbered as well as the corresponding objective. The system is updated with progress records as well as indications of each objective being met. The list is reviewed periodically by team members. This makes the survey easier while decreasing charting time.

RETENTION AND STORAGE

As an interdisciplinary team approach is used for patient care in the behavioral health-care facility or unit, it is probably most appropriate to use an integrated medical record.

CHALLENGES OF HIM PROFESSIONALS

The health information professional has special documentation issues but also has stricter release of information policies to abide by.

As for quantitative analysis and qualitative review, they are usually performed as concurrent processes because the patient lengths of stay are longer. This is sometimes more difficult to manage as some facilities feel that it requires more personnel to perform these functions on the unit.

Coding for reimbursement purposes is done using ICD-9-CM. However, additional codes for database management are added from the *Diagnostic and Statistical Manual of Mental Health Disorders*, 4th edition (DSM-IV) which is published by the American Psychiatric Association. Diagnoses are listed using the five axes:

Axis I   – principal diagnosis(es)
Axis II   – any mental health diagnosis
Axis III – medical conditions
Axis IV   – social (i.e. financial, family, etc.)
Axis V   – global assessment of functioning/severity of illness

This format looks at the person as a whole.

PERFORMANCE IMPROVEMENT AND QUALITY ASSURANCE ACTIVITIES

The JCAHO has expanded the ORYX initiative to include accredited behavioral health care to begin integrating the use of outcomes measures into the accreditation process. This gives them new opportunities to examine their processes of care and will serve to focus on performance improvement activities.

CARF has set the standard for continuous program evaluation to determine the effectiveness and efficiency of services as well as the satisfaction of the services.

References

1. Raffel MW, Raffel NK. *US Healthcare System: Origins and Functions*, 4th edn. Albany, NY: Delmar Publishers, 1994
2. United States National Institute of Health. www.nimh.nih.gov /about/index.cfm. 1998;November

Additional suggested reading

Abdelhak M, *et al*. *Health Information: Management of a Strategic Resource*. Philadelphia: W.B. Saunders, 1996

American Psychiatric Association. www.psych.org. 1998;June

Cofer J. *Health Information Management*, 10th edn. Berwyn, IL: Physician Record Co., 1994

Joint Commission introduces ORYX requirements for behavioral health and home care organizations. *For the Record* 1998;September 7

Peden AH. *Comparative Records for Health Information Management*. Albany, NY: Delmar Publishers, 1998

Personal communication

Waldon, Calla, RHIT, CCS, Manager of Clinical Records, University of Medicine and Dentistry of New Jersey, University Behavioral Health, Newark, NJ

SAMPLE FORMS IN BEHAVIORAL HEALTH CARE

Exhibit 10-1 AUTHORIZATION TO RELEASE PATIENT INFORMATION

XYZ MEDICAL CENTER

AUTHORIZATION TO RELEASE PATIENT INFORMATION	PATIENT NAME:
	M.R. #
	ADM DATE:

I hereby authorize XYZ Medical Center to release information in my medical record to:

_____

_____

_____

Specific information to be released: (MUST BE COMPLETED OR REQUEST WILL NOT BE HONORED)

☐ Discharge/Termination Summary   ☐ Physical exam and lab test
☐ Alcohol/Drug Abuse Diagnosis and/or information   ☐ HIV/AIDS Diagnosis and/or information
☐ Treatment Plans/Treatment Plan Reviews   ☐ Verbal information: specify dates of contact _____

☐ Other, please specify _____

_____

Purpose for disclosure:_____

Approx. Dates of Treatment:_____

It is understood that this consent to release information will expire, without express revocation, one year from the date signed. A photocopy, carbon copy or fax of this form is as valid as the original.

_____   ___/___/____
Social Security Number   Birthdate

_____   ___/___/____
Signature of Patient (Patient must sign if 14 years or older.)   Date Signed

_____   ___/___/____
Signature of Parent, Guardian or Authorized Representative   Date Signed

_____
Signature of Witness

DO NO COMPLETE SHADED SECTION: FOR FACILITY USE ONLY

NOTICE

This information has been disclosed to you from records protected by Federal confidentiality rules (42CFR Part 2). The Federal rules prohibit you from making any further disclosures of this information unless further disclosure is expressly permitted in the written consent of the person to whom it pertains or as otherwise permitted by 42 CFR Part 2. A general authorization for the release of medical or other information is NOT sufficient for this purpose. The Federal rules restrict any use of the information to criminally investigate or prosecute protected patients.

Information Released:_____

_____

_____

_____

_____

_____

_____   _____
Clinician Signature (If Applicable   Administrative Approval Signature

Date Sent:___/___/____   Sender's Initials_____   Total Pages_____

Exhibit 10-2 PHYSICAL EXAMINATION

XYZ MEDICAL CENTER

PHYSICAL EXAMINATION	
EXAM DATE :	ADDRESSOGRAPH

MEDICAL HISTORY	
ALLERGIES	**MEDICATIONS**
PAST ILLNESSES/SURGERIES	**FAMILY MEDICAL HISTORY**

REVIEW OF SYSTEMS

EENT_____

RESPIRATORY_____

CARDIAC_____

GI_____

GU_____

MUSCULOSKELETAL_____

NEUROLOGICAL_____

DERMATOLOGICAL_____

PEDS IMMUNIZATION (if appl) Up to date ☐ YES ☐ NO ☐ NO DOCUMENTATION - DOCUMENTATION REQUESTED ☐ YES ☐ NO

PHYSICAL EXAMINATION

PULSE	BP /	RESP	TEMP	HT	WT

GENERAL APPEARANCE

	Check If Normal	Note abnormal findings:
HEAD: NORMOCEPHALIC		
EYES: PUPILS EQUAL, REACTIVE SCLERA CLEAR, CONJUNCTIVA PINK		
EARS: CANALS CLEAR, TMs NORMAL		
NOSE: MUCOSA PINK, SEPTUM MIDLINE		
THROAT:TONSILS NML, PHARYNX NML		
MOUTH: NORMAL, DENTURES, BRACES, GOOD HYGIENE.		
NECK: SUPPLE, CERVICAL NODES NML		
THYROID: NORMAL, PROMINENT, ENLARGED		
CHEST/BACK: SYMMETRICAL, NO CVA TENDERNESS		
HEART: REGULAR RHYTHM, RATE NML, MURMUR ABSENT		
LUNGS: NML BREATH SOUNDS, ABSENT COUGH, UNLABORED		
ABDOMEN: SOFT, NONTENDER, NO MASSES, NML BOWEL SOUNDS		

PHYSICAL EXAM CONTINUED		
GENITALIA: NORMAL, DEFERRED, TANNER SCALE (ADOLESCENTS ONLY)		
EXTREMITIES: CLUBBING ABSENT, NO CYANOSIS, NO EDEMA		
SKIN: CLEAR, ACNE, SCARS, LESIONS, TATOOS, ECCHYMOSIS (DESCRIBE)		
MUSCULOSKELETAL: NML TONE, FULL ROM, NML JOINTS, NO PAIN, NO INVOLUNTARY MOVEMENT, AMES SC.		
SPEECH: NML DEVELOPMENT, NML ARTICULATION		

CRANIAL NERVES

I	OLIFACTORY	
II	VISUAL ACCUITY, VISUAL FIELD	
III,IV,VI	EOM	
V	JAW MOVEMENT, TOUCH, PAIN SENSATION,	
VII	FACIAL MOVEMENT	
VIII	HEARING, WHISPER ACCUITY	
IX, X	GAG REFLEX, PALATE	
XI	SHOULDER SHRUG, NECK MOVEMENT	
XII	TONGE MOVEMENT	

FUNDUSCOPIC EXAM: DISC OUTLINE, FUNDI	
COORDINATION: HEAL TO SHIN, FINGER TO NOSE, ROMBERG	
MUSCLE COORDINATION: 0 1 2 3 4 5	

REFLEXES: 0 = ABSENT		
1+ = DIMINISHED	BICEPS	R _____ L _____
2+ = NORMAL	TRICEPS	R _____ L _____
3+ = BRISKER THAN AVERAGE	BRACHIORADIALIS R _____ L _____	
4+ = VERY BRISK, HYPERACTIVE	KNEE	R _____ L _____
	ANKLE	R _____ L _____
	PLANTAR	R _____ L _____

MEDICAL ASSESSMENT:

AXIS III DIAGNOSIS:

PLAN:

COMPLETED BY:

SIGNATURE _____ ID#_____

COUNTERSIGNATURE _____ ID# _____

Exhibit 10-3 INITIAL TREATMENT PLAN

XYZ MEDICAL CENTER

INITIAL TREATMENT PLAN DATE_____	
STAFF PRESENT:_____ _____ _____ PRIMARY CLINICIAN_____	ADDRESSOGRAPH
PRIMARY PROBLEMS	ADD'L RELEVANT PROBLEMS

DISCHARGE CRITERIA

INTERVENTION/INFORMATION-GATHERING PLANS: If desired list provider name in space.

☐ EKG _____   ☐ Physical _____

☐ Psychiatric Evaluations_____   ☐ Psychosocial Evaluation_____

☐ Educational Evaluation_____   ☐ Therapeutic Activities Assessment_____

☐ Individual Therapy _____   ☐ Group Therapy_____

☐ Family Therapy_____   ☐ Psychological Testing/Assessment_____

☐ Nursing/Milieu (incl. Meds)_____

☐ Nursing Assessment_____   ☐ Safety_____

☐ Privileging_____   ☐ ADL_____

☐ Medical Condition _____

☐ Other _____

CONSULTATIONS/REFERRALS

Clinician Signature_____ID#_____

Physician Signature_____ID#_____

Nursing Signature _____ID#_____

Countersignature(if appl.)_____ID#_____

Exhibit 10-4 PARTIAL/IOP TREATMENT PLAN

XYZ MEDICAL CENTER

PARTIAL/IOP **TREATMENT PLAN**	
CLINICIAN_____	
PSYCHIATRIST_____	ADDRESSOGRAPH

DIAGNOSES: ☐ Admitting   ☐ Update   ☐ No Change

Axis I   _____ Code #_____

Axis I   _____ Code #_____

Axis I   _____ Code #_____

Axis II _____ Code #_____

Axis III _____ Code #_____

Axis III _____ Code #_____

Axis IV   Psychosocial and Environmental Problems (check all that apply and specify in space provided):

☐   Problems with primary support group _____

☐   Problems related to the social environment_____

☐   Educational problems_____

☐   Occupational problems_____

☐   Housing problems_____

☐   Economic problems_____

☐   Problems with access to health care services_____

☐   Problems related to interaction with the legal system/crime_____

☐   Other psychosocial and environmental problems_____

Axis V: Current GAF _____

CURRENT MEDICATIONS

NAME	DOSAGE	FREQUENCY

Discharge Criteria (to be met for termination of services)

Discharge Planning (Incl. Outside referrals, housing, financial and activity

Anticipated Length of Treatment:

Exhibit 10-5 PARTIAL HOSPITALIZATION TREATMENT PLAN

XYZ MEDICALCENTER

PARTIAL HOSPITALIZATION TREATMENT PLAN	
DATE_____ PAGE ___ OF ___	ADDRESSOGRAPH

PROBLEM # _____ _____

Manifested by:

SPECIFIC GOALS:

MEASURABLE OBJECTIVES & TIME FRAMES:

INTERVENTION(S) (Modalities, frequency and providers)

PROBLEM # _____ _____

Manifested by:

SPECIFIC GOALS:

MEASURABLE OBJECTIVES & TIME FRAMES:

INTERVENTION(S) (Modalities, frequency and providers)

PROBLEM # _____ _____

Manifested by:

SPECIFIC GOALS:

MEASURABLE OBJECTIVES & TIME FRAMES:

INTERVENTION(S) (Modalities, frequency and providers)

Exhibit 10-6 THERAPEUTIC ACTIVITIES DEPARTMENT RECORD

XYZ MEDICAL CENTER

THERAPEUTIC ACTIVITIES DEPT.	
ADM. DATE ___/___/___ **TO BE COMPLETED WITHIN 5 DAYS OF ADMISSION**	ADDRESSOGRAPH

GENERAL INFORMATION:

Age _____   Gender _____   Marital Status: S   M   D   SEP   W   Town_____

Employment/Education History _____

LIFESTYLE INFORMATION

Reason for this hospitalization/program:

Current losses/stressors:

How do other people describe you?

How do you describe yourself?

Living situation:

Are your friends/support system positive or negative?

Religious/community/cultural involvement:

Recreational, athletic and creative/interests:

Personal qualities/strengths/skills which will promote optimal level of functioning:

Physical limitations/medical conditions:

Personal goals for treatment:

Coping skill which need to be developed to achieve personal goals of treatment?

Comments

☐ Anger management   _____

☐ Assertiveness   _____

☐ Communication Skills   _____

☐ Identifying and expressing feelings _____

☐ Self-esteem   _____

☐ Stress management/relaxation   _____

☐ Conflict resolution/problem solving _____

☐ Developing leisure interests   _____

☐ Substance abuse awareness/education _____

☐ Successful/optimal adjustment to illness _____

☐ Other _____ _____

THERAPEUTIC ACTIVITIES DEPT.	
ADM. DATE ___/___/___ **Page 2**	ADDRESSOGRAPH

Therapeutic Activities Assessment/Readmission Assessment (30 days/Summary Orig. Assess. Date _____

Reason for admission/readmission:

Summary:

THERAPEUTIC ACTIVITY TREATMENT PLAN

Targeted Problem #	
BEHAVIORAL MEASURES	**INTERVENTIONS**

Targeted Problem #	
BEHAVIORAL MEASURES	**INTERVENTIONS**

Evaluator/Title_____ ID#_____ DATE_____

Countersignature_____ ID#_____ DATE_____

Exhibit 10-7 SECLUSION/RESTRAINT MONITORING RECORD

XYZ MEDICAL CENTER

SECLUSION/RESTRAINT MONITORING RECORD				
☐ SECLUSION ☐ RESTRAINT ☐ QUIET ROOM			ADDRESSOGRAPH	
DATE (m/d/y)	TIME (am/pm)	OBSERVATION/INTERVENTION(S)	STAFF SIGNATURE & I.D. #	

Chapter 11

REHABILITATION SERVICES

PART I: PHYSICAL REHABILITATION

At the conclusion of this chapter you should be able to:

Identify the various health-care providers who work in this setting

Identify and discuss the cooperative relationship between specific agencies offering accreditation to these facilities

Describe the elements of required documentation in this setting

Describe the uniqueness of medical records in this setting as compared to other health-care settings

INTRODUCTION AND OVERVIEW

This type of care is provided at various settings. Inpatient and outpatient centers have been established for the purposes of providing rehabilitative services. In addition, services are provided by established rehabilitation programs and facilities at organizations not originally established for this purpose, i.e. in NJ and NY a rehabilitation organization which has multiple facilities for physical rehabilitation is setting up services within physical fitness establishments.

TYPE OF CARE RENDERED

Rehabilitation facilities and units employ a vast variety of health-care professionals including physicians specializing in both physical rehab and internal medicine as well as the following health and allied health professionals:

- Occupational therapists
- Physical therapists/physiotherapists
- Speech/language therapists
- Psychologists
- Psychiatrists
- Acupuncturists
- Gerentologists
- Audiologists
- Chiropractics
- Developmental specialists
- Exercise physiologists

- Kinesiologists
- Neuropsychologists
- Nurses and nurse practitioners
- Orthotist/prosthetists
- Physiatrists
- Physician assistants
- Recreation therapists
- Nutritionists
- Rehabilitation counselors
- Respiratory therapists
- Social workers
- Vocational specialists

PATIENT POPULATION

Patients receiving services include those with the following maladies:

- Acquired and congenital brain injury
- Spinal cord injury
- Post fracture
- Post CVA manifestations
- Functional disabilities due to age
- Developmental disabilities
- Spinal cord injury
- Comprehensive pain management
- Brain injury
- Outpatient medical rehabilitation
- Community-based rehabilitation
- Home-based rehabilitation
- Occupational rehabilitation

LEGAL AND REGULATORY ISSUES

Licensing

States mandate licensing in accordance with the criteria and standards established by the individual state.

Accrediting agencies

The Commission on Accreditation of Rehabilitation Facilities (CARF) and the Joint Commission on Accreditation of Healthcare Organizations (JCAHO) both offer accreditation for facilities of this type. In January 1997, CARF and JCAHO joined together in a cooperative accreditation initiative agreeing to coordinate and combine some survey activities for freestanding facilities that choose this option. This could result in a simultaneous survey by both organizations. The organizations hope to eventually integrate the process resulting in one survey team for both accrediting agencies. The accreditation decisions would continue to be separate, based on the standards and findings of the accrediting body. Each organization would continue to charge separate fees. It is designed to lessen the burden of document collection and personnel involve-

172

ment in the survey process. The combined survey process would eliminate the need for two separate survey preparation efforts on the part of the organization.

One facility which opted for the combined survey states that they will not choose this option again. The two agencies (CARF and JCAHO) survey from a different focus. CARF concentrates on the rehabilitative programs provided to patients while the JCAHO has a more global survey process monitoring the organizational structure as a whole.

CARF's mission is to promote the delivery of quality services for the disabled and others in need of rehabilitation services.

Federal regulations

The Conditions of Participation for Medicare must be followed if receiving reimbursement from them.

RELEASE OF INFORMATION

Patients seem to be more involved in their own care in this setting and therefore request a review of their own record more often than you might find in other facilities. It is therefore essential that each facility has a policy and procedure for this activity which would state under what circumstances the patient may review his/her record (i.e. in the presence of a physician or HIM professional). Release of information to outside physicians, attorneys, insurance companies and others must be in accordance with applicable laws.

As with any other type of health-care facility the issue of patient confidentiality is of the utmost importance. One NJ facility which has treated several noteworthy patients has established policies and procedures for admitting patients using an alias so that their presence will remain in confidence. Also, confidentiality statements are signed by all employees.

CARF requires that persons served be informed of how they can gain access to their own records.

DOCUMENTATION GUIDELINES

Specific requirements for documenting care

CARF requires the following items be documented in the health record:

- Identification data to include the characteristics of the person served, i.e. gender, age, diagnoses, functional limitations, impairments, etc.
- Identification of patient representative (guardian, conservator, etc.)
- Pertinent history, diagnosis of disability, rehabilitation problems, goals and prognosis
- The name and phone number of the prescribing physician (if outside a hospital setting)
- Initial and ongoing assessment (see Exhibit 11-1)
- Critical incidents
- Program plan, overall plan as well as plan from each individual service
- Reports from referral source

- Reports from outside consultation including laboratory, radiology, orthotics and prosthetic services
- Designation of individual program manager
- Evidence of individual's and/or family's involvement and participation in the decision-making process
- Evaluation reports from each service rendering care
- Reports of staff conferences
- Progress reports from each service
- Appropriate release and consent forms
- Follow-up reports
- Predicted outcomes for the person services

In organizations which service pediatric patients, educational and developmental needs must also be addressed as well as providing materials and services which are developmentally, culturally and age appropriate.

Time frames for completion of specific items follow:

- History and physical – within 24 hours of admission
- Care plan – initial plan within 7 days, updated every 14 days
- Restraint order – within 24 hours of application

One focus for outpatient records is the summary of care list (problems list) which is a compiled list of all existing problems of the patient, along with previous problems and when they were resolved.

Interdisciplinary conferences were required every 7 days; however, the JCAHO has relaxed its standards so that the frequency is based on the needs of the patients rather than set at every 7 days.

At discharge it is required that there be documentation on:

- Patient outcome
- Work capability
- Disposition
- Status of impairments and disabilities
- Written discharge summary relevant to the services provided (see Exhibit 11-2)

CARF standards include information for a variety of rehabilitation programs which have different data collection requirements. Some of these programs include:

- Comprehensive integrated inpatient rehabilitation program
- Spinal cord rehabilitation program
- Medical rehabilitation program
- Occupational rehabilitation program
- Pain management programs
- Brain injury program
- Home-based rehabilitation programs
- Community-based rehabilitation program

Comprehensive and spinal cord programs are required to collect data on:

174

- Unplanned hospital transfers
- Patient achievement of goals
- Discharges to long-term care
- Patient deaths

For home-based and community-based rehabilitation programs CARF looks for evidence of the following:

- Coordination of services to meet the individual needs
- Integrated interaction and feedback such as formal meetings, written communication, faxes, etc.

Coding schemes used in rehab include ICD-9-CM as well as CPT-4. Facilities can tie in the CPT coding to the chargemaster which eliminates the need for manual coding of CPT-coded services by the health information staff.

RETENTION AND STORAGE

Rehabilitation records are unique because, although essential data are located in one record, the various service departments often maintain worksheets separate from the medical record which are included in the record at discharge or periodically throughout the patient's stay. The main medical record is therefore a combination of source-oriented and integrated information. Because therapies keep individual records on the patient, the therapy portion of the main medical record is often source-oriented as various components are added to the record by the various therapies. The progress records maintained in the main record are usually integrated for an interdisciplinary approach to allow all care-givers to keep abreast of the total treatment and care of the patient.

The facility must have policies on protection of records from unauthorized access and damage (fire and water).

CHALLENGES OF HIM PROFESSIONALS

Analysis of the record in the rehabilitation facility is often more in-depth than one would find in the traditional acute-care department. Because most of the services are provided by the various therapy services, the medical record department analyzes all of these therapy records as well as physician documentation for each encounter.

Knowing that a continuous record is present and what dates it should include is often a problem at one facility because the registration program only shows the initial date of registration and does not reflect each visit for therapy. The medical record office is advised of the presence of documentation when a report is delivered to the department. At this point, a department representative goes to the point of service and retrieves any other information.

PERFORMANCE IMPROVEMENT AND QUALITY ASSURANCE ACTIVITIES

Outcome initiatives required by CARF[1] as of 1995 include rehabilitation performance indicators to be identified to help point to key elements of program performance that can be uniformly understood.

Facilities are required by CARF to analyze the data they collect and their own effectiveness in their processes. They are also required to analyze their outcomes to establish areas for improvement and to disseminate this information to the organization's personnel for evaluation, input and action.

A sampling of clinical pertinence reviews which are conducted both retrospectively and concurrently by the HIM department are:

- Transcription turn-around time
- Request for information turn-around time
- Record completion statistics

Reference

1.   Fletcher D. Measuring up – CARF: The Rehabilitation Accreditation Commission. *J Am Health Inf Manage Assoc* 1997;February:46

Additional suggested reading

Abdelhak M, *et al. Health Information: Management of a Strategic Resource.* Philadelphia: W.B. Saunders, 1996

Commission on the Accreditation of Rehabilitation Facilities. www.carf.org. 1999;May

Peden AH. *Comparative Records for Health Information Management.* Albany, NY: Delmar Publishers, 1998

Personal communication

Taylor, Eleanor, RHIA, Director of Medical Records, Kessler Institute for Rehabilitation, West Orange, New Jersey, November 1998

SAMPLE FORMS IN PHYSICAL REHABILITATION

Exhibit 11-1 INITIAL NEEDS EVALUATION FORM

REHABILITATION FACILITY
INITIAL NEEDS EVALUATION

Patient Name_____ MR#_____

Source of Information ☐ Patient ☐ Spouse ☐ Parent ☐ Other _____

Religious/cultural practice (which should be considered in providing care:
Language/cognition: Primary Language _____   Education: ☐ Grade School ☐ High School ☐ Technical ☐ College ☐ Other _____   Impairments: ☐ Speech ☐ Hearing ☐ Visual ☐ Cognitive   Can patient understand and follow directions: ☐ Yes ☐ No, describe _____   Learning aids needed: ☐ Hearing aid ☐ Signer ☐ Interpreter
Motivation of patient/family: ☐ High   ☐ Moderate   ☐ Minimal   ☐ Not Applicable
Educational needs of patient/family: ☐ None   ☐ Homecare   ☐ Current illness/medical issues   ☐ Medications   ☐ Diet/nutrition   ☐ Access to follow up care   ☐ Rehab Techniques ☐ Equipment   ☐ Personal Hygiene/Grooming/ADL   ☐ Restraints/Safety ☐ Food/Drug Interaction   ☐ Community Resources   ☐ Other _____
Is access to schooling neeeded? ☐ No   ☐ Yes
Did patient receive **Patient Rights Brochure?** ☐ Yes ☐ No, explain: Does patient have any **questions** about his/her rights ☐ No ☐ Yes, explain:

_____   _____
            Signature   Date/Time

Evaluation: A = Achieved Learning   C = Continue Teaching

TIME FRAME DATE	TOPIC	DEPT	EVAL. A C	FOLLOW-UP INSTRUCTIONS/ REASON NOT INITIATED
ADM	ORIENT ROOM/ROUTINE/CALL SYSTEM	NSG		Signature
ADM	ORIENT TO SAFETY	NSG		Signature
ADM	ORIENT TO THERAPY AREAS	NSG		Signature
ADM	ORIENT TO WHEELCHAIR/EQUIPMENT	OT		Signature
1ST WK	INITIAL MEDICATION TEACHING	NSG		Signature
1ST WK	INITIAL TRAINING TRANSFERS	PT		Signature

INITIAL NEEDS EVALUATION FORM (continued)

TIME FRAME DATE	TOPIC	DEPT	EVAL. A C	FOLLOW-UP INSTRUCTIONS/ REASON NOT INITIATED
1ST WK	INITIAL TRAINING AMBULATION	PT		Signature
1ST WK	INITIAL TRAINING ELEVATIONS	PT		Signature
1ST WK	INITIAL TRAINING ADL	OT		Signature
1ST WK	INITIAL TRAINING COMMUNICATION	SPCH		Signature
1ST WK	INITIAL TRAINING SWALLOWING	SPCH		Signature
	MEDICAL ISSUES	NSG		Signature
	AMBULATION	PT		Signature
	ELEVATIONS	PT		Signature
	ADL	OT		Signature
	COMMUNICATION/SWALLOWING	SPCH		Signature
	NUTRITION	NUTR.		Signature
	CASE MANAGEMENT	CASE MGMT		Signature
	FAMILY TRAINING			Signature
	OTHER			Signature
	OTHER			Signature

DISCHARGE EDUCATION ☐ TRANSFERRED TO ACF   DATE _____   SIGNATURE _____

DATE	TOPIC	COMPLETED	PATIENT/ FAMILY	FOLLOW UP REQ.	COMMENTS
	MEDICATION REGIME	☐ Y ☐ N	☐ PT ☐ FAM	☐ Y ☐ N	Signature
	MOBILITY	☐ Y ☐ N	☐ PT ☐ FAM	☐ Y ☐ N	Signature
	EQUIPMENT TRAINING	☐ Y ☐ N	☐ PT ☐ FAM	☐ Y ☐ N	Signature
	ADL	☐ Y ☐ N	☐ PT ☐ FAM	☐ Y ☐ N	Signature
	COMMUN/SWALLOW	☐ Y ☐ N	☐ PT ☐ FAM	☐ Y ☐ N	Signature
	CASE MANAGEMENT	☐ Y ☐ N	☐ PT ☐ FAM	☐ Y ☐ N	Signature
	SPEC. MEDICAL ISSUES	☐ Y ☐ N	☐ PT ☐ FAM	☐ Y ☐ N	Signature
	NUTRITION	☐ Y ☐ N	☐ PT ☐ FAM	☐ Y ☐ N	Signature
	FOOD/DRUG	☐ Y ☐ N	☐ PT ☐ FAM	☐ Y ☐ N	Signature
		☐ Y ☐ N	☐ PT ☐ FAM	☐ Y ☐ N	Signature

Exhibit 11-2 INTERDISCIPLINARY DISCHARGE SUMMARY

Current problem? Y or N	Medical	Status*	Summary/follow-up
	Pt. will achieve reg/routine bowel evacuation		
	Pt. will achieve complete bladder control		
	Pt. demonstrates safe/efficient swallowing		
	Pt. will exhibit intact skin		
	Pt. nutritional intake is adequate		
	Pt. demonstrates improved pulmonary function		
	Pt. maintains therapeutic blood sugar levels and can manage diabetes		
	Pt. maintains b/p within therapeutic range		
	Pt. remains free of chest pain		
	Pt. demonstrates decreased pain behavior		
	Pt. demonstrates minimal seizure activity		
	Pt. exhibits minimal or controlled signs and symptoms of autonomic dysreflexia		
	Pt. maintains approp. level of anticoagulation		

* A = Achieved   PA = Partially Achieved   NA = Not Achieved

Signature _____ Date _____

Current problem	Disch. status	Mobility		Summary/follow-up
		Ambulation for	feet	
		Wheelchair propulsion and management		
		Sit to stand:		
		Less with elevations		
		Bed mobility		
		Transfers to bed		
		Transfers to car		
		Transfers to tub		
		Transfers to toilet		

Signature _____ Date _____

INTERDISCIPLINARY DISCHARGE SUMMARY (continued)

Current problem Y or N	Disch. status	Activities of daily living	Summary/follow-up
		Upper body dressing	
		Lower body dressing	
		Bathing	
		Feeding	
		Home management	
		Grooming and hygiene	

Signature _____ Date _____

Current problem Y or N	Disch. status	Cognitive	Summary/follow-up
		Improve pt. level of attention and concentration	
		Improve patient insight and motivation	
		Improve patient level of orientation	
		Improve patient learning and memory	
		Improve patient reasoning and creative function	
		Improve safety awareness	
		Improve perceptual abilities	

Signature _____ Date _____

Current problem Y or N	Disch. status	Communication	Summary/follow-up
		Improve speech, acoustics and alternative to speech	
		Improve functional language skills	
		Demonstrate functional hearing in communicating daily living needs	
		Grooming and hygiene	

Signature _____ Date _____

INTERDISCIPLINARY DISCHARGE SUMMARY (continued)

Current problem Y or N	Disch. status	Adjustment to disability	Summary/follow-up
		Decrease depression	
		Diminish anxiety	
		Diminish agitation	
		Improve social interaction	
		Orient toward future goals	
		Address substance abuse issues	

Signature _____ Date _____

Current problem Y or N	Disch. status	Discharge planning	Summary/follow-up
		Obtain necessary placement	
		Obtain necessary equipment	
		Obtain necessary home-care services	
		Make appropriate referral for medical, rehab and social needs	

Signature _____ Date _____

Current problem Y or N	Disch. status	Vocational education	Summary/follow-up
		Patient able to return to work or school	
		Explore vocational education options	

Signature _____ Date _____

Current problem Y or N	Disch. status	Community integration	Summary/follow-up
		Pt. obtains increased awareness of leisure activities	
		Patient comfortable with mobility in community	

Signature _____ Date _____

Exhibit 11-3 REHAB ORDER SHEET

XYZ REHABILITATION FACILITY

PLEASE DATE AND SIGN ALL ORDERS	

THE EQUIVALENT DRUG AS ESTABLISHED BY FACILITY FORMULARY MAY BE ISSUED, UNLESS NOTED TO THE CONTRARY.
NOTE: CLASS II ORDERS DISCONTINUED AFTER 48 HRS
        CLASS III, IV & V ORDERS DISCONT. AFTER 7 DAYS
        ANTIBIOTICS WILL BE DISCONT. AFTER 7 DAYS
PHONE/VERBAL ORDERS MUST BE SIGNED WITHIN 24 HRS
	ADDRESSOGRAPH

DATE/TIME	MEDICATIONS	DATE/TIME	LABS/DIAGNOSTICS/ORDERS	
		XRAY	**REASON**	
NURSE'S SIGNATURE	DATE/TIME	NURSE'S SIGNATURE	DATE/TIME	
PHYSICIAN'S SIGNATURE	DATE/TIME	PHYSICIAN'S SIGNATURE	DATE/TIME	

DATE/TIME	MEDICATIONS	DATE/TIME	LABS/DIAGNOSTICS/ORDERS	
		XRAY	**REASON**	
NURSE'S SIGNATURE	DATE/TIME	NURSE'S SIGNATURE	DATE/TIME	
PHYSICIAN'S SIGNATURE	DATE/TIME	PHYSICIAN'S SIGNATURE	DATE/TIME	

PHYSICIAN ORDER SHEET

Chapter 12

REHABILITATION SERVICES

PART II: CHEMICAL DEPENDENCY REHABILITATION

At the conclusion of this chapter you should be able to:

Describe the impact of substance abuse on society and the efforts currently being made to address this problem

List the multiple treatment settings offering care to patients and the types of care rendered

Define specific requirements of confidentiality required for patients receiving services in this setting

Describe the general requirements of documentation in this setting

Describe the bases for performance improvement activities and how information is gathered for assessment

INTRODUCTION AND OVERVIEW

Substance abuse is a major health problem in the United States. The National Institute on Drug Abuse (NIDA) and the National Institute on Alcohol Abuse and Alcoholism (NIAAA), two of the 18 institutes that comprise the National Institutes of Health (NIH), estimate that the economic cost of alcohol and drug abuse in the US was $246 billion in 1992, 60% of which was generated by alcohol abuse and 40% by drug abuse. As drug and alcohol abuse and dependence have a serious medical and social consequence to our society, the magnitude of costs associated with these conditions clearly underscores the need to find better ways to prevent and treat these disorders (Figure 12-1).

In the coming year, the United States Department of Health and Human Services (HHS) plans to spend approximately $116 million for new initiatives to improve prevention and awareness programs. This plan for spending is a response to findings in major drug surveys conducted or sponsored by HHS. The results of these surveys indicate the following:

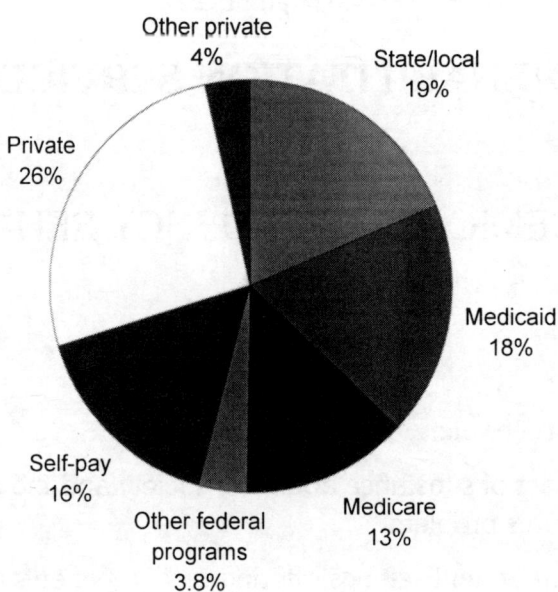

Figure 12-1 Sources of expenditure for 1996[1]

- Thirteen million Americans in 1996 were current illicit drug users. Although this number has been somewhat constant since 1992, it is a marked decrease by almost half since 1979
- A total of 51% of Americans over the age of 11 used alcohol in the previous month (prior to the date surveyed). Of those aged 12–20 years, one-half (4.4 million) were binge drinkers and 1.9 million were considered to be heavy drinkers

The HHS is making several substance abuse initiatives some of which include:

- Reduction of marijuana use among American youths through education, i.e. dissemination of free materials to parents and schools, communication through teen publications
- The Substance Abuse and Treatment Block Grant which provides funding directly to states to support state-sponsored treatment programs and prevention services
- Knowledge Development and Application Grants for evolving prevention and treatment strategies to meet the changing patterns of drug use
- An early warning system to identify potential drug problem areas and ensure that resources are targeted to areas of greatest need
- Treatment referral services which provide drug-related information to individuals seeking local treatment programs and support groups
- Drug abuse and alcohol research to further support the scientific foundation for prevention and treatment programs across the country

The National Treatment Improvement Evaluation Study (NTIES) was congressionally mandated and received support from the HHS to conduct a 5-year study on the impact of drug and alcohol treatment. The study showed the positive impact of treatment. Participants in treatment programs were able to reduce their drug use by about 50% for as long as 1 year after leaving treatment (Figure 12-2).

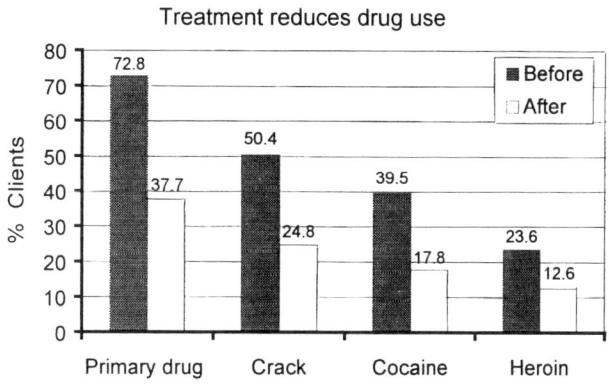

Figure 12-2 Changes in illicit drug use, 12 months before versus 12 months after treatment exit (*n*=4,411), 1997[2]

Substance abuse is known to be a major contributor to poor physical and mental health which results in abusers consuming a disproportionately high percentage of the health services. Figure 12-3 demonstrates improvements in the health of clients after treatment.

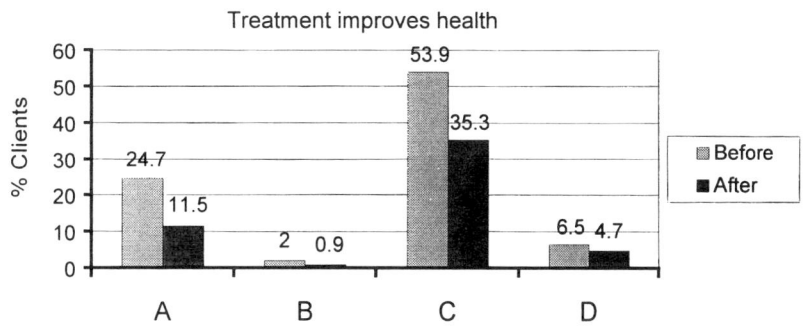

Figure 12-3 Changes in physical and mental health, 12 months before versus 12 months after treatment exit (*n*=4,411), 1997[2]. A, had alcohol/drug-related medical visit; B, TB problems; C, somewhat bothered or bothered by mental health problems; D, had inpatient mental health visit

A multitude of changes in health care have had significant changes on all aspects of medical care. Changes in the US health-care system include the following:

- Changes in the structure of health-care delivery from small independent units of production (cottage industry) to more centralized, integrated, large-scale delivery systems
- Changes in additional treatment philosophies, from program-model treatment to clinically driven treatment
- Changes in the relationship between addictive medicine services and psychiatric services
- Changes in the relationship between general health-care services and behavioral health services
- Changes in addictive disease

- Changes in disease progression models for alcohol, nicotine and other drug addiction (from acute disease models to chronic disease models)
- Changes in understanding about the spectrum of alcohol, nicotine and other drug problems
- Changes in modalities of treatment for addiction (pharmacotherapies, specific psychotherapies)

All of these changes have affected addiction medicine. A broader continuum of service delivery is emerging including residential and partial hospitalization services, brief and continuing care outpatient therapy, and outpatient detoxification and home health care. New modalities of addiction care are also emerging, and the relative roles of specialist physicians, general physicians and non-physicians, are likely to undergo even closer scrutiny by health planners and clinical administrators. The biomedical components of addiction care are being addressed to an increasing degree by physician assistants and nurse practitioners, and the psychosocial components of addiction care are continuing to be addressed by non-physician counselors, clinical social workers, and psychologists.

Substance abuse facilities can be free standing or a part of an acute-care facility. Comprehensive health and social-service facilities provide treatment with a goal of lasting rehabilitation from substance dependence.

Treatment settings[3]

- *Outpatient substance abuse facility* Clients receive regularly scheduled outpatient treatment
- *Intensive outpatient substance abuse facility* Clients spend at least 9 hours per week in treatment but do not stay overnight
- *Medically monitored inpatient substance abuse treatment facility* Clients are treated in a non-medical residential facility
- *Medically managed inpatient substance abuse treatment facility* Clients are treated under the direction of a physician in a facility which includes all the services of an acute-care hospital
- *Substance abuse education and prevention program* Designed to prevent substance abuse problems in individuals and families
- *Self-help recovery groups* Support groups established to assist individuals in maintaining sobriety and a drug-free lifestyle

One facility may have a combination of the above treatment settings.

TYPE OF CARE RENDERED

The types of services provided at chemical dependency facilities vary as greatly as the type of facility in which they might be offered. These services include the following:

- Substance abuse detoxification (which is considered to be subacute care in a freestanding facility)
- Identification and treatment of medical problems related to substance abuse
- Therapy and counseling directed at motivating patients to complete detoxification and enter into or continue long-term treatment

188

- Education to patients of the facility, their families and also educational programs within the community as requested for prevention
- Pro-social skill development
- Recreational activities
- Pastoral care
- Grief therapy
- Legal services

The above services are aimed at treating the patient as a whole whereby not only is the addiction disorder addressed, but the causes of the dependency are explored. The attention is to personal stressors which will overshadow treatment, as well as ensuring a continuum of care to maximize the potential for success.

Care may be rendered at different levels or phases through which the patient/client would progress beginning with full-time residential treatment, and progressing through residence in a group facility and outpatient treatment, and job counseling. It is essential that each program is individualized to meet the needs of the patient. This individualization will also depend on the drug/substance of choice which will have differing manifestations.

A patient arrives at the facility on his/her own, transported by a family member or responsible person, or in some cases through transportation provided by the facility that makes extra efforts to ensure that the patient's recovery is not delayed due to lack of transportation. Upon entry into the facility, immediate efforts are made to address immediate outside issues which need to be resolved in order for the patient to be able to focus fully on the problem at hand. This may include arranging for the patient's family to receive public services or even ensuring that the patient's automobile, if left somewhere away from home, be moved to a more secure location or returned home.

The initial assessment must also determine if medical or behavioral health problems are present which will prevent success in overcoming the addictive problem. If the facility is unable to address these overshadowing problems, they will discharge the patient to a facility which has the capacity to treat the medical/behavioral concerns.

While at a facility the patient and the family/significant other will be provided with a variety of services. The patient who is physically withdrawing from chemicals will first go through detoxification and receive primary medical and nursing care specific to substance abuse. The patient is evaluated by an interdisciplinary team of addiction professionals who determine the optimal plan to best manage the biomedical, emotional and behavioral conditions of the patient. A program which serves to provide rigorous motivational strategies is essential.

Not all patients require inpatient care. Intensive outpatient treatment can be designed to allow the patient to remain a part of their own community while being part of a structured treatment protocol. These services are coordinated with established systems and services available in industry, hospitals, schools and churches, as well as various self-help groups.

The care and treatment of addictions does not end with detoxification and/or inpatient therapy. Post-discharge care is essential. The patient may continue treatment and therapy in either a partial hospitalization program or an outpatient day program. Partial hospitalization is a full-day program where the patient is required to attend every day but does not stay overnight. In an outpatient day program, the patient attends less often, perhaps 2 or 3 days per week.

The patient will also be included in a program which provides group therapy and individual therapy to meet the individual's needs as a component of aftercare and relapse prevention. Linking the patient with a sponsor from a support group such as Alcoholics Anonymous or Narcotics Anonymous affords them the opportunity to receive the support they need while working through specific problems in daily living and/or employment.

To ensure continuity of care, a facility may follow up on patient referrals to monitor the patient's arrival and completion of recommended treatment plans.

Health-care professionals employed in chemical dependency facilities are dependent on the type of facility and the level of care provided. These often include the following:

- Physicians, preferably with certification in addictive medicine. One particular facility finds that some of the physicians employed are those who have retired from their active private practice and have decided to accept salaried positions in other areas which are not as demanding (time-wise). Through continuing education programs a physician can become certified in addictive medicine
- Nursing personnel with training in addictive medicine
- Counselors who specialize in areas such as chemical dependency, physical abuse, sexual abuse and family therapy
- Midwives to address the concerns of pregnant females as well as issues not relating to pregnancy for female patients who cannot discuss certain topics with ease with other counselors
- Nutritionists/dieticians who often have certification in eating disorders
- Nurse practitioners and physician assistants are used where permitted by law; however, as with other types of facilities, their use may be limited because of physician opposition in areas where physician supply is not limited

PATIENT POPULATION

Referral for treatment comes from many sources. These include referral from the following:

- Acute-care facilities for detoxification or following detoxification for continued therapy
- Patients themselves: although patients do seek needed treatment on their own, there are instances, especially in inclement weather, where the patient is merely seeking shelter but knows how to 'play the game' to get admitted to the facility
- Family members and significant others
- Court systems
- School counselors
- Employee assistance programs through employment

- Insurance companies and managed-care organizations

Patients who are receiving treatment or therapy through pressure of legal or outside sources have a decreased level of success. A facility's catchment area may be quite extensive covering several states.

LEGAL AND REGULATORY ISSUES

Licensing

Chemical dependency programs of all types are licensed in most states by the state health agency of that state.

Accrediting agencies

Substance abuse treatment facilities are governed by many outside regulatory agencies. The regulations are numerous and often conflicting. These organizations include:

- Joint Commission on Accreditation of Healthcare Organizations (JCAHO)
- Commission on Accreditation of Rehabilitation Facilities (CARF)

Some facilities seek accreditation from both organizations; however, this may be cost-prohibitive to some.

The JCAHO felt that their existing standards for health-care facilities may not be sufficient for substance abuse facilities and formed a task force to determine whether additional standards were needed to survey programs for alcoholism and other drug dependencies. Based on the study, principles to guide the development of new standards were established.

CARF provides standards that promote quality of care and continuous outcome evaluation for alcohol and other drug programs. CARF accredits programs which are organized and designed to provide services primarily for persons who have, or who are at risk of having, harmful involvement with alcohol and other drugs.

Federal regulations

Facilities authorized to receive Medicare payment must meet the Conditions of Participation in all areas. A freestanding facility that does not receive federal reimbursement from Medicare or Medicaid may opt to subcontract with hospitals for provision of services to referred patients. In these cases the acute-care facility bills for federal reimbursement directly while a payment arrangement is made between the two organizations.

RELEASE OF INFORMATION

One important consideration in managing records at a substance abuse facility is that these records are protected by federal law. (General hospital records for the most part are not.) Federal law protects the confidentiality of any records of patients who have ever been treated/enrolled in a methadone program, all detoxification records, and general medical records which include references to the patients having been enrolled in a substance abuse program.

Not only would it be illegal to provide unauthorized medical records of these patients, but the facility must also take precautions against the inadvertent release of information by telephone or through visitation. Persons calling for information on patients should not only be denied that information but the response to the call should not give any indication that the individual is even at the facility.

Because of these mandatory restrictions on information release it is essential that extra precautions be taken to ensure patient privacy.

The following authorization procedures are followed at one particular facility:

Patient privacy

Upon admission to the facility, the patient must complete and sign the following:

- A telephone list which indicates the names of persons who will be calling the facility and may be provided with limited updates
- A visitors list of persons who may arrive at the facility at designated times to see the patient
- An authorization for release of information to the insurance or managed-care company or authorization for release of information to the employer (when needed to ensure that the patient retains a position of employment as well as to facilitate the completion of disability forms)

The telephone and visitors lists are reviewed by the patient's counselor for approval before being provided to those within the facility who would need the information.

In addition, visitors to all areas of the facility must sign a confidentiality statement.

The prohibition on communication of information does not extend to the staff members of the facility who, in the course of duty, will need information to adequately treat the patient.

Occasionally, the patient themselves will request their own record. As the information within the record is legally the property of the patient this request cannot be denied. The record should be reviewed by the physician and/or the Department of Risk Management. A decision is made whether the record may be reviewed with the medical record staff, a professional staff member, or with the physician present. The patient may challenge or object to information contained in the record and has a right to write an addendum to that information which describes the factual errors in the record. The objectionable information cannot be expunged or removed from the record. The author of the information may then write a rebuttal to the patient's addendum. The patient should be assured that by federal law any information contained in the record that they may have disclosed during the course of treatment and therapy cannot be used against them.

Some states require that facilities report positive findings on HIV testing. In states with confidential testing centers, such as New Jersey, intravenous drug users may be sent for voluntary testing so they may be assured of the results remaining confidential.

Records of juveniles must be given special consideration. A child over the age of 12 years may seek treatment for chemical dependency without parental consent. The law generally follows the premise that if the patient is old enough to consent to the treatment they are to receive, then they also have the right to control the release of the information within the record. If a parent requests to review the record of a child over the age of 12, the child must consent to the review. If the health-care worker feels that the parents' review of the record would be detrimental to the relationship of the child and the health-care provider, the request for review may be denied. This situation might arise if the child has shared information with the health-care worker that they would not want the parents to know. It should be noted that at certain facilities the juvenile patient will only be accepted for treatment if the family agrees to participate in the treatment plan, provide the support necessary for successful outcome, as well as providing financial support as the patient is usually covered under the insurance plan of the parents. The agreement to be a part of this process and to take financial responsibility does not outweigh the patient's rights to privacy.

Alcohol and drug abuse records protected by federal law may only be released without an authorization if requested by subpoena *and* court order. By requiring a court order there is an opportunity for a hearing at which the request for records without the patient's consent is weighed by the courts against the reason the records are needed.

DOCUMENTATION GUIDELINES

Content of the medical records as required by the JCAHO for inpatient care are as follows:

- History: must include history of drug use by the patient according to age, first year of use, type of drug and route of drug administration. Current drug use is also documented, as well as indications of last use and duration. Review of systems for other health problems must also be included
- Physician exam: to include plans for continuing treatment. This report along with the history is required to be on record within 72 hours
- Psychosocial assessment: sex, ethnicity, marital status, education and referral source as well as background information on the number of detoxification admissions, substance abuse history, drug and alcohol treatment history, education and legal and psychiatric history with respect to significant problems or hospitalizations. This assessment is required within 72 hours of admission
- Progress notes are the same as those found in other record systems. One exception might be that there is a significantly higher amount of documentation by persons other than physicians and nurses, i.e. counselors and therapists. Like hospice records and mental health records, they use the interdisciplinary approach. Patient plan and strategy is discussed and developed by the members of the team which include the physician, nursing personnel, therapists, activity coordinator, as well as quality improvement or utilization case manager

- Medication records are sometimes kept separately on drugs related directly to alcohol and drug dependency, i.e. methadone administration; however, whether maintained on one document or on separate documents the medications provided for chemical dependency are most often classified as narcotics by the US Food and Drug Administration (FDA) and therefore require meticulous documentation as controlled substances
- Preprinted treatment protocols may be developed based on the specific drug dependence as long as they are adapted to the needs of the individual patient with additions and deletions
- Physician's orders not only include orders for treatment, but whether visitors will be permitted, and whether permission to go on pass will be given. As stated previously, some facilities handle this by using phone and visitor lists which are reviewed by the patient counselor and approved for use after an initial 'blackout period' during which time the patient's intensive treatment does not permit interruption
- Counseling documentation also will include information on the support system available to the patient as determined during family (significant other) counseling
- Discharge résumé includes a summary of facts and findings from treatment as discharge summaries do in other settings

RETENTION AND STORAGE

Many facilities of this type process discharge records in much the same way as the inpatient records are processed in the acute-care facility. The records are assembled after discharge in the predetermined order. Records are analyzed for deficiencies by medical record staff and flagged for completion. Analysis in chemical dependency programs is often more extensive than in the inpatient setting as the various therapy records are also reviewed and compared to ensure consistency in documentation across the various disciplines. Records are coded using ICD-9-CM as well as DSM-IV. As was stated in an earlier chapter the diagnoses are listed using the five axes.

    Axis I – principal diagnosis(es)
    Axis II – mental health diagnosis
    Axis III – medical conditions
    Axis IV – social (i.e. financial, family, etc.)
    Axis V – global assessment of functioning/severity of illness

Following completion, records are stored in open file areas (which must be secured from unauthorized use) using color-coded folders, and depending on the size of the facility, either alphabetical filing or numerical filing often utilizing the terminal-digit or middle-digit method.

For freestanding chemical dependency facilities in many states, there is no specific requirement for retention of records before destruction. As with all medical records, the American Health Information Management Association (AHIMA) recommends a retention period of at least 10 years.

The progression of records from a paper format to a paperless format has already been accomplished at some facilities as demonstrated below.

The electronic record

Sunrise House in Lafayette, NJ is utilizing electronic records while patients are at the facility. The majority of their health-care professionals record documentation directly into the record which is protected by sign-on codes and individual passwords. The system has a decision-support system designed for substance abuse facilities. Ancillary providers, such as pharmacy and laboratory, receive or submit data via modem, through facsimile (faxing) or by hard-copy paper reports.

The discharge summary is compiled by the transcriptionist from the documentation located in the electronic record (by basically using 'cut' and 'paste' transfers). This is reviewed and signed by the physician.

Presently, the electronic portion of the record is printed out in hard copy after discharge so that the facility has a paper record on every patient. After the next JCAHO survey, they will begin making the transition to a full electronic record pre- and post-discharge.

CHALLENGES OF HIM PROFESSIONALS

Besides the Health Information Services Department's performance of post-discharge processing, their responsibilities include safeguarding federally protected information. In managing these records, they are requested to retrieve information for the purposes of:

- Patient treatment and care
- Review of the quality of patient care
- Educational and research activities
- Administrative planning
- Medical–legal review
- Accreditation and regulatory review

PERFORMANCE IMPROVEMENT AND QUALITY ASSURANCE ACTIVITIES

There are noted changes in process and accountability such as changes in[1]:

- Utilization-management and care-management processes and structures including the growth of managed-care behavioral health-care organizations (MBHCOs)
- Performance measurement – comparison of care process to established practice guidelines, increased practice profiting and performance assessment of physicians
- Accountability – demands from private sector and public sector purchasers and fiscal intermediaries for fiscal and clinical outcome data
- Assessment of treatment outcome for addiction problems – increased use of functional outcome measures other than absolute abstinence

As with any type of service, it is important to assess the satisfaction of the clientele receiving the services. This is usually done through post-discharge (or exit) surveys to determine the client's 'perception of care' which will be used to identify areas which may need improvement. These questionnaires are reviewed for complaints, compliments and suggestions. Although every response is shared with the appropriate department or service, patterns are assessed to provide areas for organizational improvement.

Quality improvement reviews are often based on what is optimally achievable for each individual. Since the 1980s, facilities have been concurrently reviewing care. This is very significant since the introduction of managed care, which represents a majority of admissions. With the advent of managed care, facilities were required to get pre-admission approval to certify the necessity for the admission. This can present a problem for this type of facility. Chemical dependency facilities know that if they do not get the patient into the program immediately they may loose them. With managed care, there can be a delay, sometimes of 2–3 days, in getting the pre-admission certification because many managed-care organizations want a full clinical assessment with recommendations prior to approval. Due to the public awareness of delayed treatment pending managed-care organization approval in other aspects of medical care, this issue may very well be addressed by forthcoming legislative efforts.

In one western state, there are law firms who are challenging denials by managed-care organizations because denial and certification decisions are being made by physicians who are not necessarily specialists in addictive medicine.

References

1. United States National Institute of Health, National Institute of Mental Health. Sources of expenditures 1996. www.nimh.nih.gov. 1998
2. National Treatment Improvement Evaluation Studies. http://www.health.org/nties97/drug.htm. 1998;November 18
3. Peden AH. *Comparative Records for Health Information Management*. Albany, NY: Delmar Publishers, 1998

Additional suggested reading

American Society of Addictive Medicine. www.asam.org. 1999;April

Press Release, National Institute on Drug Abuse and National Institute on Alcohol Abuse and Alcoholism. www.nih.nih.gov. 1998;May 13

Personal communication

Aldredge, Patricia, RHIT, Director of Quality Assurance, Sunrise House Foundation, Lafayette, NJ, December 1998

SAMPLE FORM IN CHEMICAL DEPENDENCY

Exhibit 12-1 NEW JERSEY PROBLEM-ORIENTED TREATMENT SYSTEM

New Jersey Problem Oriented Treatment System

Review previous Treatment Plan and Progress Notes, if any... Carry forward all unresolved problems. Use original date on all problems. Use Index Number for each problem/goal/
Intervention strategy: 1=Health/Drug Use; 2=Legal; 3=Employment/Vocational; 4=Educational; 5=Psychological

Treatment Plan		Client Name:
		Record Number:

Date Revised _____ _____ _____ _____ _____ _____

Date Identified	Index No	Statement of Problem	Statement of Goal	Intervention Strategy	Date Resolved	Target Date	Long-Term	Short-Term
	1	Due to chemical dependency client is in need of residential treatment.	To achieve a chemically free lifestyle	28 day evaluation				
	2	Legal status as presented intake has been verified.	Confirm legal status in accordance with regulations concerning confidentiality of patient information	Contact appropriate persons to confirm legal status within 28 days				
	3	Effects of chemical dependency interfere with work performance	Adequate vocational adjustment	Assess work performance and vocational plans/needs				
	4	Client needs continued life skills education	Enter into educational program designed for the individual	Develop educational plan within the first 28 days of admission				
	5	Client has neglected daily responsibilities for routine maintenance of clothing and living quarters	Demonstrates consistent responsibility for daily maintenance of self and living quarters	Client will be responsible for personal living quarters and personal laundry. Client will be assigned housekeeping duties on a rotating schedule				

Signature of Primary Counselor

Signature of Client

Chapter 13

REIMBURSEMENT METHODOLOGIES AND ISSUES

At the conclusion of this chapter you should be able to:

Compare and contrast the reimbursement issues found in the various health-care settings

Describe several methods of reimbursement to the physician and individual practitioner

Describe the various prospective payment systems currently utilized or planned for future implementation

INTRODUCTION AND OVERVIEW

The financing of health care in the United States has been influenced over time by many factors including the providers of health care, employers of those accessing health care, purchasers or payers of health care, consumers who use health-care services and political factors[1]. These various influences have resulted in today's vast collection of reimbursement mechanisms and will continue to foster debates on responsibility toward the provision of care, escalating costs of care and maintenance of quality services.

Health-care expenditures continue to escalate. This can be seen in Figure 13-1 which shows the rise in costs over a number of years as well as projections for future expenditure[2]. Some of the factors which have contributed to this rise in costs are[3]:

- Rising expectations about the value of health services
- Rapid development of technology
- Government financing
- Third-party reimbursement
- Growth in the proportion of the elderly to the total population
- Lack of competitive forces which might increase efficiency and productivity
- Maldistribution of health-care providers

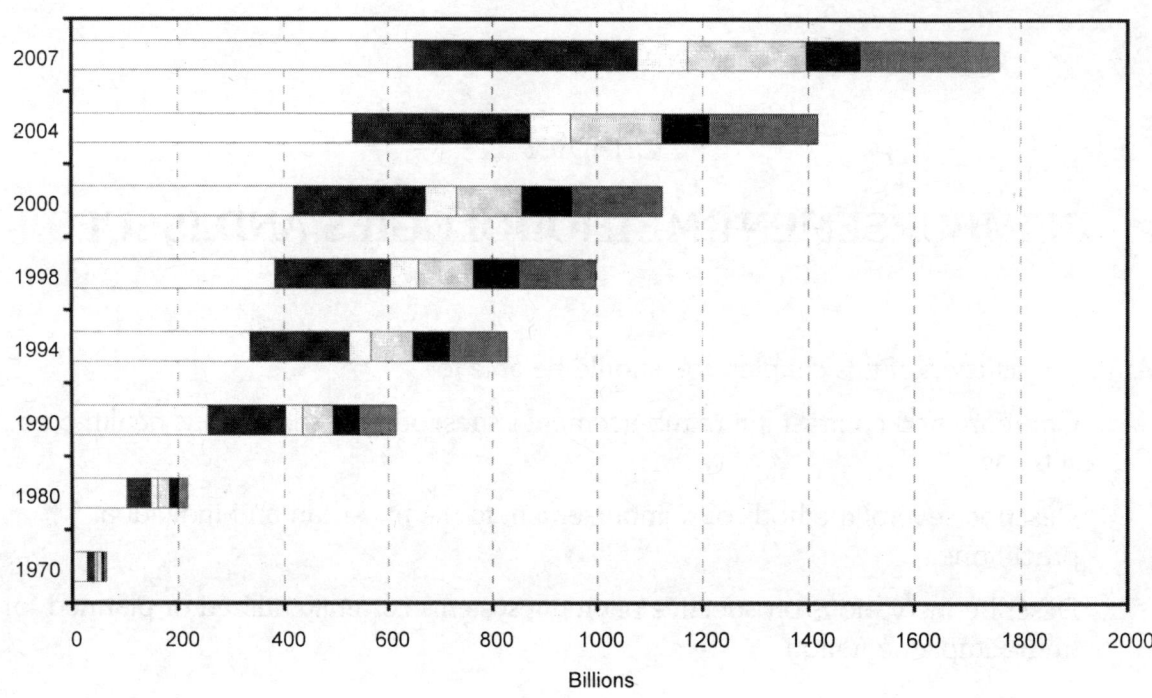

□ Hospital care ■ Physician services □ Dental services □ Drugs and non-durables ■ Nursing home care ▨ Other services

Figure 13-1 National personal health expenditure dollars, selected years

The source of these funds also have a profound influence on the rise in health-care costs. These changes can be seen over time in Figure 13-2.

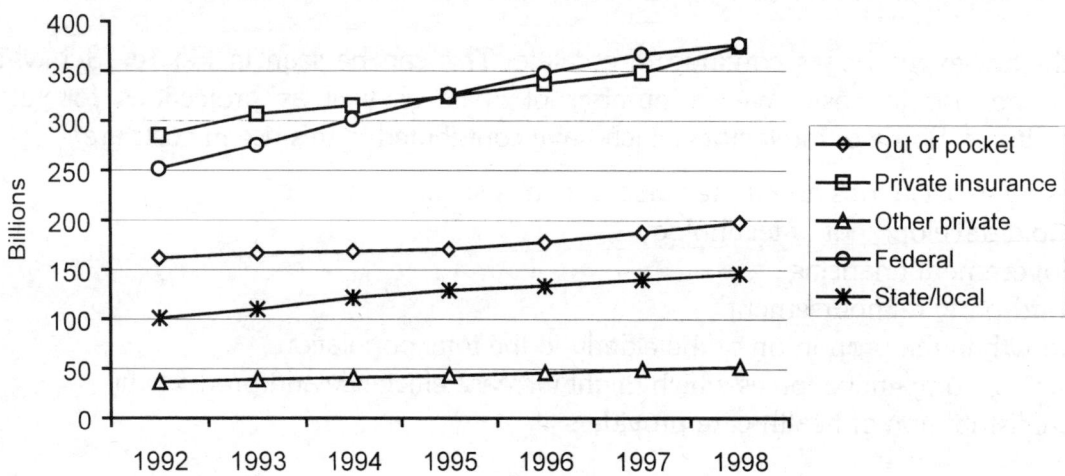

Figure 13-2 National health expenditures by source of funds 1992–1998[2]

Of the items listed above, one major issue which will continue to increase is the proportion of the elderly in the population of the United States. The United States Bureau of Census estimates that, by the turn of the millennium, the population will consist of 76.1 million persons over the age of 50, with those over 85 representing the largest-growing segment. Increased age results in an increase of chronic illnesses and therefore increased spending. It is estimated that more than half of all inpatient days are consumed by those over the age of 65[1].

HEALTH-CARE REFORM

National health insurance has been studied for decades as a possible solution to escalating expenditures. Several legislative attempts have been made to institute such a plan since the 1930s with no success. In the 1990s, health-care reform has been one of the hottest domestic political issues. President Clinton's Health Security Plan (1993) called for the formation of regional alliances (or purchasing cooperatives) as a cost-saving mechanism as well as a separate risk pool for the uninsured (of which there are over 40 million[1]). Because the plan required financing on a national level it did not succeed. However, private industry has moved toward these alliances for organizational survival and containment of costs[3].

Much effort is expended in finding ways to reduce, or at least slow down, the rise in health-care costs. Over the last few decades, cost-containment incentives have been debated, designed and/or implemented such as Diagnosis Related Groups (DRGs), Prospective Payment System (PPS), Ambulatory Patient Categories (APCs), Resource Utilization Groups (RUGS), Health Care Reform and Resource Based Relative Value System (RBRVS).

Diagnosis Related Groups

The DRG payment system was a cost-containment project developed at Yale University. The system was implemented in a few states, including New Jersey, in the late 1970s for hospital inpatient reimbursement for non-federal patients. Initially there were approximately 450 DRGs into which patients were grouped based on diagnosis, procedure, length of stay, sex, age and discharge disposition. The facility was reimbursed the same amount for each patient in the numerical group unless they were considered to be an 'outlier'. An outlier was a patient that did not meet the homogeneous criteria of the group because of either length of stay or discharge disposition. Because the reimbursement was determined prospectively, hospitals were aware of the amount they would be paid in advance and therefore had to learn to work within this pricing structure. Critics of the system claim that facilities compromised quality of care by discharging patients early or withholding costly treatment in order to improve their financial standing. New Jersey gave up this system as a basis of reimbursement in 1992; however, all non-federal cases must still be assigned a DRG which is then in turn reported to the state.

Prospective Payment System

PPS is the prospective payment system developed by HCFA for hospital reimbursement on all Medicare patients. Enacted in 1983, this system was initiated as an amendment to the Social Security Act in 1986. This system is similar to the DRG system. Patients are grouped into one of approximately 700 groups based on the same criteria as stated previously. In addition to a length of stay outlier, the Medicare system also has a cost outlier. As an outlier the payment would be based on a per diem rate or a combination of the per diem rate with the DRG rate.

Facilities which use a DRG system for non-federal reimbursement and the PPS system mandated for Medicare reimbursement are considered to be 'all-payer' DRG states. One problem with being an all-payer state is that the systems are often updated at different times of the year because of differing fiscal calendars at state and federal levels. This can create a problem with the computerized billing, particularly if using a shared (or leased) system, as the groupers (the programs that assign the DRG) are updated at different times.

Ambulatory Patient Categories

APCs were initially developed by HCFA and 3M/Health Information Systems as APGs (ambulatory payment groups).   This system, scheduled for implementation on August 1, 2000, groups services provided by hospitals on an outpatient basis into payment groups which determine the reimbursement for services provided to Medicare beneficiaries. The primary purpose of this system is to simplify payment and encourage hospitals to provide services efficiently while at the same time ensuring that the facilities receive adequate compensation for legitimate costs. Tested by six payers, the system has been shown to reduce hospital outpatient costs, reward lower-cost facilities, and simplify contract negotiation.

The APC system encompasses nearly all hospitals with few exceptions. These exceptions include Maryland hospitals (paid under a cost containment waiver), critical access hospitals (paid at cost) and certain facilities in the Indian Health Services. Small rural hospitals will also be given special consideration through 2003.

Services subject to reimbursement in this system include:

- Surgical procedures
- Radiology
- Radiation therapy
- Clinic visits
- Emergency Department visits
- Diagnostic services and other diagnostic tests
- Partial hospitalization for the mentally ill
- Surgical pathology
- Cancer chemotherapy

Services excluded from the system are:

- Ambulance services
- Physical therapy
- Occupational therapy
- Speech/language pathology
- Some end-stage renal disease services
- Laboratory services paid under the clinical diagnostic laboratory fee schedule
- Durable medical equipment[4]
- Chemotherapy and current orphan drugs

APCs bundle clinically related services within a patient visit, including the cost of most drugs, anesthesia, labs and X-rays. Unlike the DRG system, where a hospital bill will be assigned a single DRG, the APC system may result in each patient encounter being assigned multiple APCs. Each APC is given a status indicator which determines which APCs will be paid at 100%, discounted to 50%, or not reimbursed.

Resource Utilization Groups

The Balanced Budget Act of 1997 mandated the implementation of a prospective payment system, effective July 1, 1998, which would result in the facility receiving a per diem rate for Medicare Part A patients based on the acuity and resource utilization. Fixed reimbursement will cover all routine, therapy, ancillary and capital-related Part A costs. On August 5, 1997, section 1888 of the Act was amended by adding a subsection which required implementation of a Medicare SNF prospective payment system (PPS) for all skilled-nursing facilities (SNFs) for cost-reporting periods beginning on or after July 1, 1998. Under the PPS, SNFs will be paid under a PPS applicable to all covered SNF services. This system is known as Resource Utilization Groups (RUGS). These payment rates will encompass all costs of furnishing covered skilled-nursing services (that is, routine, ancillary and capital-related costs) other than costs associated with operating approved educational activities.

RUGSIII resident's case-mix classification group[5] utilizes information from the minimum data set (MDS) resident assessment instrument to classify residents into one of 44 groups, which account for the relative resource use of different patient types. RUGSIII has seven major classification groups:

- Rehabilitation
- Extensive services
- Special care
- Clinically complex
- Impaired cognition
- Behavior problems
- Reduced physical functions[5]

SNFs complete these assessments according to an assessment schedule specifically designed for Medicare payment (see Table 13-1). Facilities will send each patient's MDS assessments to the State and claims for Medicare payment to the fiscal intermediary on a 30-day cycle. Payment will be made according to the RUGSIII group(s) recorded on the claim.

Table 13-1 Medicare assessment schedule

Medicare MDS	Reason for assessment type (AA8b code)	Assessment reference assessment date	Number of days authorized for coverage and payment	Applicable Medicare payment days
5 day	1	Days 1–8*	14	1 through 14
14 day	7	Days 11–14**	16	15 through 30
30 day	2	Days 21–29	30	31 through 60
60 day	3	Days 50–59	30	61 through 90
90 day	4	Days 80–89	10	91 through 100

*If a patient expires or transfers to another facility before day 8, the facility will still need to prepare an MDS as completely as possible for the RUG-III classification and Medicare payment purposes. Otherwise the days will be paid at the default rate[2].
**RAPS (Resident assessment protocols) follow federal rules; RAPS must be performed with either the 5-day or 14-day assessment

The purpose of resource utilization groups is to have a systematic method to show the variation of nursing-care time among residents, specifically nursing-care time by type of nursing staff.

Resource Based Relative Value Scale (RBRVS)

On January 1, 1992, Medicare initiated a new system for reimbursing physicians using a resource-based relative value scale. This method divides resources needed to produce physician services into three components: physician work, practice expense and malpractice insurance costs. For each procedure, each of the three components is characterized by a numerical value representing its relative contribution to the expenses incurred in delivering service. The components are each adjusted for geographic cost variations[3].

REIMBURSEMENT METHODS BY PROVIDER TYPE

Physician reimbursement[3]

The method of payment to physicians in practice can vary greatly depending on the type of setting in which the physician is working. Discussed below are various methods of payment.

Fee-for-service is the preferred method of payment although it is becoming less common because of managed care. In fee-for-service the unit of remuneration is the medical act, either a service or a procedure. In the absence of health insurance, some physicians have a sliding-scale fee wherein the fee charged is based on the patient's income. With insurance it became more regulated and physicians adopt one schedule of fees and charges for all payers. However, fees often vary by type of insurance.

Indemnity is a method of payment that stipulates a certain dollar value per procedure, usually based on a table of allowances. Traditionally, the provider can charge the patient for any amount above the allowance. The allowance is based on the relative value unit (RVU), that is, the relative technical difficulty and time cost of the service.

Service benefits pay a percentage of the procedure, usually 80% of the usual, customary and reasonable (UCR) fees. This protects the insurance carrier from unlimited liability for high charges. Patients are often surprised to find that 80% of the total charge is not being covered when the total charge is higher than the UCR fee determined by the insurance company. (Usual = in that doctor's practice, customary = in that community, reasonable = distribution of all charges for that service in the community.) If the physician is 'participating' in the insurance plan, the UCR fee is accepted and the patient pays the remaining percentage. If the physician is 'non-participating', the patient can be charged the remaining balance not covered by the insurance plan.

Hybrid fee-based systems are systems developed by preferred provider organizations (PPOs) which combine the features of indemnity and service benefits. The intermediary contracts with the provider to accept a discounted version of the UCR table of allowances. The plan considers these allowed amounts to be the maximum covered expense.

Fixed fees in some plans require that physicians only charge a specific amount for the services provided, and will only be paid according to the fixed fee with little or no cost sharing on the part of the patient. The physician accepts the fee schedule when agreeing to participate with the plan.

Prepayment or capitation is when the person served is the unit of remuneration. The capitation payment takes care of reimbursement for a stipulated length of time, usually a year. Advantages to prepayment plans, such as health maintenance organizations (HMOs), is that it is administratively simple and it gives physicians an incentive to control the costs of medical treatment.

Salary is payment to doctors for time consumption, irrespective of the units of service or number of patients. Highly organized networks almost always have salaried physicians as well as many urban hospitals in areas which service indigent patients.

Long-term care reimbursement

An overwhelming majority of patients in long-term care are insured through federal programs, namely Medicare and Medicaid. (Medicare generally serves a more post-acute resident population while Medicaid generally serves a longer-term custodial care population.) These programs are regulated by the Health Care Finance Administration. Until very recently reimbursement to these facilities was on a retrospective payment system. The RUGS classification system discussed earlier in the chapter is now the basis for reimbursement to long-term care facilities. As different patients have different nursing-care needs, a financial reimbursement system must reflect these differences. Case-mix has become a familiar term in health care. In a nursing home the 'case' refers to the home residents; 'mix' refers to the mixture of different types of residents' care within a facility. The cases are classified based on their characteristics, i.e. functional status, clinical condition, etc.

The regulations on the application of the PPS also apply to extended-care services furnished in hospital swing-bed units, which are acute-care beds used intermittently as long-term subacute care beds. However, this requirement is to be implemented no earlier than cost-reporting periods beginning on July 1, 1999 and no later than cost-reporting periods beginning in the 12-month period starting on July 1, 2001.

Because a skilled-nursing facility's (SNF's) traditional patient population is primarily the elderly and many patients discharged from the hospitals to a subacute care setting receive Medicare and/or Medicaid, the SNF is faced with the challenges of:

* Providing high-acuity care and increased therapy hours
* Managing increased costs that are more than the SNF's routine cost limit as determined by HCFA
* Ensuring adherence to the Medicare requirement – charging the same for all types of payers across the board for similar services rendered

Hospital-based ambulatory care reimbursement

On April 7, 2000, HCFA published the final rules for PPS for all hospital-based ambulatory care services. In August 2000, this will replace the cost-based system with one using APCs. A challenge to facilities is determining the CPT Evaluation and

Management code for services which were previously reimbursed based on ICD-9-CM code assignment. There are no guidelines currently available for the assignment of E/M codes to services other than those provided by the physician.

Rehabilitation reimbursement

Currently, facilities which are determined to be rehabilitation institutions are not reimbursed based on any prospective reimbursement system except for services which are provided as a component of care rendered at a facility not exempt from RUGS, DRGs or APCs. However, for these facilities, functional related groups (FRGs) are scheduled to be implemented as the method of reimbursement in 2002. This system is based on a patient care assessment system called functional independence measurement (FIMS).

Ambulatory-care reimbursement

Payment for services in ambulatory-care settings not covered previously is most commonly by fee-for-service but this is rapidly changing. As many ambulatory-care centers are becoming predominantly organized through some type of managed-care arrangement, their method of reimbursement is outlined in the contract or arrangement as either capitation, fixed or a hybrid system.

Correctional care facilities reimbursement

Health services provided in prisons, jails and detention centers are not subject to the issues of reimbursement imposed by health insurers because the facilities cannot presently bill for services provided. There has been some discussion of requiring inmates to pay for services in some way; however, critics of this contend that the services provided are a basic right which should not be denied. Should a payment system be implemented, one must consider the consequences to the inmate who is unable to pay for services.

Home-care reimbursement

Medicare is the largest payer of home services and currently covers home care only when skilled services, ordered by a physician and administered by a licensed nurse or therapist, are required. Home care is still cost-reimbursed[6]. The Medicare Home Health PPS (HHPPS) is scheduled for implementation on October 1, 2000.

Many private insurers will cover home service if they immediately follow hospitalization. In fact, in some states, such as New Jersey, it is required by law that early discharge on some diagnoses be followed by home care as a covered service.

Hospice reimbursement

Many hospices were unable to secure reimbursement from third-party payers for many years because these types of services were not included as benefits. They existed primarily on donations, limited patient revenues and the generosity of their parent organizations. To resolve this, many states passed legislation requiring insurance carriers to offer some type of hospice benefit. Reimbursement is currently cost-based unless otherwise specified by the insurance contract.

Subacute-care reimbursement

Subacute-care patients covered by Medicare are subject to the regulations under the Resource Utilization Groups (RUGS) developed for long-term care discussed earlier. While RUGSIII may not address all of the medical/surgical cases that are considered subacute, it is a useful tool for patients who need rehabilitation, complex care and extensive services. If the patient is not clinically assessed appropriately or classified in the appropriate level negotiated in the managed-care contract, the facility may lose an opportunity to maximize reimbursement and may even risk losing money[7].

Under Medicare PPS, the government and other third-party payers (primarily managed-care organizations) tell the subacute providers what services they want provided, how often they will be provided and how much they will pay for them.

Subacute services provided to Medicaid patients are not usually reimbursed, unless special subacute rates were pre-negotiated with the states Department of Public Aid or Department of Public Welfare. If an SNF is providing subacute care which increases its routine costs, it should apply for an exemption from the limits.

HIM PROFESSIONAL AND REIMBURSEMENT

The health information manager has a pivotal role in the financial success of any health-care organization. The documentation contained in the medical record defines the accuracy and completeness of services provided and the conditions treated which will be submitted for reimbursement.

In these changing times in health care, the importance of the financial aspects of each health-care organization has increased for good management decisions. The health information manager must be acutely aware of all regulatory changes in the financial environment[8].

References

1. Sultz HA, Young KM. *Healthcare USA*. Gaithersburg, MD: Aspen Publications, 1997
2. Williams SJ, Torrens PR. *Introduction to Health Services*, 5th edn. Albany, NY: Delmar Publishers, 1999
3. Health Care Financing Administration, Office of the Actuary: National Health Statistics Group. www.hcfa.gov. 10-29-98
4. Frawley K. HCFA publishes proposed rule for hospital outpatient services PPS. *J Am Health Inf Manage Assoc* 1998;69:14
5. Zbylot S, Job C, McCormick E, Boulter C, Moore A. A case mix classification system for long-term care facilities. *Nurs Manage* 1995;April
6 . Chidley E. Home healthcare prepares to automate. *For the Record* 1997;May11:8–11
7 . Stahl D. Maximizing reimbursement for subacute care. *Nurs Manage* 1995;April
8. Abdelhak M, *et al. Health Information: Management of a Strategic Resource*. Philadelphia: W.B. Saunders, 1996

Additional suggested reading

Cofer J. *Health Information Management*, 10th edn. Berwyn, IL: Physician Record Co., 1994

Medicare program: prospective payment system and consolidated billing for skilled nursing facilities; final rule. *Federal Register* 1998;May 12. http://www.frwebgate2.access.gpo.gov/cgi-bim/waisgate.cgi?waisdocID=7371442340+0. 1999;93:no. 91, October

Peden AH. *Comparative Records for Health Information Management.* Albany, NY: Delmar Publishers, 1998

Stahl D. Reengineering: the key to survival and growth under PPS. *Nurs Manage* 1998;March

Appendix: Abbreviations list

AAHC	Association for Accreditation of Ambulatory Health Care
ACF	Acute-care facility
ACHSA	American Correctional Health Services Association
ADL(s)	Activities of daily living
AHEs	Average hourly earnings
AHIMA	American Health Information Management Association
ALOS	Average length of stay
AOA	American Osteopathy Association
APC	Ambulatory patient category
ART	Accredited record technician
BBA	Balanced Budget Act of 1997
BEA	Bureau of Economic Analysis
BLS	Bureau of Labor Statistics
CABG	Coronary artery bypass surgery
CAH	Critical access hospital
CARF	Commission on Accreditation of Rehabilitation Facilities
CCHP	Certified Correctional Health Professional
CCS	Certified Coding Specialist
CCS-P	Certified Coding Specialist-Physician Office
CFR	Code of Federal Regulations
CHAP	Community Health Accreditation Program
CHF	Congestive heart failure
COP	Conditions of Participation (Medicare)
CPC	Certified Procedural Coder
CPI	Consumer Price Index
CPI-U	Consumer Price Index for All Urban Consumers
CPT	Current Procedural Terminology
CVA	Cerebrovascular accident
DO	Doctor of Osteopathy
DOH	Department of Health
DRG	Diagnosis-related groups
DSM-IV	*Diagnostic and Statistical Manual of Mental Health Disorders*, 4th Edition
ECI	Employment Cost Index
ECT	Electroconvulsive therapy
ED	Emergency Department
ER	Emergency Room
FDA	Food and Drug Administration, United States
FI	Fiscal intermediary
FTE	Full time equivalent
GPIN	Group Practice Improvement Network
HCFA	Health Care Financing Administration
HCO	Health-care organization
HCPCS	HCFA Common Procedure Coding System
HHA	Health and Human Administration, United States Department of
HIM	Health Information Management
HIPAA	Health Insurance Portability and Accountability Act
HIPDB	Healthcare Integrity and Protection Data Bank
HMO	Health Maintenance Organization
ICD-10	*International Classification of Diseases*, 10th Edition
ICD-9-CM	*International Classification of Diseases*, 9th Edition, Clinical Modification
ICU	Intensive care unit
IPA	Individual Practice Association Model
JAMA	*Journal of the American Medical Association*

JCAHO	Joint Commission on Accreditation of Healthcare Organizations
LOS	Length of stay
LPN	Licensed Practical Nurse
LTC	Long-term care
MBI ICO	Mental and Behavioral Health Care Organization
MCO	Managed-care organization
MD	Medical Doctor
MDS	Minimum data set
MEDPAR	Medicare provider analysis and review file
MGMA	Medical Group Management Association
MPI	Master patient index
MR	Medical record
MSA	Metropolitan statistical area
MSO	Managed services organization
NCCHC	National Commission of Correctional Health Care
NCQA	National Commission of Quality Assurance
NECMA	New England County Metropolitan Area
NH	Nursing home
NIAAA	National Institute on Alcohol Abuse and Alcoholism
NIDA	National Institute on Drug Abuse
NIH	National Institutes of Health
NLN	National League of Nursing
NP	Nurse practitioner
NTIES	National Treatment Improvement Evaluation Study
OIG	Office of Inspector General
OT	Occupational therapy
PA	Physician assistant
PCE	Personal care expenditures
PHN	Public health nurse
PI	Performance improvement
POMR	Problem-oriented medical record
PPI	Producer price index
PPO	Preferred provider organization
PPS	Prospective payment system
PT	Physical therapy
QA	Quality assurance
RAI	Resident Assessment Instrument
RAPs	Resident Assessment Protocol Guidelines
RAPS	Resident Assessment Protocol Summary
RBRVS	Resource based Relative Value System
RN	Registered nurse
RRA	Registered record administrator
RUG	Resource utilization group
RUGS	Resource utilization groups
SCAMC	Symposium on Computer Applications in Medical Care
SDS	Same day surgery
SDS	Same day stay
SNF	Skilled nursing facility
STM	Staff time measure
SW	Social worker
UACDS	Uniform ambulatory care data set
UCR	Usual, customary and reasonable (fees)
UTI	Urinary tract infection
VNA	Visiting nurse association

INDEX